The Search

for an
Australian Paradise

Bill Hornadge

e t t

*The Search
for an
Australian Paradise*

Also available from IMPRINT *by the same author:*
The Hidden History of Australia
Lennie Lower: He made a nation laugh

An IMPRINT book

IMPRINT is a division of
Gumquest Pty Ltd (ACN 072 443 611)
Trading as ETT Imprint
PO Box 1388
Bondi Junction NSW 2022
Australia

First published 1999

Copyright © Bill Hornadge 1999

This book is copyright. Apart from any fair dealing for the
purpose of private study, research, criticism or review, as
permitted under the Copyright Act, no part may be reproduced
by any process without written permission from the publishers,
to whom all enquiries should be addressed.

ISBN 1875892 70 21

COVER ART AND DESIGN by Sharni Allen

PRESTIDIGITATION by Mike Connolly
PRINTED by Sands Print Group, Western Australia

CONTENTS

CONTENTS

PREFACE

It would seem that when Homo sapiens developed on earth he came equipped with itchy feet, and an insatiable sense of curiosity allied to a fervent belief that the grass was always greener in the next valley.

As a result of these attributes he seemed from the earliest times engaged in a perpetual search for Paradise, Utopia, Arcadia, Shangri La or any of the other names allotted to places of beauty, peace and plenty - and nowhere have these quests been in more evidence than in Australia.

This book is all about the eternal quest for Paradise, including some ambitious plans for Utopian settlements in the Great South Land (as Australia was once known), long before white settlement in 1778.

An interesting thing about this quest is that it seems these Utopian yearnings were perfectly normal, even included in Thomas Jefferson's original draft of the American Declaration of Independence:

We hold these two Truths to be Sacred and Undeniable: that all men are created equal and Independent, that from that equal Creation they deserve rights inherent and unalienable, among which are the preservation of Life, Liberty, and the pursuit of Happiness.

There we have it – THE PURSUIT OF HAPPINESS - or the search for one's own Paradise. This was quite a noble and interesting idea, though Jefferson seems not to have given any thought to the fact that on his plantation he owned many Negro slaves who certainly did not have any freedom to go in search of their own Utopia.

The major part of this work is given over to the very many plans for, and actual experiments with Utopian style settlements, communes and cooperatives, endeavours by both secular and spiritually oriented groups in their many different forms.

Alas, despite the high hopes of the participants, the failure rate of such ventures has been very high indeed.

It is interesting to note that the success rate for single or family Paradise-seekers is far higher than it is for the organised groups. There are some quite remarkable stories of this sturdy band of solo Utopians and these provide a nice balance to the many failed cooperative efforts.

In researching these stories I was struck by the great diversity of thought about what Paradise exactly means to different people. What some consider Paradise others take for granted.

For example, for many of the new settlers who came to Australia from the migrant camps of Europe immediately after World War 11 with its unimaginable horrors and deprivations, their new home must have seemed a paradise of abundance and tranquillity in many ways. Few Australians at that time would have been happy living in the Bonegilla refugee camp, for instance, but in 1997 the noted industrial magnate Sir Arvi Parvo summed up his impressions for *Sun-Herald* journalist Simon Kent thus:

Here, in the middle of the Australian bush, was a camp that embodied all the things I craved. Food, shelter, warmth, clothing, peace, sheer unadulterated luxury. It was like standing outside Aladdin's Cave and being waved towards an armchair inside.

Not all people have their sights set on a life in some far off island setting. For some a modest home of their dreams can represent their idea of paradise. For others it might be a job that provides soul-satisfying work; for many other seekers the answer is found within a happy family grouping or a good personal relationship or marriage.

For a few, Paradise can be found in the ending of marriage, though not all take it to the extreme of Patrizia Reggiani, former wife of Maurizio Gucci. Heir to the global fashion fortune, Gucci was murdered in 1995 in a plot organised by his ex-wife. At her trial in 1998 when she was found guilty of this deed and given a 29 year gaol sentence, it was revealed that in her diary on the day her ex-husband was shot dead, she had written just a single word, in Greek: PARADEISOS

Paradise may have come for her that day, but she was always a bit unorthodox in her thinking. Reggiani had already described her divorce settlement of $1.6 million as little more than a "bag of lentils", proclaiming that she would always rather cry in a Rolls Royce than be happy on a bicycle.

Yet not all seekers of Paradise are built in the mould of Patrizia Reggiani, and some do make considerable efforts within the law to achieve their Utopian aims. I hope you will enjoy reading about some of these achievements in the following pages.

Bill Hornadge
Dubbo, 1999.

1

In the Beginning

The current thinking of anthropologists seems to be that Homo sapiens originated in Africa some 200,000 years ago and then migrated north to the great land mass that embraces Europe, the Middle East and Asia about 150,000 years ago.

But their migrations did not stop there. They continued in a most unlikely fashion further north, then across the then existing Siberian-Alaskan land bridge, and right down the whole length of the Americas to the tip of Tierra de1 Fuego.

Later there were also thrusts east and south out of Asia, resulting in the arrival of several different groupings to Australia - migrations that in time spread right across the island continent to the southern most tip of Tasmania, then joined to the mainland. Here, many of these hardy travellers survived right through the last Ice Age.

What caused these massive ancient migrations of nomadic type people is not clear. Since populations of the various family and tribal groupings must have been small, and the territories they inhabited in their wanderings quite vast, population pressures seem an unlikely explanation for these movements. Climatic changes affecting the food chains, arising out of the collision between the planet and some massive object(s) from outer space is a possible but unproven theory still awaiting scientific evidence.

On the other hand, there is the possibility that man's natural curiosity took over and that he started his long trek out of Africa in the belief that the grass is always greener on the other side! These uncoordinated wanderings continued in most parts of the world until around 10,000 years ago when two changes in the patterns of life of the majority of the earth's inhabitants brought about a dramatic change of direction for Homo sapiens.

The first change was when the nomadic groupings started to domesticate animals that restricted their wanderings. The second, and major, development was when they started to manage and harvest the fruits and the plants of the earth. This forced them to stay put in one place for considerable lengths of time, resulting in the development first of villages, then ultimately, towns and cities which in turn led to nations, states and empires.

The mass migrations were brought to a halt, except when some natural or man-made catastrophe overtook a whole community, forcing it to uproot and settle elsewhere.

By 5000 BC most of the world's population had settled into some form of urban lifestyle, leaving only a minority of indigenes in isolated areas of the globe, including Australia, to continue their nomadic roaming. The fate of these nomadic remnants of Homo sapiens was sealed in 1492 when Christopher Columbus discovered what was to become known as the New World - the Americas.

When gold and silver was found in these new territories, a positive orgy of empire building resulted with all the major European states, led by Spain and Portugal, setting out to acquire by any means every spare piece of turf around. They totally ignored the rights of the indigenes and wiped out entire civilisations such as the Aztecs, Incas and Mayans.

This new breed of piratical adventurers was not driven by

11

desires to discover Gardens of Eden, they were driven by the basest of motifs; the greed for gold and the lust for power through possession of territory. Australia was perhaps fortunate to have escaped the original empire-building stampede of the 16th and 17th centuries.

Although the early cartographers were well aware of the existence of a Great South Land (which initially they thought to be part of Antarctica) they had no idea of its shape or actual size, nor any clear idea of the nature of its geography or inhabitants. The early reports of 'Terra Australis' were unfavourable, from early European mariners who had touched lightly on some inhospitable areas of the north west-coast of Western Australia.

The Dutch explorer Francois Pelsaart made such a landing in 1629, followed by the English pirate William Dampier in 1699. Both damned the place as being a desert wasteland inhabited only by hordes of persistent flies and ignorant and hostile natives. Dampier branded the latter as 'the miserablest people in the world'. Perhaps to the great luck of the inhabitants, both reports of Pelsaart and Dampier recorded the fact that the natives wore no ornaments. This meant that Empire builders back in Europe believed that Terra Australis lacked gold and silver.

Had they had any glimmering of knowledge of the vast mineral wealth of the Australian continent they would have been "in like Flynn". Perhaps we owe a great debt of gratitude to both Pelsaart and Dampier for their reporting deficiencies.

In 1625 a prominent London merchant, Sir William Courteen, presented a petition to King James 1 seeking permission to establish colonies in what he called Terra Australis. Sir William was the owner or co-owner of more twenty ships and had an extensive trade in the West Indies. What he sought was Royal assent to a monopoly of trading posts in the Great

South Land.

Although he had lent large sums of money, which gave him some claim on Royal favours, the King turned a deaf ear to the petition, though he did grant Courteen a title to the island of Barbados, in the West Indies.

In 1713 a Captain John Welbe, who had been with William Dampier in the South Seas, yet not turned off by the flies and the natives of, suggested to the British Government that he should explore the continent and establish a colony there, but received little support in any official quarter.

In France however, the idea of such a settlement was receiving much more careful consideration.

2

Early Settlement Plans

The earliest detailed plan for a settlement in the Great South Land was put forward by Jean Pierre Purry, who was born in Neufchatel, Switzerland about 1670, and who had seen service as Batavia with the Dutch East India Company.

Finding both the Dutch Government and his employer uninterested in plans for colonies to the south in what he called Peter Nuyt's Land, he moved to Paris, believing the French Government would be more receptive to his proposals.

The Purry proposal is very interesting because, unlike other 18th Century plans, it had a solid scientific base. Purry took as his guide the lands of Africa and South America between the latitudes of 33 and 66. He provided detailed figures of climatic conditions, rainfalls, soils, fruits, crops and flora in these latitudes on both continents, reasoning that conditions would be the same in these latitudes of the Great South Land.

Purry put aside the idea that because the world so far contacted west and north were unsuited, the Continent must be like this:

Why should one, then, if one has seen only the inferior parts of New Holland, make no distinction between these parts and the good Land of Nuyts, which must be the best part?... Who knows what there is in New Holland, and whether that country does not, perhaps, contain richer mines of gold or silver than did Chili, Peru or Mexico.

Why should all the countries of the world which are situated within this climate be good, and this one alone worthless?

Purry then addressed himself as to how the attempt to colonise New Holland should be carried out. Being a cautious individual, he suggested that the advance scouting party should comprise at least 500 to 600 well-armed soldiers to spy out the land, because the unknown Indians might prove to be better equipped to fight than the Indians of North and South America. He posed the question:

Why, for instance, should they not have fortified towns; and if we have discovered the use of (gun) Powder only since 200 or 300 years, why should not those people also have invented other machines of war yet more terrifying than our bombs and cannons?

He went on to speculate that it was even possible the land was peopled by giants of prodigious intelligence and knowledge! Monsieur Purry had a very vivid imagination. One can only speculate on what he would have thought of that remarkable machine of war, the boomerang, had he known of its existence. Perhaps for our own good health, the French authorities did not take Monsieur Purry's questions on climate, or his plans for colonisation seriously and nothing came of his proposals.

More credence appears to have been given to a later detailed plan put forward in 1756 by Monsieur Charles de Brosses, President of the regional Parliament of Dijon. His proposal differed markedly from that of Purry as it proposed that Terra Australis should be used by France as colonies for the foundling beggars and criminals of the Motherland. This proposal was actually adopted in part for a period after the French Revolution on the French island of New Caledonia. Like Purry, de Brosses believed that Terra Australis had both bad and good features and climates, and that the best ones should be sought out and settled.

De Brosses pointed to the great loss of life on long sea voyages, mainly due to scurvy, and suggested that the expeditions should make first for India, where they should be re-victualled completely. After resting at Pondicherry, they should take a route that avoided contact with any port held by the Dutch, which he regarded as an enemy of France.

He advocated an initial expedition of at least three vessels that should take aboard ready cut pieces of wood for quick. assembly ashore of wooden forts. As soon as the expedition had established itself ashore at some point, one of the ships would return to Pondicherry to report progress and return with fresh supplies. A second ship would explore up and down the coast around the new settlement, while the third ship would remain at the new colony in case of trouble.

One of the most interesting parts of this plan is that great care should be taken with the choice of crew for the expedition. His candid observations on the faults and failings of the various nationalities of Europe would have resulted in some heated exchanges among French allies if they had been publicised at the time:

The officers chosen to command the three vessels should be mild of character, so that they may gain the esteem of their crews; *firm, without being* arrogant, *not subject to fits of ill-temper, impatience or brutality. The greatest obstacle that our nation finds to preventing their making substantial gains in these far distant lands derives from this fact: that the French, so companionable in their own native land, cannot agree together when in foreign countries. The general failing of each and every nationality reveal themselves more during a long extended* voyage *than in any other circumstances. The Spaniard is always revealed as arrogant and cruel through his pride in himself and his contempt of others; The Englishman, as reserved, lawless, piratical; The anger of the Spaniard is that of the lion; the fierceness of the Englishman is that of the bull-dog. The injustice of the Spaniards, born of the exalted opinion they hold of themselves, nevertheless still preserves signs of the greatness of their souls; that of the English, engendered of the hatred they have of others, reveals only frenzy and ferocity. In expeditions such as these is there not to be seen at every moment the Dutchman greed of gain, and suffering without a murmur every kind of degradation, provided it is accompanied by profit; the Frenchman impatient, undisciplined, presumptuous, inconsistent in his views, without any feeling of inferiority, infatuated with a false idea of honour, always complaining and full of pretensions? Whereas the failings of other people turn against those with whom they have dealings, those of our own nation turn against themselves. History teaches us how these weaknesses have brought about the failure of many fine commercial enterprises. Some of these are far too recent to need recalling here.*

Phew! One wonders whether de Brosses had in mind the recruitment of Eskimos as leaders of his expeditions! Of all the pre-settlement plans drawn up in the 17th and 18th Centuries, that of de Brosses was the only one to deal in a humane manner with the natives they planned to dispossess of their lands. His suggestions were full of commonsense and a model for would-be Empire builders - a model that, alas, was seldom put into practice. Here are some of his suggestions:

Every possible effort should be made to gain the goodwill of the native. It is , of course, expected that difficulties will occur, and that the greatest possible discretion will have to be used. One cannot wonder at finding them scared at the sight of so many objects, strange and unknown, and so extraordinary to them. We ourselves whose mentality and knowledge are so much above those of the savages would not make a much better showing on the appearance of a horde of Australian natives who made a descent on our shores... one must proceed carefully, await a favourable moment, not grow impatient, gain them over gradually by offering small presents, leave on the ground what is offered to them if they refuse to accept it from hand to hand, avoid any display of violence and make sparing use of firearms ... neither their fruits, nor their animals, should be taken by force, nor their own persons should be taken by force ... a little time will bring them familiarity with the strangest things. When, after they have come forward, they receive good treatment, they will return voluntarily. In a word, everything depends on self-control at the outset.

And can it be asserted that the Australians are so unintelligent that they do not care a straw about what we take from them? Let only two of them become possessed of some of European attire, then all the others will immediately wish to do the same. Do not the great passions hold sway in far distant solitudes just as they do in our great world? Do not these great passions make themselves felt in the midst of poverty as in the lap of luxury? Vanity, curiosity, the desire to equal or excel one's fellows, are qualities inherent in man in every land.

De Brosses also strongly recommended that missionaries should only be allowed into new colonies after harmonious relations had been established with the natives. As he pointed out, their zeal could sometimes be too enthusiastic, adding that to bring reconciliation with the spirit of the people, it was foolish to show at the outset opposition towards matters that the natives hold most dear, adding:

That he should hold the false belief *that his religion is the* only *true one will not serve as an excuse. It is well known that each individual believes his own faith to be the only true one. If there is any one point concerning which the: natural liberty of man does not wish to be constrained, it is that of religion. Idolatry does not deprive those who have the misfortune to be given up to it, of the liberty of their persons or the ownership of their goods. We have no right to render miserable those whom we have not been able to convert to our own way of thinking.*

When Charles de Brosses put forward his proposal to colonise Australia, France was in state of political turmoil, so nothing came of his grand plans.

At this late stage, we can only idly speculate on the course of Australian history had Paris acted on the de Brosses proposals and settled the continent, say around 1760, a decade before Captain Cook came on the scene. Would the French have declared the continent terra nulius (empty of natives) as the British did in 1788? And would the inhabitants of the Land Down Under now all be playing boule instead of cricket and Aussie rules?

3

The Matra Plans

The English authorities were well aware of the two French plans for settlement of The Great South Land outlined in the previous chapter. After Jean Pierre Purry found little interest in his 1718 plan, he moved to London where he published *A Method for Determining the Best Climate of the Earth* which was the basis of his colonial proposal. The English proved to be as disinterested as the French in his climate based theories.

The authorities must also have been aware of the more detailed and ambitious proposals of Charles de Brosses because between the years 1766 and 1768 John Callander published in Edinburgh his three volume treatise, being an English translation of the de Brosses proposals, plus his own commentaries. In the third volume there was an additional chapter: *Of the method of forming Colonies in the Terra Australis, and the Advantages that may be expected to result to Great Britain from such Establishments in that Hemisphere*. The Mandarins of Whitehall were still unmoved.

But two subsequent events caused a sudden change of heart at the highest levels of the English Establishment. The first was Captain James Cook's exploration of the East Coast of Australia in 1770 (along with his act of proclaiming British ownership of the whole continent at Possession Island); the second was the unexpected loss of the American Colonies in the

American War of Independence of 1776.

On the one hand they had nominally gained a huge unexplored island/continent, while on the other they had lost the North American colonies where they had been shipping vast numbers of convicts.

They started to look at the possibility of a settlement in Terra Australis with entirely new eyes and several plans were advanced by men who hoped to personally profit from such ventures, The first of these proposals came from James Matra in 1783 and immediately received consideration at the highest level because it was supported by Sir Joseph Banks, and because Matra had actually been to Terra Australis as a member of Cook's crew on the Endeavour. Thus his plan came with first hand knowledge of the proposed colony or colonies, an ingredient lacking in all other proposals up to that time.

James Mario Matra was a colourful individual with an unusual background. He was born in New York in 1746, the son of James and Elizabeth Magra, His father was the scion of an ancient Corsican family of Matra. Seeking a better life James Matra went first to Ireland (in the early 1730's) where for some unexplained reason he changed his name to Magra, and where he studied medicine. He migrated to America in the late 1730's and settled in New York where he gained a reputation as an eminent physician. Fame brought with it wealth and he was so shrewd in his choice of investments that when he died in 1774 he was a wealthy man. However, most of that wealth vanished in the turbulence of the American Revolution, The Magras had three sons, Redmond, James and Perkins. The elder son Redmond was an unprincipled adventurer who was in and out of trouble with the army and other authorities most of his adult life. His younger brother Perkins followed Redmond into the army where he had a distinguished and apparently blemish-free career.

Little is known of the early years of the middle brother

James, the subject of this story, other than the fact that he was, at least partly, educated in England and saw some service in the British navy in the Seven Years War. After the war he had signed on again and was transferred to the North American station at New York (probably at his behest to be near his parents).In 1768 he was back in England and on July 25 of that year signed on with the Endeavour for its epic around the world history making voyage.

Despite his above average education and fairly extensive naval service up to that time his rank was that of a lowly midshipman. He appears to have been much given to drunken pranks and was not held in high regard by his Captain. In the Middle Watch of the night of May 22, 1770, somewhere off the Queensland coast, Captain Cook's clerk, Mr Orton, fell into a drunken stupor and someone cut all the clothes off his back and not satisfied with that proceeded to cut off parts of both his ears. The incensed Captain strongly suspected Midshipman Magra to be the culprit and suspended him from duties. However, lacking proof of the matter, he was forced to reinstate Magra. Recording the incident in his Journal Cook noted:

He (Magra) being one of those Gentlemen frequently found on board King's Ships, that can very well be spared, or to speake more planer, good for nothing.

If Cook had a poor opinion of Magra, it seems the feeling was mutual. Two months after the Endeavour reached England on its global voyage Becket and De Hondt published anonymously in direct contravention of the Admiralty ban on such a publication. *A Journal of a Voyage Round the World*: in which much praise was heaped on Banks and Solander, and castigating Cook's vacillation on the New Zealand coast. Although proof was lacking at the time, it appears certain that Magra was the author of this work. Maybe he felt it evened up the score a little to counter Cook's scorn and hostility.

After the return of the Endeavour, Magra did a further stint in the Navy as lieutenant until Joseph Banks, who had befriended him on the Endeavour, obtained a post for him as British Consul in the Canary Islands in 1772.

In 1775 Magra returned to London and petitioned the King to be allowed to change his name back to the origin clan name of Matra, and this was approved in 1776. In the years 1778-80 the newly named James Mario Matra was British Embassy Secretary at Constantinople.

Returning to London in 1781 he dreamed up an ambitious proposal for British settlements in Corsica and the Canary Islands which attracted no attention, before turning his thoughts to Botany Bay, a place he had visited in his younger, wilder days.

The result was *A Proposal for Establishing a Settlement in New South Wales - to atone for the loss of our American Colonies*. This proposal was presented on August 2 1783 to the British Coalition Government of Fox and North. As it had Sir Joseph Banks' endorsement it received immediate attention, but was never going to get off the ground because of one key element.

The centrepiece of this Matra Plan was that it should be primarily a settlement of colonists from America, some of whom had been seriously disadvantaged by the American Revolution, and whose loyalties still remained with Britain. After British forces had established military bridgeheads along the New South Wales coast, the disgruntled American colonists were to be resettled. There they could establish plantations, worked by indented coolie labourers brought from China (he made no mention of Negro slaves that were such as feature of the North American plantations of the time).

Matra felt it would be necessary to have permanent garrisons of troops to guard the plantations and he put forward an ingenious scheme to meet the physical needs of such troops.

This was that one of the first fleet ships should go to New Caledonia, Otaheite and other neighbouring islands to procure there a few families, and *as many women* as *may serve the men left behind.* (my italics). He added that there was every reason to believe that such women could be obtained without difficulty.

To bolster his main theme of the settlement of ex-American colonists, Matra stressed that the Cook Expedition of 1770 had traversed some 2000 miles of the New South Wales coastline. They had seen every variety of soil and with moderate climates suitable for all types of produce such as sugar cane, tea, coffee, silk, cotton, indigo and tobacco. All these crops could be grown for export to the markets of Asia, especially China. He added that New South Wales would be a good place to establish a British Military Base from which Britain could annoy Holland or Spain if war eventuated with either country!

And the natives - the Aborigines who had occupied the continent for some 50,000 years! What had Matra to say about them? Very little actually as they were mentioned in only one dismissive paragraph:

This immense tract. peopled only by a few black inhabitants, who, in the rudest state of society, knew other arts than such as were necessary to their mere animal existence, and which was almost entirely sustained by catching fish.

In his initial plan Matra made no mention at all of convicts. They simply didn't enter into his scheme of things. However, after he had been granted an interview with Lord Sydney, he became acutely aware that the plight of Loyal American colonists was very low on the priority list of the Government. Their major problem was the huge number of criminals then sweating it out in prisons and even more overcrowded prison hulks moored in various British waterways.

Being quick to see which way the wind was blowing, Matra did an about turn and produced an amended proposal that concentrated on transferring the inhabitants of the prisons and hulks to Botany Bay.

Some of the statistics presented by Matra to support this revised plan are quite startling. He revealed that in the years 1775 and 1776 a total of 746 convicts had been sent to Africa, of which 334 had died, 271 had managed to escape, while of the others no account could be given by the authorities charged with their care.

He disclosed that upward of a thousand felons, many of whom were under the age of eighteen, were convicted each year and that the Government paid to the contractors holding them in the hulks, the sum of twenty six pounds fifteen shillings and tenpence per prisoner per year. When the convicts were being sent to the American Colonies, the Government made a profit on them as they were sold to the plantation owners for a servitude of seven years.

Matra was not in favour of the old American system. His plan was simple and to the point:

Give them a few acres of ground as soon as they arrive in New South Wales, in absolute property, with what assistance they may need to till them. Let it be here remarked that they cannot fly the country, that they have no temptation to theft, and that they must work or starve. I likewise suppose that they are not, by any means, to be reproached for their former conduct. If these premises be granted me, I may reasonably conclude that it is highly probable they will be useful; that it is very possible they will be moral subjects of society.

Matra concluded by stating that the expense to the nation of implementing his plan would be imperceptible compared to what the convicts were then costing the Government, thus blending what he called the "desirable and beautiful union" of economy to the Public, and humanity to the individual! Despite the obvious implausibility of many of Matra's ideas, he was called to give evidence on his proposals in 1785, before the House of

Commons Beauchamp Committee on Transportation.

From the tenor of the questions, it is quite clear that the committee did not see any place for free settlers in proposed colonies in New South Wales. If established they would be for convicts only, under military supervision at all times.

Matra was asked how many convicts could be sent to a colony to which his answer was 500 subject to there being sufficient guards. In response to another question, he also thought a number of such convict colonies could be established along the New South Wales coastline without any intercourse between the convicts.

The Committee seemed greatly interested in Matra's plan to import women from various South Seas Islands for use of the troops, and the following exchange took place (Matra's response in italics):

Are the inhabitants of New Caledonia, Otaheite and the other neighbouring islands a happy people?

They appear to be so as much as human Nature generally are. They are of a quiet Nature.

Do you think Women could be induced to go from thence for Use of the European Men at the New Settlement?

Yes, in any Number. They are more partial to Europeans than to their own Countrymen.

At that stage of the questioning, Matra's hidden agenda for putting the proposal forward emerged. It became clear that he was seeking a senior post in the whole operation, possibly that of Governor of the colonies:

Have you offered or desired to have any concern in the Execution of this Plan?

I have not yet, but rather than the Plan should fall to the Ground for want of a proper person I will, if the Administration choose it, undertake it not on the footing of a Contractor but as an Officer under the Government to be the Conductor and Governor.

Have any others offered?

Not as I know of.

Do you mean you will undertake it as a sober regular Colony or as a Colony of Convicts?

Both or either.

In response to further questions, Matra said he would need 200 Marines and a Guard Ship for each colony. There would have to be a system of Justice established and several Ministers of the Gospel should be at each Colony.

Matra believed that all seeds and livestock for the enterprise could be obtained at the Cape of Good Hope or in the Moluccan Islands where the Dutch Agents were so corrupt that they would supply anything.

In all the lengthy questioning by the Committee not one mention was made of the Aboriginal inhabitants of New South Wales.

Matra was given gentle treatment by the Committee and probably came away from its questioning with a belief that his proposal had a fair chance of success. If so, he was to be disappointed as the Government did not offer him any position, in their finally adopted anonymous "Heads of a Plan" of 1786,which had no truck with the idea of American Loyalists, or even free settlers. In the words of Alexander Dalrymple, a close friend of Matra, the name of the new colony should be *The Intended Thief-Colony of Botany Bay*.

Matra spent the rest of his life in the service of the British Foreign Office as Consul at Tangier (1787-1906), a posting that was more a poisoned chalice than a golden reward. The Emperor of Morocco's insatiable demands for bribes and presents had bankrupted more than one previous holder of the British Consular post, forcing the unlucky holder of the post to dig deep into his own pocket to maintain favour with the Emperor and his Court.

Matra managed to survive this hurdle but struck another one when the Emperor expressed concern at Matra's single state and ordered him to send to England for a wife, on the grounds that a single state was a state of sin! The Emperor had no such problems, having a large harem.

Matra for some time paid court to a widow named Lucinda but his suit was not successful. In October 1793 he married Henrietta Maxwell, the daughter of the British Army's victualling agent in nearby Gibraltar. Henrietta was no stranger to his bed as he explained in a letter to his old friend Sir Joseph Banks, penned immediately after the ceremony:

…the permanent support you have so long afforded me would make me sorry that you should hear from any but myself - that I am married - seeing no chance of a remove from this unhappy Country & being heartily tired of the very unsociable Life we lead in Tangiers was the sole motive that lead me to that measure. The Girl I have been intimate with since I left England, and with other Visitors, she has occasionally resided in my House so that at least we know each other rather better than the general run of People do before marriage. She knows what She is, & what She is not to expect, & is content. For my expectations, I am content to run the risque like others that have gone before me.

There were no children to the union.

Matra served the British Government for twenty years at his post in Tangier, without ever returning to his adoptive land of England. In that period he complained incessantly about the burdens of the post and sought a transfer to some more hospitable place in vain. The truth was that he had become so expert in the devious machinations of Moorish politics that he was indispensable at ensuring a constant flow of Moorish products into the Gibraltar garrison. Without this the Mediterranean Squadron could not have operated effectively, and Nelson's victory at Trafalgar was largely due to this support.

With the coming of the new century, Matra's health began to deteriorate. By 1805 he was bedridden and unable to carry out his duties and the following year his eyes failed entirely. The Pitt Government finally agreed to his retirement and notification of a pension was on the way when he died at Tangier on March 29 1806.

He had failed in life to find a personal Paradise but served his adoptive country so well, for so long, that others may have done so due to his efforts.

4

Paradise Lost

The first European explorers to venture into the South Seas in the 17th and 18th Centuries brought back highly coloured tales of the island paradises they had found there, tales which were lascivious in their descriptions of the sexual appetites and customs of the wahines of these islands.

It is little wonder that the folk back home in their staid and sober homelands gained an entirely erroneous impression of life in that distant part of the globe. These misconceptions clearly coloured the expectations of those planning settlements in the Great South Land, more commonly referred to as Terra Australis. Their reasoning perhaps went along the lines that as this great unexplored land mass was located in what was loosely described as the "South Seas", then life there would not be all that much different from that in the smaller islands. The image seems to have been only dented slightly by reports of Cook's discoveries along the east coast in 1770. In the matter of daydreams, hope usually triumphs over reality.

The hardheads in the British Admiralty who planned the First Fleet expedition were practical men who had experience of similar operations in other parts of the world, with few illusions about the difficulty of setting up such a convict outpost. Less informed would have been the general public and many of the participants in the venture, since for months before the fleet sailed the newspapers of the day had been full of stories about the bold experiment to be thrust upon Botany Bay. The convict participants would have had few expectations other than of severe doses of the lash if they disobeyed orders.

Little thought was given at the time to the innate conservatism of human nature; the natural instinct to stay with tradition, to resist change and to only feel at ease with familiar things and surroundings.

They were never going to see as Paradise, a place that was so vastly different to anything they had experienced "back home".

Not only different in landscape and climate but in every aspect of life. In Brian Penton's novel *Landtakers* (1934), one of his characters complain bitterly about this new land in which he had found himself:

It's a long way from your merry old England out here, and it's a funny sort of place, where nothing happens like it should. Christmas comes in the middle of summer. The north wind's hot and the south wind's cold. Trees drop their bark and keep their leaves. The flowers don't smell and the birds don't sing. The swans are black and the eagles white. You burn cedar to boil your hominy and build your fences out of mahogany. Aye, it's not the same as the Old Country at all.

The newcomers to this strange country found it hard to cope with the blistering heat of summer and with a land that seemed to defy every effort to tame it. This was certainly no paradise and most of the arrivals, whether free or in chains, would have warmly agreed with the sentiments of TB Macauley that "an acre in Middlesex is better than a principality in Utopia."

But one man's poison is another man's meat. The First Fleeters, had they only known it, HAD arrived in a Paradise, but, because of their upbringing and perceptions, were unable to see it as such. As a result, most of them cursed their gods for having landed them in such a hell-hole as Sydney Cove.

The Eora people, who had long occupied the area, held a quite different view to the newcomers. To them it WAS Paradise. To the north lived the Camaraigal People, the Gayimai People, the Gwiyagal People and other people of the Dharuk language group (who occupied all the magnificent waterways which we know as Pittwater and the great Hawkesbury basin area with its breathtaking coves and inlets); these people all knew they lived in Paradise.

They knew this because they had been occupying it for thousands of years, knew everything about its seasons and rhythms and its moods. It also provided them with all their needs in the form of plentiful fish in the waters, and plentiful wildlife on land, and a temperate climate that required only rough shelters. There was no need for grand plantations or any type of agriculture, since a bountiful nature provided all their needs. So great was the bounty in the Sydney basin that present day dietitians believe that the indigenes of the area in 1788 would have had a better, more balanced, diet and a higher intake of nourishing foods, than most new settlers which arrived on the First Fleet.

This Paradise was shattered by the arrival of the newcomers who were blind to its existence and its virtues and within a few decades, the original inhabitants and nurturers were almost completely wiped out by diseases brought by the white settlers. For them it was Paradise lost forever, by bullet if not by disease to which they had no immunity.

In the two centuries that have elapsed since then, the white newcomers to these shores have also succeeded in destroying much of the physical beauty of this ancient Paradise. Bricks and mortar have inched their way into almost every corner of this old Paradise - always of course in the name of Progress and Profit.

A few isolated spots retain their virginity, mainly because

the rugged terrain has defied the efforts of the bulldozers. No doubt they too will succumb in time to new gee-whiz technology, so that some time in the 21st Century some adventurous developer will be able to stand on some hill and look down and say with the pride of his calling. "Look Shirl! I've done it! I've finally done it. Destroyed the last segment of their stupid old Paradise."

Congratulations, Mate, on your great achievement.

5

An Island Paradise

Whole forests have been chopped down to provide the paper that Australian travel agents consume in producing brochures describing Lord Howe Island as "the Island Paradise of the South Seas".

Travel agents use adjectives with total abandon when they come to describe various holiday destinations, but in the case of Lord Howe Island their superlatives are probably justified. Lord Howe IS something special in the way of islands despite the buccaneering charges often made by its accommodation providers.

It must be one of the few truly scenic spots on earth to have managed to keep at bay the worst depredation of the developers, and for that we should be thankful, though acknowledging that along the way some (non human) inhabitants of this island gem suffered dearly.

Perhaps the real mystery of the island is how it came to escape human attention before 1788. The Polynesians overlooked it during their expeditions, and Captain Cook failed to sight it on the two occasions he was in the area. On his second voyage he did discover Norfolk Island and this in itself led indirectly to the discovery of Lord Howe.

Cook was much taken with two things on Norfolk Island, the magnificent stands of Norfolk Pines which he thought would make great ship spars, and the flax which he believed could be woven into sails.

When his report eventually reached the Admiralty back in England they were more than interested because war seemed to be looming with their old enemy France. If that occurred their main source of spars, Scandinavia, might be cut off by the French. A new source of flax was always of interest to the admirals.

Such importance was attached to Cook's findings that when the First Fleet sailed, Captain Arthur Phillip carried secret orders to secure and occupy Norfolk Island immediately he had established the convict settlement at Botany Bay.

Following the successful settlement in Sydney Cove, Phillip sent Lieutenant Philip Gidley King off in the Supply to establish a colony on Norfolk Island. As Lord Howe Island stands in a direct line between Sydney and Norfolk Island, it is not surprising that three days out of Sydney the Captain of the Supply spotted what he thought were two islands in the distance. He named one Lord Howe Island, after the First Sea Lord of the Admiralty, Lord Howe, but delayed investigating his discovery until the return trip.

Norfolk Island was found and settled without incident but it did not prove to be the bonanza their Lordships of the Admiralty had been seeking. The Norfolk Island pines proved to be totally unsuitable for converting into spars and all efforts to turn the Norfolk flax into cloth failed. At a later date they even went to the extreme of going across to New Zealand and kidnapping two Maori chiefs from the Bay of Islands, to instruct the locals into processing the stubborn flax plants. Of course the Chiefs were unable to oblige, never having had any experience at such lowly labour - this being women's work. The dim-witted Norfolk Commander who thought up the idea should have had the raiding party kidnap the wives of the chiefs. However this would not have solved the issue as later experiments showed that the Norfolk flax was of a different species to that growing in New Zealand, making it useless for sail making.

Had the Admiralty known this they probably wouldn't have bothered to occupy Norfolk in the first place and many years may have elapsed before Lord Howe Island was discovered by Lieutenant Henry Lidgbird Ball, captain of the Supply.

Returning from Norfolk Island on March 13 1788 he landed a party there and found no sign that humans had ever set foot on the island. The waters around the island abounded with turtles and the island itself was densely populated with swamp hens, gannets, pigeons and other birds.

As the birds had never had experience of predators, they stood their ground when approached and were thus slaughtered in great numbers, providing excellent food for the crew. Considerable numbers were taken back to Sydney along with a quantity of huge turtles, some of which weighed upward of 150 pounds.

The fresh meat was very welcome in Sydney where scurvy was rife, and Governor Phillip quickly sent Lieutenant Ball back to Lord Howe Island for further supplies. In the coming months the island was to become a regular source of supply of food for the inhabitants of Sydney Town. While this mainly benefited the officers of the Settlement, the effect on the island's bird life was tragic.

In the early days of colonisation food was so scarce that it was a case of "if it moves, eat it". Flavour or quality was not all that important, and survival of many species depended almost entirely on how fleet of foot or wing they were.

The descriptions of the slaughter of birds by the early Sydney settlers, and later by crews of whalers who quickly learned of this new Pacific larder, are quite stomach-churning,

Surgeon Arthur Bowes, of the Lady Penrhyn, in his journal of May 16, 1788, wrote of his recent visit to the island:

...when I was in the woods amongst the Birds I cd not help picturing to myself the Golden Age as described by Ovid - to see the Fowls or Coots some white, some blue & white, other all blue wt. large red bills and a patch of red on top of their heads & the Boobies in thousands, together wt. a curious brown Bird abt. the sixe of the Land Reel (Rail) in England walking totally fearless & unconcerned in all part around us, so we had nothing more to do than to stand still a minute or two & knock down as many as we pleas'd wt. a short stick - if you thro'd at them & miss'd them, or even hit them without killing them, they never made the least attempt to fly away & indeed wd. only run a few yards from you & be as quiet & unconcern'd as if nothing had happen'd. The Pidgeons also were as tame as those already describe'd & wd. sit upon the branches of the trees till you might go & take them off with yr. hands or if the branch was so high on wh. they sat, they wd. at all times still till you might knock them down with a short stick, many hundreds of all sorts mention'd above, together wt. Parrots & Parraquets, ,Magpies & other birds were caught and carried on board our Ship & the Charlotten

Thus did the birds of Lord Howe Island lose their innocence and, in time, their existence because the slaughter was so great that many species unique to the island became extinct.

In time the birds of Lord Howe Island were replaced by humans but fortunately for the other flora and fauna their numbers were small and their stay usually brief, at least in the early years.

At one time there was talk in Sydney Town of establishing a convict settlement there along the lines of that on Norfolk Island but fortunately that bit of nonsense did not get off the drawing board.

Records are scanty about early settlers. In the mid-1830's several men from whalers stayed awhile with their Maori wives, mainly growing vegetables for whaling ships, and an escaped convict and even an itinerant aborigine were recorded as short term settlers in the same period.

Eventually the itinerant whalers were bought out by Captain Poole, a retired officer with the British East India Company, who settled on the island and, with the aid of a silent partner in Sydney, carried on a trading venture supplying passing ships, mainly whalers. By the early 1840's he had engaged two families named Hescott and McAuliffe to run the business, while Captain Poole ruled over the island as a "benevolent dictator" though he had no land rights or any official sanction to a title.

In June 1844 Captain Poole brought ten new settlers to the island with thirty packages of household goods and settlement of a kind was under way at last. They included a Dr Foulis who settled at Windy Point with his wife and his servants. His two daughters were the first children born on the island.

Some of the early settlers had colourful backgrounds. One was a freed American slave named Perry Johnson, who liked the island so much he went off to Sydney and got himself an African fiancee who he brought back to the island and married. Fifty years later they discovered the original island marriage had not been legal, so they repeated their vows in 1913. Perry died in 1915 and his wife in 1918, aged 100.

Another batch of interesting settlers arrived around 1853 led by an American Nathan Chase Thompson, who was born in 1823 into a well-connected Massachusetts whaling family. He had spent some years on whaling ships in the Pacific. As captain of a ship sailing in the Gilbert Islands group he had encountered a canoe containing a Islander with the daughter of an Islander chief, and two women who were attendants of the girl. He was told the girl was fleeing to another island to avoid marrying an old man to whom she had been betrothed at birth.

Captain Thompson took the three women on board, but

shortly afterwards his ship was wrecked on Wreck Reef. Accompanied by the chief's daughter, Bogue and her two attendants Boranga and Bogaroo, and two crew members, George Campbell and Jack Brian; Captain Thompson finally made it to Lord Howe Island where he decided to settle with his new found family.

He took Boranga as his wife and they had a son Hugh, who died on the island aged 11. Boranga died soon afterwards, so Thompson then married the fleeing princess Bogue, then in her early twenties. They had five children, and many of the present-day islanders are descended from this union. Thompson died in 1895 and Bogue in 1897.

By most standards, Lord Howe Island has always had a small population for its size and natural resources, but this is the way the islanders have always wanted it. They have always regarded their island as a little corner of a fairly bountiful paradise and are so determined to keep it that way that today it is impossible for an "outsider" to buy land or settle and the number of visitors are strictly controlled.

Paradise, it seems, is for sharing, but only for stays of five or seven days at the few resorts available to visitors.

Back in 1940 Harold Rabone wrote a small book, *LORD HOWE ISLAND: Its Discovery and Early Associations 1788-1888*, which also covered in some detail the island's geographical features, flora and fauna. Rabone loved the island he had visited on so many occasions and this shone through in his prose. Scattered through the book were the verses of a long and detailed poem devoted to the island. In the text no mention is made of the poem, or any provenance provided for it, so I assume the author was its creator. I thought the final verse summed up to perfection what an island paradise can be, and should be, and why the Travel Agents may be right when they insist on calling Lord Howe an "Island Paradise":

Happy they were without a care,
Who made their home forever there;
Happy they were, and calm and free,
Living upon their island home,
Whose beach was girt with a silvery sea,
That sprinkled it ever with starry foam,
Their life was a moving melody,
Their seas a long serenity.

6

Van Demons' Land!

When the Dutch explorer Abel Janszoon Tasman (1603-1659) discovered the island we now know as Tasmania in November 1642 he named it Van Diemen's Land after the Governor General of the Dutch Indies, Anthony Van Diemen.

Given the events that followed white settlement of the island some one hundred and sixty years on, a more appropriate name might have been Van Demons' Land since no place on earth has been so plagued with the forces of human evil, even unto this decade, as has the place we now call Tasmania. And even nature seems to have lent a hand to the human desecration by presenting as the largest surviving mammal of the island surely one of the most repulsive species of the animal kingdom - Sarcophilus harrisii - known to us as the Tasmanian Devil.

To the students of history, the island is the embodiment of human evil, the dark side of Homo sapiens. Yet, the island that has been host to these demons for close on two centuries is also one of the most beautiful places on the planet. A beauty and the beast combination it would be difficult to duplicate elsewhere.

And yet, before 1803 it appears to have had no dark side -at least nothing the archaeologists have been able to discover.

Indeed, the very first archaeologist to set foot on the island found it a magic place of innocence and delight.

His name was Francois Peron, a noted naturalist of his era who was born in France in 1775. In October 1800 he sailed on the Le Geographe as naturalist in the South Seas expedition organised by the Institut de France and led by Nicolas Baudin. The expedition touched on a number of places in Australia, and the then-unsettled island of Van Diemen's Land, a name it officially retained until 1855. When the expedition returned to France in 1804 it brought with it 100,000 specimens collected by Peron and his colleagues, a vast collection which is housed in the Museum of Natural History in Paris. Peron died in 1810 before he could finish the cataloguing of his collection, but he did leave behind a considerable amount of work on his anthropological studies in the South Seas, including a remarkable account of a visit he made to tribe of aborigines in the D'Entrecasteaux Channel on the south east coast of Tasmania, in January 1802.

This is his account of the meeting of the two vastly differing cultures:

Responding to our gestures of friendship, one of them bounded down and was with us in an instant. He was a young man of 22 to 24, of robust constitution, and having no defect other than the characteristically thin legs and arms of his race. His facial appearance was neither stern nor fierce, his eyes were lively and intelligent and his manner expressed both goodwill and surprise.

What first interested him was the whiteness of our skins.

Wishing to see if our bodies were the same colour, he opened our waistcoats and shirts, demonstrating his amazement by loud cries and by rapidly stamping his feet. His curiosity then switched to our boat. Disregarding the sailors it contained, he jumped in totally absorbed by its construction. Silently and excitedly he closely examined the thickness of the ribs and timbers, the strength of its construction and the form of the rudder, oars, masts and sails.

It was not long before we saw the same family coming toward us along the beach. As soon as they saw us they gave shouts of joy and ran to join us. Their number was now increased to nine members by the addition of a young girl of sixteen, a small boy of four and a girl of about three years of age. They were returning from a successful fishing trip, being weighed down with shellfish of the large type of 'sea ears' (abalone) found on these shores. The old man took de Freycinet by the hand and indicating that we should follow, led us to the dwelling which we had recently found.

A fire was quickly lit and after ordering several times 'Medi, Medi' (sit down, sit down) which we did, the natives squatted on their heels and prepared to enjoy the meal. Their method of cooking was simple - the shellfish being placed directly in the fire and baked in the shells. We tasted some and found them very tender and juicy.

While these kind people were eating, we decided to treat them to some songs. At first the natives appeared more puzzled - than surprised, but they began to listen attentively. Their meal was soon forgotten as they showed pleasure with such fantastic facial contortions and gestures that we could hardly refrain from laughing. The young man especially was beside himself, catching hold of his hair, rubbing his head with his hands and throwing himself all over the place, accompanied by loud screams.

The young Ouray Ouray, like her parents wholly naked, yet entirely unselfconscious, drew herself to our attention by subtle glances and an affectionate expression. De Freycinet, seated next to her, became the focus of her attention and smiles. Taking some charcoal in her hands, she crunched it into a very fine powder.

Holding this in her left hand, she then rubbed some of it with her right hand, first on her forehead and then her cheeks, seeming very pleased with the results.

Ouray Ouray alone carried an elegant rush bag of such unique construction that I was keen to have it. As the girl had previously given me a favouring eye, I took the risk of asking if she would give it to me. Immediately, and without hesitation, she put it in my hand,

43

accompanying her present with a pleasant smile and some affectionate words which, sadly, I could not understand. In return I gave her a handkerchief and an axe, the effectiveness of which astonished her brother and excited the whole family.

Gradually they became accustomed to us, such that by the end they behaved as familiarly as if we had been old friends. We loaded them with presents but the only one that produced pleasure was a plume of real feathers presented to Ouray Ouray. She leapt with joy, calling the attention of her father and brothers, made loud shouts, laughed, and in short, seemed transformed with delight.

They all rose to accompany us, but after a few words from the head man, the older woman, the baby and all the children except the eldest, remained at the hut. De Ereycinet gave his arm to Ouray Ouray, while the head of the family was my mate. Charles Lesueur (the expedition artist) was accompanied by the young man and the Midshipman led the child. The undergrowth scratched their naked skins and although Ouray Ouray was especially badly scratched, she did not seem to notice. She was completely absorbed with chattering with de Freycinet, accompanying her conversation with seductive gestures and smiles, so gracious and expressive, that they were like the most polished coquetry.

As we pushed our two boats from the shore their sadness was most moving. By means of signs they invited us to visit them again. Thus ended our first interview with the inhabitants of Van Diemen's Land. All the descriptions which I have given are exactly true, and without doubt it would have been difficult to deny oneself the sweet emotions which such circumstances ought to inspire. This gentle confidence of the people in us, these affectionate evidences of benevolence which they never ceased to manifest towards us, the sincerity of their demonstrations, the frankness of their manners, the touching ingenuousness of their caresses, all concurred to excite within us sentiments of the tenderest interest. The general union of the different individuals of a family, the sort of patriarchal life of which we had *been spectators, had strongly moved us. I saw with an inexpressible pleasure the realisation of those brilliant descriptions of the happiness and simplicity of the state of nature of which I had so many times in reading felt the seductive charm.*

Alas, the veritable Garden of Eden described so vividly by Peron was about to end for all its inhabitants. Ouray Ouray's ancestors had survived the onslaughts of nature in the wilderness and wilds of Tasmania for thousands of years, including the perils of the last Ice Age, only to fall easy prey to a new threat from without.

Barely a year after Peron's visit, white invasion came to the island, first in the form of one of the most vicious and inhumane convict outposts, followed quickly by settlers intent on depriving the original inhabitants of their lands. These new white skinned invaders came to Van Diemen's Land with a gun in one hand and the Bible in the other, the latter providing the clearest of instructions of how the former should be used, for it was outlined in detail in Deuteronomy how they should act:

1 When the Lord your God brings you into the land you are entering to possess and drives out many nations.

2 …and when the Lord your God has delivered them over to you and you have defeated them, then you must destroy them totally. Make no treaty with them, and show them no mercy.

3 You must destroy all the peoples the Lord your God gives over to you. Do not look on them with pity.

And being good Christian folk, the new settlers obeyed these instructions to such good effect that within a few decades they had exterminated every last Tasmanian native in one of the most efficient examples of genocide and ethnic cleansing in modern history.

And to balance the loss of (black) numbers which this

operation caused, the new rulers of Van Diemen's Land brought in approximate numbers of (white) convicts which they proceeded to incarcerate and torture in such hell holes as Port Arthur and Macquarie Harbour.

When the prison settlement of Macquarie Harbour, was set up on the west coast in 1821 by Lieutenant Governor William Sorell (1775-1842) he made no bones about its purpose. In his standing orders to its first commandant, Lieutenant John Cuthbertson, he wrote:

...the constant and active, unremitting employment of every individual in very hard labour is the grand and main design of your settlement... They must dread the very idea of being sent there ...you must find work and labour, even if it consists in opening cavities and filling them up again ...Prisoners on trial declared that they would rather suffer death than be sent back to Macquarie Harbour. It is a feeling I am most anxious to be kept alive.

Little wonder that demons continue to haunt such places as Macquarie Harbour and Port Arthur, even to the present day! And yet, there is another side to the island we once called Van Diemen's Land, but now know as Tasmania. For all its history and enduring testimony to the inherent vileness of Homo sapiens, it always was and still remains a place of incredible wild, untamed beauty, which even the most determined efforts of the woodchippers and the vandals of the Tasmanian Hydro Commission have only managed to partly extinguish. Much of the original remains, though how long this continues seems a matter of conjecture. Almost two centuries ago, it was an outsider, a civilised Frenchman, Francois Peron, who first brought to the attention of the world the charm and natural beauty of the original inhabitants. A century and a half further down the track it was left to another remarkable civilised "outsider" to draw the attention of the world to some of the long-hidden natural beauties of the island.

His name was Olegas Truchanas and like Francois Peron he was from the other side of the world, and came to this part of the globe in his manhood to devote the rest of his remarkable life to his adoptive land. Truchanas was born in 1923 in Siauliai, in the tiny Baltic state of Lithuania. In his early years he saw his country invaded and occupied first by the Russians (1940) and then by the Germans (1941), and by the Russians again in 1945. He lived to see almost a third of his countrymen killed or sent to concentration camps, and to experience the humiliation of seeing his country handed over to the Russians in the carve up of Europe hammered out by the Stalin, Churchill and Roosevelt at the Yalta meeting in 1945. Unfortunately he did not live to see Lithuania achieve independence again after the collapse of the Soviet Union in 1991.

After the Yalta fiasco Truchanas and members of his family fled to West Germany (then under Allied occupation) where he gained admittance to a University to study law. However, rioting forced the Americans to close the University campus and the foreign students were sent to camps for displaced persons.

In 1948 he came to Australia under the Government Immigration scheme which called for him to undertake two years service in public works as directed. These two years he served with the Electrolytic Zinc Company, near Risdon, in Tasmania, in labouring work pushing trucks loaded with metal along old worn out rail lines. During this time his father, mother and sister had also arrived as migrants and the Truchanas clan was a family again.

Somewhere along the way he had developed quite remarkable photographic skills and, allied with his love of mountaineering, he began the exploration of the wilderness of his new land.

He had read an old 1928 newspaper account of an exploration of The Splits in the Gordon River, and this inspired him to build a special demountable kyak to attempt to ride the Serpentine River from Lake Pedder to the Gordon in 1954. He had almost reached the junction with the Gordon when he lost his kyak and most of his equipment, forcing him to abandon the venture.

In 1956 he married Melva Stocks, a keen member of the Launceston Walking Club, who he had met some five years earlier.

After building a house for his bride at West Hobart, he turned his thoughts again to the challenges of the Gordon River. This time he built a more substantial kyak and in 1957 succeeded in reaching The Splits area of the Gordon which had been explored by the 1928 expedition. But this only posed a greater challenge: could the Gordon be followed to the sea? In 1958 he succeeded in this seemingly impossible task with a new aluminium kyak and an ambitious and exhausting plan to climb a mountain with his kyak and heavy packs to avoid the treacherous Splits, finally making it to the convict remains of Macquarie Harbour, and down to Strachan. The first white man to undertake such a hazardous expedition.

In this period Truchanas was working for the Tasmanian Hydro-Electric Commission, and for several years he devoted his attentions to his growing family (two daughters and a son) and to general photography work in his spare time.

In 1965 he was dismayed by the announcement of the Tasmanian Government that the Lake Pedder National Park would be "modified". Dismay turned to disbelief and anger when in 1967 the plans for this 'modification' revealed that in fact Lake Pedder was to be obliterated with its famous beach submerged under fifty feet of water.

Another great personal tragedy engulfed him later that year when bushfires swept through eastern Tasmania destroying (amongst many others) the home he had built. Also destroyed was his precious collection of photographs and records so meticulously built up over almost two decades of exploring wilderness areas.

As a senior employee of the Hydro Commission, he could not publicly criticise their actions, but with fierce determination and energy he set about building up another collection of photographs of the vast Pedder, Franklin and Gordon areas to show the public what they were in danger of losing. And these photographs did provide the basis for the unsuccessful campaign to save Lake Pedder which raged for the next few years.

With the battle for Lake Pedder lost, Truchanas knew that it would only be a matter of time before the planners started to plot similar destruction of the next great untouched area of Tasmania's south west, the Lower Gordon, which he had explored and photographed back in 1958.

At the end of 1971 he applied for and secured a post he had dreamed about - the position of Senior Tutor in the School of Education and General Studies at the Tasmanian College of Advanced Education, to commence in the New Year. It was a position that not only would employ his talents and knowledge to the full, but would free him of restraints imposed by his job with the Hydro Commission.

He was due to start teaching in February, and decided to use the January holiday break to once again explore the Gordon and capture its rare beauty on film again.

He left on this final expedition on January 6 1972, but never did make it to the Splits and the Lower Gordon. In a relatively calm stretch of the Gordon, his kyak overturned and, while hauling it in, he slipped on a water-worn rock and vanished into the turbulent waters. Frantic searchers found his body three days later, thrown against a sunken tree. He had perished at last in the river he had fought for so long to save.

In one sense it might be said that Olegas Truchanas lost the battle for Lake Pedder, but in a broader sense he may have won the war because the magnificent photographs that he took in the years he spent exploring Tasmania's magnificent wilderness areas remain. They have now gained world wide circulation in such books as *The World of Olegas Truchanas,* published in 1975 by the Olegas Truchanas Publication Committee, Hobart, as a tribute to this great visitor to our shores.

Australia is much, much richer for his presence amongst us, and all Australians owe him an enormous debt for his efforts in showing us a glimpse of the Paradise still to be found in that troubled island which might well have been called Van Demons' Land.

7

The Early Settlements

There were few experiments of communes or settlements, secular or spiritual, in the first half century of white settlement of Australia, which is not surprising given that in this period the various outposts were under military control and governed by rules imposed from far off England.

The first privately organised settlement, which had communal overtones, was almost wholly planned and sponsored in London for Western Australia - the ill-fated Australind Settlement.

After the successful establishment of the Swan River Colony at Perth in 1829, much thought was given to opening up the country both north and south of the embryo settlement.

One of the early pioneers in this field was Colonel PA Lautour who had obtained a grant of 103,000 acres on the mouth of the Collie River, on the Leschenault estuary, some ninety miles south of Perth. Lautour had ideas for a private settlement scheme but was unable to get it up and running, and eventually his land, and adjoining lands granted to James Stirling, were acquired by the Western Australia Company, constituted in 1840.

Their plans for the new settlement in the Antipodes were very grand indeed. The whole scheme revolved around the establishment of a town to be called Australind, all properly laid out on 1000 acres with public buildings, schools, churches, parks, markets, hospitals and quays. Adjoining the town were to be 100 acre lots which would be sold to settlers. The idea was that the settlers would live in comfort in town supervising work to be carried out on the farms by hired labour. As there was no hired labour available at the time, or ever likely to be, the whole scheme was so crazy that it is incredible it ever got beyond the drawing board stage. But hope seems to spring eternal in human hearts seeking paradise at the end of distant rainbows and the company did enlist a considerable number of starters for this antipodean dream - families who parted with good money to buy from the company house blocks in the then non-existent Australind and farmlets in the surrounding countryside.

The first of these hopeful settlers departed from England on September 2 1840 on the Parkfield, a barque of 600 tons. On board were 125 souls, including captain and crew of 32. Among the travellers was Marshall Waller Clifton, whom the Western Australian Company had appointed as Chief Commissioner, to get the new settlement started. Clifton had with him his wife and eleven of his fourteen children.

Chief Commissioner Clifton put on a brave face to his small flock of hopefuls, but his private diary indicated that all was not well in the matter of supplies for this considerable undertaking on the other side of the world:

...From the slovenly manner in which the shipments of provisions, stores, implements and utensils had been conducted, the liberal intentions of the directors had been altogether frustrated: and, while I had positive knowledge that many of these indispensable articles had been left on the docks. I had, in fact, no certainty that the expedition was completely provided with a sufficiency of any of them... We even knew not whether our fishing nets and guns and powder, on which we were to depend for all means of support beyond the articles of salt, meat, and flour, were aboard, but we knew too

well that we had neither ploughs, horses, sheep nor cattle (excepting two cows), with us. No expedition so little calculated for the first formation of a colony had certainly ever left the shores of Britain; unarmed myself with either naval, military or civil authority, and not having any people with me who were under my command, I could only hope to obtain authority over them by acquiring during the voyage a moral influence sufficient to control them on landing.

On the voyage Chief Commissioner Clifton gave a series of lectures in which he outlined to his charges the rules and regulations which they would be expected to obey when they reached Australind. In the initial formation period they would work without wages but would be provided with the necessities of stores and supplies from the depot. The men would also form a private militia force to maintain order. The women were not left out of the scheme of things as they were to do the washing for the whole community with the settlers having to pay a suggested charge of sixpence per dozen items washed, this amount being paid into a general fund to buy soap and starch as needed.

The new settlers arrived at the site of Australind in April 1841 to find no grand buildings awaiting them - only lightly, wooded plains. On this they proceeded to hastily erect a store to house their provisions and supplies, and tents to house the settlers themselves. It was the beginning of a wet and bleak winter during which the settlers experienced much suffering but at least they had food from the store. Luckily for them, the natives in that part of Western Australia were not hostile though they didn't endear themselves to Chief Commissioner Clifton, who recorded in his diary: *A corroboree of natives at tea-time by the store which we all attended but it* was *degrading to human nature to see men in such a state of monkeyish action.*

When the original food supplies ran out the would-be settlers were in dire straits. No hired labour was available to work their "farms" as had been promised, and most of them had no farming experience back in England, and were ill-equipped to tackle the much more difficult Australian bush conditions. The land around the tiny settlement was still virgin bushland and remained in this condition for many years. Some settlers attempted to work their farms, but few made any progress. By 1843 the whole scheme collapsed when the Company withdrew financial support.

The majority of the original settlers drifted away, but Chief Commissioner Clifton stayed on and even built himself a stylish mansion, Upton House, which survives. Australind is now a small but popular seaside resort with only Upton House and a monument engraved with the original ambitious Town Plan marking the folly of the 1840's settlement. It does however, boast a unique tourist attraction, Australia's smallest church, St Nicholas Church (size 8.2 metres by 3.6 metres) converted from an old workman's cottage in 1848. Cramped Sunday services are still held there.

Although Australind was a private enterprise, entered into with the blessings of officialdom, a whole string of Governments failed to take the lessons of the experiment to heart; ignoring history and using taxpayers' money, engaging in various ill-conceived and ill-executed settlement schemes.

The last major scheme to attract this tag occurred in the 1920's when the then Western Australian government brought some 6000 Britons out to settle on dairy farms in the south west corner of the state. As the vast majority of these new settlers had no rural skills to offer, they found that the misleading government promises of a land of milk and honey turned sour, providing little milk and no honey. Only an estimated 300 settlers of the 6000 recruited for this scheme survived to tell the tale.

And this experience has been matched by government

sponsored settlement schemes in almost every Australian state, with some notable failures in Queensland and South Australia.

8

Communes

Commune: Any community of like-minded people choosing to live independently of the state, often cherishing ideals differing from those held in the state: Hippy Commune.

MACQUARIE DICTIONARY

As communes, large and small, ancient and modern, will feature quite a lot in this work, perhaps it would be wise to look at the origins and meaning of the word, and take a quick look at such groups in general.

The word commune derives from Medieval Latin Cunununia (things held in common) and came into general use in France as Commoner, a term for what we generally define as Local Government, an assembly of villagers or others united by common interest. It was a sop thrown by the Barons to their serfs to keep them quiet.

Lloyd's Dictionary of 1895 summed it up very neatly thus: *The commanality as opposed to the Nobility.*

The system was later adopted by Switzerland and Italy.

It gained new meaning and notoriety in the French Revolution when the Paris Commune was formed to rule, and later terrorise the city.

It passed into the English language unchanged when Robert Owen published his *New View of Society* in 1813. Owen attempted to found a commune on the banks of the Wabash in 1825, but it failed, as did subsequent communal attempts at Orbiston (1827) and at "Harmony Hall" in Lanarkshire in 1843. After that Owen. gave up the search for a personal Utopia. Many years on, Fydor Dostoyeveski was to pertinently note:

All the Utopias will come to pass only when we grow wings and all the people are converted into angels.

One important point to note is that communes fall into several quite distinct categories which may be summarised as follows:

A: Groups of people living together in a herd situation for common protection and food gathering without any sense of personal property or possessions.

B: Communes organised on communist principles with all property and assets held in common.

C: Communes based on common interest and co-operative principles but allowing individual ownership of goods or property.

There is a further division of all the above three types of communes between those established on a purely secular (or self-interest) basis and those with what I call a spiritual (or religious) basis, though in some cases there may be a mix of secular and spiritual motives.

When the ancient ancestors of Homo sapiens decided to come down from the trees to explore the open savannas of Africa for a better style of living they brought their communal system with them to their new cave-based method of living.

The original lifestyle of Australian aboriginals prior to and for a long period after white invasion of 1788 was also purely Type A communal, as were (and are) most nomadic groups.

What kept these groups together over such great spans of time was the sheer necessity of staying and working in tandem to survive, particularly in times of food shortages and adverse climatic conditions.

Most monasteries and nunneries of various religions have organised themselves along purely communist (Type B) lines for centuries, even the modern ones who fiercely oppose state communist systems.

The many religious communes which sprang up in the United States of America in the 19th Century, and which continue to proliferate there even in this modern secular age, have purely communistic systems of one kind or another.

Likewise, all the Australian communes from the 19th Century rural settlements and co-operatives to the modern "Hippie", communes have organised themselves on (B) or (C) systems. In doing so all seem to be responding to some primeval urge to get back to basics - to Cave Men style living - taking some modern amenities with them to soften the physical pain involved in such changes of living style.

Modern Paradise seekers who form communes fall back on written rules, often of a complex and unrealistic nature, in place of the missing glue factor. And these seldom work, at least not in Australia where individualist attitudes are deeply embedded in the national psyche, and where the average Australian. has a deep aversion to rules and regulations of all kinds.

("Rules are made to be broken, aren't they", is almost a national war cry).

The history of Australian communes is littered with examples of schemes that fell apart under the weight of ill-conceived rules. The best examples are those where organisers of a commune have attempted to impose their own narrow religious beliefs or moral standards on their followers. William Lane's socialist colonies in Paraguay (covered in a separate chapter) foundered on one unrealistic rule - total prohibition of liquor.

Most compilers of such rules act as though all men are

equal and will respond the same way in all circumstances. But, as the Chief Pig in George Orwell's *Animal Farm* put it so succinctly: *All pigs are equal but some are more equal than others.*

The real sticking point in most communal experiments is in its input and output. That is the amount of energy each member is supposed to contribute, and the sharing up of any dividends that may accrue to combined energy input of members; "I'm working harder than he is" and "I deserve more than that lazy bastard" seem to be cries ringing out around Australian communes for a century or more. And so far as I can determine, no set of commune *rules* has managed to solve this basic communal whinge.

Perhaps the compilers of these rules would have more success if their heeded the words of the 16th Century philosopher Michel Eyquem Montaigne:

I*t is noteworthy that among nations where the laws regulating propriety are fewer and more elastic, the fundamental laws of common sense are better observed.*

A large number of Australian communes have foundered on the false idea that the seeker after Paradise prefers freedom to possessions. The records of failed communal experiments are quite overwhelming on this point.

Many of the pure communistic (no ownership) communes only managed to survive by changing over to co-operative structures which permitted the participants to buy their own little plots of land to become the mini capitalists they previously despised. Homo sapiens it seems has not only developed a territorial imperative, but he seeks to own his piece of turf as well as dominate it.

Any commune which operates otherwise would seem to be heading for extinction in this consumer driven age.

9

New Italy

Back in the 1879-80 period four shiploads of (mainly) French and Italian peasant men, women and children sailed from Europe to establish what they thought would be a South Seas Island Paradise only to find they had sailed quite literally into the Jaws of Hell. Many perished, before the remnants were rescued and taken to Australia where most of the Italian survivors established their own (second grade!) Paradise and called it New Italy.

The victims of this ill-fated South Seas Bubble venture owed their plight to one man, Charles Bonaventure du Breil, the Marquis de Rays, descendant of a long line of French noblemen who traced their line as Signeurs back to the fourteenth century.

In the French Revolution the then Marquis de Rays was forced to leave his native Brittany for Holland, and then England. After the Restoration the family returned to France only to find their beautiful castle sacked and in such decrepit condition that it had to be razed. But the family made a partial recovery and it was left to young Charles Bonaventure du Breil, born in 1832, to try and restore the family name to the position it held before the Revolution. Alas, he failed quite signally to do so, and ended up bringing considerable shame and disgrace to the family. When he was twenty he set out to conquer the world but only succeeded in leaving in his wake a trail of failed ventures: ranching in America, a venture into commerce in Senegal, and attempts to found colonies in Madagascar and Indo-China. It seems that he was the eternal dreamer, seldom an achiever.

Back in France in his late thirties, married and with time on his hands, his thoughts again turned to wild dreams of establishing an empire in some part of the world where as overlord he could exercise power to live up to his family's motto:

I spare the week I humble the mighty.

The problem was to find a place to do all this sparing and humbling as by that time there weren't that many vacant bits of land around the globe given the wild stampede of European nations to found empires after Christopher Columbus discovered the Americas in 1492.

For months and years the Marquis pored over maps, charts and travellers' tales in search of a suitable place to found an outpost of Empire in the name of France. Initially he favoured the north-west part of Australia, which we today know as the Kimberleys, but then virtually a wilderness area. However, enquiries showed that the British would take unkindly to any attempt at a French settlement in this part of its far flung empire.

Finally his focus settled on Port Praslin at the southern tip of the island of New Ireland, mainly because Commander Duperry, making a brief visit there in command of the Coquille in 1823, had described it as a veritable Eden.

His decision made, the Marquis de Ray, proceeded to proclaim in the name of France the annexation of New Ireland, New Britain, portion of New Guinea, the Solomon Islands and all adjacent islands, which henceforth would be known as La Nouvelle France (New France). The declaration attracted little attention in France at the time because the nation was only just recovering from the excesses of a minor civil war (1871) during which some 17,000 Communards perished and another 13,000 were exiled to the convict colony of New Caledonia.

In the next two years the Marquis devoted all his energies to getting his grandiose scheme of a private Empire off the ground, his opening shot being an advertisement in the July 26 1877 issue of *Le Petit Journal* offering land at two francs an acre at the Free Colony of Port Breton. The advertisement had a nice carrot for investors "Fortune rapid and assured without leaving one's country".

He followed this up with meetings in various French cities at which he outlined his plans for La Nouvelle France, a colony to be run by a mutual society to handle the general management of the new colony. His detailed plan for the settlement had three tiers to it:

1. At the top of the heap were the stay-at-home investors who would put up the finance for the operation and would reap huge profits and would be given titles according to the size of their contribution; ie. those who purchased twelve square mile acreages became aristocrats first class (dukes or marquis), those who only purchased six square mile holdings became aristocrats second class (the French equivalent of Earls, viscounts or barons).

2. Agricultural labourers, who were required to pay a thousand francs per family, would receive passage to the colony, a house and land and rations for five years until they became settled, after which they would own the land and house.

3. Workers would be brought in from China, the Dutch East Indies and other places on short term contracts to do the hard work.

Missionaries would accompany the expedition to tame and convert the natives who were said to be friendly!

At the head of this great enterprise, of course, was the

self-proclaimed first King of La Nouvelle France, King Charles 1, the Marquis himself.

The Marquis de Ray's family name, some expensive advertising and the turbulent political times were enough to confirm Barnum's famous dictum that there is a fool born every minute, and in no time the Marquis had 3000 subscribers to the Society and funds estimated at half a million pounds sterling - a vast sum in those days.

He purchased a vessel, the Chandernagore, at the Havre, but had a major setback when the French Government, who had opposed the crazy settlement scheme from the start, stepped in and forbad the manning of the ship. The Marquis found himself with a ship but no crew. He managed to assemble an illegal crew and slipped away to Belgium which he thought might be more friendly. This was not so and they threatened to seize the ship so he took it on to Flushing in Holland, from whence it finally departed with a new rag-tag crew at 3am on September 14 1879, with 150 colonists. A multicultural mix of French, German, Italian, Belgian and Polish would-be settlers and searchers of Paradise.

At Madeira the ship was quarantined, but managed to defeat this by again slipping out of port in the early hours of the morning. After a four months nightmare journey the ship finally arrived at Port Praslin (then renamed Port Breton) on January 16 1880. That's when their troubles REALLY started.

Port Breton proved to be an attractive tiny bay backed by rocky cliffs and a high mountain range, totally unsuited for any type of settlement. Some hardy colonists went ashore and attempted to establish a foothold on the only tiny strip of arable land. The majority wisely refused to disembark.

On the night of January 30 a fierce storm blew up and the Chandernagore hastily headed for open sea and anchored at a place they named Liki-Liki, some twelve miles to the north-east of Port Breton. Aided by natives, the few settlers who had been left behind, managed to re-unite with their fellow colonists by making an exhausting overland trek through dense bush which left them with bleeding hands and feet, more dead than alive. At Liki-Liki the settlers acquired 50 acres of land from the natives for a string of beads. They built a blockhouse but had no luck in attempts to cultivate vegetables or crops on the sand and mud flats on the place.

They decided to re-board the Chandernagore and seek a more hospitable area for settlement, but Captain Seykus had other ideas and greeted them at revolver point, refusing them permission to embark. On the morning of February 20 1880 the stranded settlers awoke to find that their ship once again had stolen away in the night. Their position was desperate as they had only 3 weeks supplies of food. A group set out to try and reach a Mission Station at Port Hunter on the other side of New Ireland, but most perished on the way and only three made it to the mission. In the meantime an island trading vessel happened to call at Liki-Liki and seeing the plight of the settlers, alerted 2 missionaries on the nearby Duke of York Island. The missionaries managed to rescue the 20 survivors, then reduced to mere walking skeletons, in their vessel the Ripple. The Missionaries were in no position to support such a large group, and most went back to Liki-Liki with the HMS Conflict which gave them fresh supplies, but when these ran out they took to foraging in the jungle for food and simply disappeared. Of 5 who managed to make it to Buka in a small boat, 4 were eaten by cannibals, and the sole survivor was demented when later rescued.

Meanwhile the Marquis de Ray, having found the French, Belgian and Dutch Governments so hostile, moved his headquarters to Barcelona from where he organised his second expedition on the Genil, a 350 ton vessel flying the Liberian flag, followed closely by a third expedition vessel India, an old sailing vessel fitted with an engine, which departed from Barcelona on July 7 1880 with a crew and 350 colonists. News of the disasterous first expedition had not filtered back to Europe.

Both the Genil and India arrived about the same time at the New Ireland beach of Port Breton below the towering 2500 feet high Mount Vernon. The Doctor on the India, Dr Goyon, immediately saw that this was an unhealthy place, but the ship captains refused his pleas to seek a more suitable site. Both were afraid to override the instructions of the Marquis de Ray (King Charles I) who had personally chosen this spot on his atlas from the safety of his study at the other side of the world.

The results were entirely predictable. In addition to the appalling climate with its many tropical diseases, the area was populated with fierce cannibal tribes. By the end of November the small colony was so decimated by fevers, dysentery and malaria that Captain le Prevost was dispatched in the Genil to try and get supplies of food and medicine from Sydney, where the Marquis had established his Pacific base. In charge of the Society of Farmers General in Sydney was Monsieur Henri Niau, who with his wife and small daughter Josephine, had travelled to Sydney direct on an English vessel, and who knew nothing of the tragedies which had occurred at Port Breton and Liki-Liki. Monsieur Niau immediately organised a relief party with supplies of food and medicines and with a new captain on the Genil (Captain le Prevost having suddenly claimed to have heart trouble) the ship sailed from Sydney on February 2 1881, only to have its boiler burst after a week on its journey north. It made it to Maryborough under sail, and weeks were lost in repair.

When they reached their destination they found the settlement deserted except for a few emaciated dogs. Of the colonists and the India there was no sign.

After waiting 125 days for the Genil to return, Captain

Robardy, who was in charge of the settlement, made the decision to abandon the settlement because of escalating deaths and an acute shortage of food. He embarked all the survivors and headed for Noumea in New Caledonia where the authorities refused to let the India proceed further because of its unseaworthiness. Learning of the plight of the (mainly) Italian passengers stranded at Noumea, the New South Wales Premier Sir Henry Parkes sent a steamer, the James Patterson to bring them to Sydney. To cover the cost of the rescue mission the Government took a bill of sale over the stricken India and it was auctioned at Noumea for the bargain basement price of 35,000 francs (about 1500 pounds, or a quarter of its original cost.)

The James Patterson arrived in Sydney on April 7 1881 with the 200 surviving members of the Marquis de Rays ill-fated expeditions. The deathroll of the Lambourn settlement was 46 men, women and children.

And on the very same day, April 7 1881, the fourth and final Marquis de Ray expedition left Barcelona on the Nouvelle Bretagne with its crew of thirty and another 200 colonists totally unaware of the fate of the those sent on the first three expeditions, though the Marquis himself was briefed on the facts as a result of cables sent from his agents in Sydney.

At Colombo , Ceylon, (now Sri Lanka) the Captain of the Nouvelle Bretagne, Captain Henry, received a long cable from the Marquis de Ray advising that the Port Breton settlement was abandoned and advised him to seek another place on New Ireland to land his passengers. The astute Captain Henry suspected a large size rodent in the whole adventure and tried to persuade the colonists to abandon ship at Singapore, even then a thriving port, and seek suitable employment. The colonists refused point blank to adopt the Captain's suggestion, believing he was only trying to deprive them of the land they had already paid for on New Ireland.

The Captain gave in to the wishes of the colonists, and in Singapore purchased a small back-up supply ship, the Nettie Merriman, which he re-named Marquis de Rays, and the small fleet of two set off for Port Breton.

Arriving at that infamous hell-hole they found awaiting at anchor the Genil, which had returned from its Sydney rescue mission only to find the settlement deserted. When Captain Robardy of the Genil came aboard, the news he had of the first three expeditions shattered the would-be colonists. Before their eyes was the proof in the shape of a few huts and abandoned gardens, along with the crosses marking the graves of the many victims who came before them. As Captain Robardy was reluctant to abandon Port Breton, a meeting of settlers decided that Captain Henry would take those wishing to abandon the adventure to Manila, and return within 3 months with fresh supplies, when a final decision would be made about staying on at Port Breton or seeking another site along the New Ireland coastline.

While Captain Henry sailed off on his mission, Captain Robardy remained behind in the new settlement of Port Breton, soon revealing himself as a despot. He insisted that all the colonists go ashore and make do the best they could while he remained safely aboard the Gentil, refusing at gunpoint any attempt by a settler to board the ship.

When Captain Henry reached Manila he expected to find awaiting the sum of 8000 pounds, being 4 monthly payments that the Marquis de Ray had pledged to meet the needs of the colonists. Instead, only 1000 pounds was there, insufficient to pay the debts already incurred. He sent urgent cables to the Marquis in Barcelona, explaining the plight of the latest expedition and in return the Marquis promised to cable 6000 pounds.

Acting on this, Captain Henry provisioned the ship. The

promised money never came. The ship's agents in Barcelona, sent a cable stating that no money was available and instructing him to return all supplies and, if necessary sell the ship. Word of this spread in Manila and the authorities placed an embargo on the Nouvelle Bretagne and seized the boiler for good measure.

On December 10 a cyclone appeared to save the Captain. Fearing they might embroil Spain with a foreign power if they left the ship to the elements, port authorities returned the boiler, but put 6 soldiers on board to guard it. Captain Henry fed the guards with a rich supper and much wine and when they were hopelessly drunk, sailed out of the harbour into the teeth of the cyclone, thus committing an act of piracy.

He put the sailors ashore at Isle Panay, then hastened back to Port Breton with all his unpaid-for provisions and medicines, well aware that the Spaniards would send a warship after him. His arrival back at Port Breton was greeted at first with great joy by the rapidly dwindling numbers of unhappy settlers, only to be tempered by despair when they realised the respite was only temporary. On January 12 1882 the Spanish warship, the Legaspi, cast anchor at Port Breton and took Captain Henry prisoner. When he saw the condition of the colony, the Commander of the Legaspi agreed to take on board 60 desperately ill colonists plus the crew of the Gentil (except the cook) who sought to escape from the the crazed Captain Robardy. Many of the colonists died on the voyage back to Manila.

In Manila the Governor Don Primo de River was determined to make an example of Captain Henry, all to no avail as successive courts proved very unwilling to convict. Eventually Henry was freed and continued a successful maritime career well away from the Marquis de Ray. The Nouvelle Bretagne was sold to meet the demands of the Manila merchants and that strand of the Marquis' operations was brought to a close.

Back at Port Breton the tiny colony continued to

disintegrate due to fevers and other tropical diseases until mid-February 1882 when the remnants of the tragic fourth expedition were moved on the Gentil to Makeo. Captain Robardy, realising at last the game was up, took his own life.

With a new crew and skipper, Captain Boore; the Gentil slipped out of Makeo for what was to be a thirteen day voyage. After a mishap with a reef off Cooktown, it reached Cairns, where its desperately ill passengers and ship were patched up. They continued down the coast to Sydney, where the ship was immediately seized at the order of 2 Frenchmen who held mortgages over it. The colonists were allowed ashore, most of them destitute, and were helped to find work by their fellow nationals.

The collapse of all 4 expeditions to New France - the Great South Seas Bubble - as the press of the day called it, caused enormous scandal in France, Italy and other countries whose nationals had so cruelly been deprived of their fortunes and often their lives.

There was a general baying for blood, of Marquis de Ray in particular and in July 1882 he was extradited from Spain and imprisoned at Mazas, France, on charges of homicide through criminal imprudence.

When finally brought to trial in March 1883, the Marquis tried to talk his way out of trouble by putting all the blame on incompetent or criminal subordinates. He had few explanations though for the fact that of the estimated 200,000 pounds subscribed to his schemes, no less than 80,000 pounds had found their way into his own pockets mainly for high living and expensive gifts for his wife and his two mistresses.

He was found guilty and given a sentence of 4 years imprisonment, on top of the 2 years he had spent in custody, and a modest fine of 3000 francs. He appealed against the sentence but lost. On release from prison he embarked on a new enterprise conducting passengers on luxury cruises, including an around the world cruise in the Tyburnia. This venture also ended in disaster due to his extravagence and on July 29 1893, the Marquis de Ray died as he had lived, in debt, no doubt untroubled by the ruin he had brought to so many who believed his promises of Paradise.

Of the 4 expeditions of the Marquis de Ray, 230 survivors eventually found their way to Sydney in the 1881-2 period. Did any of them find the paradise that eluded them on the island of New Britain? Some of the survivors found their way back to their native lands, while many others dispersed widely around Australia,. Little is known of the ultimate fate of this very mixed bag of unwilling migrants.

However, we do know a fair bit about one particular group of Italians from the South Seas Bubble scam because they started a small colony in Australia which they named New Italy.

There is a fairly widespread impression in the Northern Districts of New South Wales that the New Italy Colony, as it was often referred to, was the initiative of the Government of the day, but this was not so. It is true that when the two hundred survivors reached Sydney in April 1881 there was considerable public discussion on settling this unexpected influx of migrants.

Since they were almost all people with agricultural backgrounds and skills in their original countries, suggestions were made that the Government should initiate some land settlement scheme. The Premier, Sir Henry Parkes, backed away from this proposal probably fearing that he would attract the same unfavourable publicity then being accorded the Marquis de Ray if any settlement venture were to fail. Very little Government assistance came their way after they landed and it was left to the respective consulates and fellow countrymen to find them refuge and jobs.

But most of them yearned for a piece of land to till. After

all it was what attracted them to the Marquis de Ray scheme in the first place, and their terrible experiences in New Britain did not dampen their feelings for the land. In April 1882 one Rocco Comminitti reported that he had found a vast tract of land between the Richmond and Clarence Rivers available at only a pound an acre, and that he had taken up a holding of 40 acres.

This was fairly heavily timbered land in the parishes of Donaldson, Bungawalbyn and Evans, in the county of Richmond, south from the small settlement of Woodburn. Early settlers in the district had considered the soils in this area too poor for traditional farming, and the tracts had only been used for timber cutting purposes. Comminitti had come from a wine growing area of Italy, and believed the soils in the Richmond area were very similar to those of his home country, and therefore would be suitable for viticulture.

He was joined by other survivors of the New France who had similar backgrounds in Italy. They too shared Comminitti's opinions of the soil and quickly took up adjoining selections of land. In the year 1882 nine other survivors joined Comminitti, each taking up selections ranging from 40 to 90 acres. They were: Pietro Mazzer, Antonio Melare, Guiseppe Martinuzzi, Antonio Nardi, Giovanni Rusolen, Antonio Pezzuti, Phillippe Palis, Angelo Rodero and Dominic Spinaze.

News of New Italy quickly spread among the other stranded families who flocked to join them in the next few years. In 1883 a further 1000 acres were taken up by new or old settlers: Liugi Antonelli, Maria Batistuzzi, Giovanni Batistuzzi, Antonio Bazzuzza, Natali Fava, Maria Gava, Angelo Nardi, Agoin Pelizier, Antonio Piccoli, Giacomo Piccoli, Nicholas Pezzuti, Francesa Rodero, Giovanni Rodero, Lorenzo Spinaze and Michel Scavrabellotto. There was a slowing down on expansion of the settlement in succeeding years but the following selections were recorded. For 1884: Giovani Bertoli, Aadrian Palis, Lorenzo

Roder, Giovani Spinaze, Guiseppe Tedesco. In 1885 Giovani Batistuzzi expanded his original holding and in 1886 there were more expansions by Giovanni Bertoli and by the three Roder brothers Giovanni, Lorenzo and Candido. Additions in 1887 were Cathernia Comminitti, Dominico Merandini and Antonio Melaro, while to July 1888 the following new land holdings were recorded: Antonio Resolen, Giacomo Martinuzzi, Guiseppe Martinuzzi, Peter Resolen, Antonio Morandi and Pietro Sanot. Up to that point, the peak of the settlement the total expanse of the New Italy colony was 3030 acres.

The early settlers all planted grape vines, which flourished and New Italy rapidly gained the reputation of being a progressive wine producing area. The settlers also planted a wide variety of vegetables for their own consumption, the main crop here being sweet potatoes, as well as maize and other cereals and experimental crops of tobacco.

From the beginning the settlers relied heavily on outside work to supplement the income from the products they were able to grow and sell, usually timber cutting, seasonal cane cutting and other farm work.

By 1887 the population of New Italy was 202 comprising 34 married males, 35 married females, 22 single males, 8 single females and 103 children under the age of 16. More than 20 of these families were from the James Paterson arrivals of 1881, supplemented by other Italian families attracted by the idea of farming alongside their own countrymen.

In the period 1884-7 Frederick Chudleigh Clifford of Coraki made a number of visits to New Italy and compiled extensive reports on the soil, native timbers and progress of the settlement for the New South Wales Department of Agriculture. His report was published by the Department in 1889 under the ponderous title of *NEW ITALY: A Brief Sketch of a New and Thriving Colony Founded and Established by the Italian Immigrants who were Sufferers by the Marquis De Ray's New Ireland Colonisation Scheme.*

Clifford noted that until Rocca Comminitti appeared on the scene in April 1882 the area was:

comparatively a howling wilderness, sacred to the timber getter and the dingo, and the land thereabouts generally being described as not fit to keep a bandicoot.

He found an extensive range of timber located along the western boundary of the New Italy colony running right through to the Clarence River, heavily populated with ironbark, mahogany, spotted gum, oak, tallow-wood, pine, beech, teak and stringy-bark. Clifford heaped great praise on the New Italy settlers for their industry and initiatives and high moral standards, noting: *So healthy is the climate of New Italy, and so frugal and abstemious are the people, that a doctor would starve there.*

He also predicted that within another decade the colony might grow to a thousand souls, given the success of the venture to date and the fecundity of the settlers (20 babies were born in the settlement in 1888).

As timber was so plentiful, the settlers built themselves wooden houses, and a Roman Catholic church. By 1887 they had a school and teacher's residence supplied by the state, and at the entrance to colony on the Woodburn Road, there was erected a substantial two storey pise (rammed earth) building for Luigi Antonelli's wine bar and guest house - for many years the communal meeting place. It must have seemed to the survivors of the Port Breton tragedy that at last they had found their little corner of paradise, but changing economic conditions were against them and gradually New Italy faded away. Younger members drifted away to larger centres and more productive lands along the Richmond and Tweed rivers; a trend hastened by the loss of young men in World War 1 (when Italy was on side of the Allies) and by the onset of Great Depression in 1929.

When Josephine Hyacinthe Niau, daughter of Henry Niau, who in 1881 had journeyed from Sydney to Port Breton to try and rescue the stranded settlers, visited New Italy in 1933, the Great Depression had taken a grim toll on the community and only 3 families remained in the colony. Only half a dozen houses remained standing in the once-thriving settlement.

Mme Niau, wrote a book about the Marquis de Ray's expeditions and her family's involvement, *The Phantom Paradise*, published in 1936. In 1945 I was sub editor of the *Northern Star* newspaper in Lismore and was given a copy of Mme Niau's book by the grandson of one of the original New Italy settlers. I learned from him that an old man Giacomo Piccoli - who had come to the colony as a child more than 60 years earlier – was still living on the old settlement.

My journalistic instincts were immediately aroused and I was determined to make a visit to New Italy to interview him. War-time transport was restricted and I did not possess a car - even if petrol had been available for such an enterprise so one Sunday morning I caught a bus from Lismore to Woodburn, with my bicycle on a rack at the back of the bus. There I unhitched the bicycle and rode the six miles to New Italy.

It wasn't difficult to find as a bedraggled sign stood at the track into the old colony. Not far behind the sign were the remnants of the old rammed earth wine bar building.

A small search located the old school and schoolmaster's building where the last schoolmaster, Mr Davies, had been allowed to stay on after the school closed in the 1930's. He directed me to Giacomo Piccoli who was a bit astonished to find a journalist on his doorstep seeking an interview.

Then well into his seventies (he declined to reveal his exact age), he had embarked at Barcelona with his parents on the decrepit old ship India on July 7 1880 on the third of the

Marquis de Ray expeditions. As a child he had vivid recollections of the Marquis de Ray ("a fat handsome man") coming aboard before the sailing to farewell the colonists.

In his long life he had made 3 trips around the world, each time returning to New Italy. He strongly rejected the idea that New Italy was an Eden that had failed, and was certain that it would be revitalised after the war. He pointed to a stand of towering spotted gums, remarking that no trees would grow like that on poor soil.

Giacomo Piccoli showed me his Park of Peace - in 1937 he had dedicated 55 acres of his land on the 55th Anniversary of the settlement of New Italy and planted 63 trees, each one commemorating some person or event associated with the colony. Picolli insisted that I sample one of his fine wines and impressed me with his enthusiasm and vigour, and the way he went about tending his vines, his poultry and his silkworms with which he had carried off high honours at district Agricultural Shows.

Giacomo Piccoli was to live another 10 years, although I was not to know it that day as I shook hands with him and cycled off to catch the afternoon bus back to Lismore. I thought that at last I had found an individual, well satisfied with his long life and still holding firm to the belief that he had found his own little piece of earthly paradise.

And what more of life could you want than that?

10

The Paraguay Colonies

The most publicised and criticised settlement experiments of the 19th Century were William Lane's two Utopian Socialist Colonies in the South American Republic of Paraguay, the New Australia settlement and its later rival Cosme.

William Lane was born in Bristol, England on September 6 1861, the eldest of five children born to James Lane, an Irish Protestant, and his wife Caroline. James Lane was a landscape gardener who at one time employed twenty men, but his business foundered because of his intemperate drinking habits. The fall in the family fortunes made such an impression on the young Lane that he became a lifelong temperance advocate, a stance that led to the collapse of his Paraguayan ventures.

William Lane was lame in one leg, possibly due to polio, but this did not hold him back, as he was a brilliant student at the Bristol Grammar School. At the age of 16 he left home and worked his way on a ship to Canada as a cabin boy.

He found work on a newspaper as a printer's devil and progressed to linotype operator and then to journalist on several Canadian and American newspapers.

In 1884 at the age of 24, he met and married Anne McQuire, who was working on the same newspaper in Detroit.

In 1885 the couple returned to her native England with their newborn daughter, only to find that Will's younger brother

John was about to migrate to Australia to join two other brothers, Frank and Ernest. Lane decided to take his wife and child with John Lane on his adventure to the Antipodes.

Will Lane's term as a journalist had politicised him, and on his arrival in Brisbane he wrote socialist orientated articles for the *Courier Mail* and the *Observer*. He played a leading role in the formation of the Brisbane Trades and Labour Council, editing and partly funding a radical weekly journal in 1887 called *The Boomerang*. In that year he also founded the Bellamy Society, based on the Utopian ideas of the American, Edward Bellamy.

This period was a time of great political and social unrest in Australia, particularly in Queensland where there was considerable unemployment, arising out of a prolonged drought, a collapse in the Victorian land boom and failure of the banks.

Lane played a dominant role in the formation of the Australasian Labour Federation in 1889, a body created with the aim of achieving state socialism. The following year he founded *The Worker*, a Queensland Labour newspaper with the motto *Socialism in our time*.

Lane had began floating the idea of promoting a Utopian Socialist Colony in north or south America around this time. Such ideas weren't exactly novel, as numerous experiements had tried and failed since the 1850s. He was attracted to two North American colonies as models for his own. The first was the Utopian colony of Icaria which the French radical Etienne Cabet had founded in northern Texas in 1848, where the 280 settlers had experienced a year of great hardship before moving to Nauvoo, in Illinios. Here Cabet's dictatorial style caused such dissension that he was forced out of the colony in 1856, and the project subsequently collapsed. Had Lane studied this experiment a little more carefully, he might have learned some useful lessons in leadership of Utopian colonies.

Lane's other example for guidance was the Topolobampo Communal Settlement recently established in 1886 in the north west corner of Mexico by an American engineer named Albert Kimsey Owen. When Lane contacted Owen seeking details of the colony, it had a population of 400 at Topolobampo Bay and 5000 subscribers scattered throughout the United States and Canada.

It operated on a system of credits instead of money and Owen reported that the experiment was going well. Alas, his optimism was somewhat misplaced as within a few years Topolobampo was also destined to disappear in to that great Black Hole of Utopian dreams.

Whilst Lane found many followers sympathetic to the concept a of such a colony, few were interested in following Lane or anyone else into any overseas wildness. Most advised him to find some place in Australia to realise his dreams, but this was not easy to achieve as by 1890 most of the good lands had been snapped up at the usual going rate of a pound an acre for workable Crown Lands.

Frustrated in his search for suitable Australian lands, Lane in 1892 formed the New Australia Co-operative Settlement Association, which dispatched Alfred Walker, the former business manager of *The Boomerang*, to South America to open negotiations with the Argentine Government on the possibility of establishing a settlement.

In the same year Lane published his novel *The Working Man's Paradise* under the pseudonym of John Miller, devoting the proceeds from the book to a fund to help shearers imprisoned as a result of the prolonged strikes of 1890-l.

Today the novel reads as fairly amateurish propaganda, but it fitted the mood of the times and was widely read, not the least by militants trying to identify themselves and their friends in the various characters assigned by Lane.

The character of Arty, the "people's poet" in the book, was clearly Henry Lawson, a good friend of Lane. It was Lane who had published Lawson's first contribution to *The Worker*, 'Freedom on the Wallaby' with its provocative lines:

> *So we must fly a rebel flag*
> *As others did before us -*
> *They needn't say the fault is ours*
> *If blood should stain the wattle.*

The novel's hero Ned was clearly David Russell Stevenson, a bushman who accompanied Lane to Paraguay, but some of the other characters were more difficult to identify. Rumours abounded that the heroine Nellie was modelled on another of Lane's close friends, Mary Cameron (later Mary Gilmore) then a Brisbane schoolteacher. It was quite a few years before Mary Gilmore publicly "outed" herself as Nellie, adding that every incident, every person and every conversation in the book was real.

As Alfred Walker was not making any progress in Argentina, Lane arranged for two prospectors, William Saunders and Charles Leek, to scout for land in South America. They looked at land in Patagonia, but it was too windswept and barren. When they returned to Buenos Aires they found that Walker had received some favourable correspondence from the Government of Paraguay, a small land-locked republic bounded by Argentina, Bolivia and Brazil. A sub-tropical country about half the size of New South Wales, located almost in the centre of the South American continent, it had achieved independence from the original Spanish conquerors, but was a backward, impoverished country wracked by corruption. It had barely recovered from the disastrous Chaco war against an alliance of Brazil, Argentina and Uruguay whereby its population had been reduced from 800,000 to 250,000 of which only 14,000 were men.

The Chaco War had been fought from 1865 to 1870, and successive governments realised that recovery could only come through outside help in money and manpower. In 1881 they passed a law authorising the formation of agricultural colonies and the right to cede lands to private companies, but there was little interest from the outside world apart from two relatively small groups in Germany. The first of these was a Socialist Utopian group from Berlin who settled themselves on the shores of Lake Ypacarai.

This was followed in 1887 by another group of German Socialists led by Dr Bernard Foerster and his wife Elizabeth, sister of the German philosopher Friedrich Nietsche. They established a colony called Nueva Germania in the north-eastern corner of Paraguay and in a foretaste of German things to come, proclaimed itself to be an Aryan colony "uncontaminated by Jews".

Both these colonies eventually abandoned the Socialist principles and faded from the history books.

When Saunders and Leek ventured up to Asuncion, the capital of Paraguay in 1892, they were greeted with open arms by the Government, anxious to make available to them vast tracts of arable land on the most favourable terms.

Saunders and Leek couldn't believe their luck and quickly travelled up on Paraguay's only railway line to Villarica, located 110 miles south-east of Ascunsion. Here they inspected the. promised land which comprised forty square leagues (185,240 acres) of well-watered land only fifteen miles from the railway line.

After returning to Asuncion, they communicated the news to Walker in Buenos Aires. Walker cabled the information to Lane in Australia, and this was followed up by a 4000 word report on the land, climatic conditions, and political situation in Paraguay - information which was not entirely correct.

While Saunders returned to Australia, Walker joined Leek in Asuncion and started negotiations with the Paraguay Government for even better and more land than that offered, who reserved for the Association a total of 100 leagues (463,000 acres) of unoccupied land, surveyed and free of all charges. The Association in return was to agree to settle 1200 families within six years. It would receive half the land immediately and when it had established 600 families, would receive the other 50 leagues. As a bonus the Government offered to provide all the settlers with free rail transport from Asuncion to the site, and would exempt the colony from property tax for ten years.

Governments don't make offers like that any more! Back in Brisbane Lane was convinced that at last his dream of a Socialist Utopia was near to fruition.

Lane set about the task of organising the venture with enormous zeal and energy, mainly utilising the pages of a small newspaper *New Australia*, which he had launched in November 1892. Funds for the enterprise came mainly from subscribers to the association. Each subscriber paid an initial ten pounds, with an additional fifty pounds to be paid if they were actually going to Paraguay. Lane himself put up one thousand pounds and quite a few of the more enthusiastic supporters of the proposal donated much more than nominal fees, some even selling up their houses and donating the proceeds.

Total subscriptions were claimed to be around thirty thousand pounds, and with these funds the Association purchased (for thirteen hundred and fifty pounds) a 598-ton sailing ship the Royal Tar. She had been built as a freighter, not a passenger ship, so alterations used up considerable time and money.

While the Royal Tar was being re-fitted and provisioned, Lane and his team were busy organising the initial team of two hundred settlers to proceed in the advance party to Paraguay.

While all this activity was going on, the venture was understandably receiving massive coverage in the newspapers and magazines of the times. While some commentators reserved their judgment, others were highly critical of the fact that Lane was taking his followers away from Australia. Perhaps the sternest critic was the *Bulletin* magazine which described the venture as *one of the most feather-headed expeditions ever conceived since Ponce de Leon started out to find the Fountain of Eternal Youth, or Sir Galahad pursued the Holy Grail.*

Under the rules of the Association, there was to be communal ownership of the means of production and distribution, communal conduct of production and distribution, communal maintenance of children under the guardianship of their parents and communal saving of all capital. Wives and single women had equal rights of the men, though not required to make any financial contribution. There were a few taboos. No person of colour could be a member of the Association, nor could any one married to a coloured person. Membership was also barred to anyone not having a sound knowledge of English, or was living in a relationship that was not a lawful marriage. Membership was also barred to anyone had been disloyal to the Labour movement.

Freedom of religion and speech was upheld but every member had to pledge to teetotalism.

After lengthy delays the Royal Tar sailed from Sydney harbour on Sunday, July 16 1893 with a final passenger count of 220 (80 men, 40 women and 100 children). Of the adults 43 men and 7 women were single.

The voyage to their first port of call (Montevideo) lasted fifty seven days and was marked with dissension and quarrels, often over petty matters. Right from the start, Lane displayed a lack of leadership in the manner of handling these trivial upsets. It was a forewarning of the trouble to come on land and an indication of dissension amongst of the seekers of Utopia.

At Montevideo several of the males defied Lane and went ashore, returning late at night very much inebriated and in open revolt against the temperance rules. A stronger leader, would have sent the renegades back to Sydney for such blatant breaches of the rules. Lane did nothing and sowed the seeds for his own eventual destruction.

From Montevideo the passengers embarked on another vessel upstream to Asuncion, where the women and children were housed in the Municipal Theatre while a party of fifty men went ahead to prepare shelters on their settlement of New Australia. The whole expedition had been poorly planned and they were short of tents and basic tools, but they set to work to erect rough bush shelters for the arrival of the community.

By October 10, New Australia was sufficiently shipshape for a Foundation Day ceremony to take place, attended by the Paraguayan Minister for Colonisation, Dr Lopez. The rest is best summarised by Gavin Souter in *A Peculiar People:*

Having managed to impress the Minister for Colonisation with their industry and unity, the New Australians knuckled down to the serious business of disintegration.

Whilst work on the settlement continued for the next two months, the colony seethed with quarrels, sometimes settled by fisticuffs, and divided into two warring factions, Royalists led by Lane and the Rebels. Lane held the trump card as he was recognised by the Paraguayan Government as the leader of community, and had been appointed a magistrate.

The Rebels themselves were divided into two camps, the stirrers who consistently thumbed their nose at Lane and who broke the rules, particularly the temperance rule, on a regular basis, and many others who obeyed the rules but were increasingly disenchanted with the whole venture . Much of the discontent came from the women, who had been persuaded to go to Paraguay against their own better judgement and who bore the brunt of the exceedingly primitive bush conditions that prevailed. Those who had come from city backgrounds were the most vocal in their complaints.

The main leaders and rule breakers in the rebel camp were Fred White, Tom Westwood, Arthur Brittlebank and Louis Simon. The leader of this group was White, then in his mid-thirties, who was said to have served as a special constable during the Queensland shearers' strikes of the early 1890's. Some of the Royalists suspected that he had joined the Association with the deliberate attempt to sabotage it, which is unlikely, but whether deliberate or not, this is what he managed to achieve.

With Christmas 1893 approaching the colony was in a state of crisis and matters were brought to a head on December 15 when Lane issued a proclamation expelling White, Westwood and Simon for consistent breaches of the temperance rules. White was away in Asuncion at the time and never did return to New Australia. Westwood and Simon refused to leave the colony and were forcibly removed by Paraguay troops summoned by Lane.

The expulsion only resulted in further upheaval with a third of the population of New Australia (thirty men, seventeen wives and thirty four children) leaving the colony for Villarica or a Government Colony, Colonia Gonzalez.

The Paraguayan Government was concerned at this rift in the colony and enlisted the aid of Mr M de Findlay (later Sir Mansfeldt de Cardonnel Findlay), the Second Secretary of the British Legation in Buenos Aires, who happened to be making an official visit to Paraguay at the time. Findlay was brought in to reconcile the differences of the colonists, but he had little luck. In his subsequent report to the Paraguay Government he found that most of the complaints were exaggerated or false. He was less than impressed with Lane, who he found to be cold and dogmatic and "remarkably deficient in the tact and human sympathy so necessary in a leader of men." However, he had a grudging respect for Lane's idealism though he thought his administration too strict for ordinary men.

There was to be no reconciliation between the two camps and the dissenters went their own way, most eventually finding their way back to Australia.

At New Australia things should have been rosy. Lane had got rid of most, but not all of the rebels but any rejoicing about Peace in the Promised land was to prove short-lived. More trouble was on the way in the shape of a new batch of settlers.

On December 31 1893 the Royal Tar departed from Adelaide on its second voyage to South America with 199 passengers. There should have been 204 but two were denied passage because they had turned up drunk at Christmas, two others pulled out when they realised that the temperance rule really WAS going to be enforced, and one simply missed the boat. Shortly before leaving Adelaide the passengers had received a cable advising that eight colonists had left New Australia. The original cable lodged at Asuncion had correctly stated the number of defectors as 80 but in transmission the nought had been "lost" possibly at the instigation of the Paraguayan authorities who had a motif for concealing the bad news of the split in the colony.

On arrival of the Royal Tar in Montevideo the passengers were given the facts and the option of returning to Australia on the Royal Tar. Seven single men decided to opt out of the venture but the rest, proceeded on to New Australia.

It was an opportunity to wipe the slate clean and start afresh and had Lane taken the lessons of 1893 on board this might well have happened. But Lane seemed impervious to his own shortcomings and soon the expanded colony had split into Royalist and Rebel factions, and this time the Royalists were in the minority.

The new colonists were a sober lot, mainly rural workers

from outback Queensland. On this occasion there were no problems over the temperance rules, but continuing friction over administrative rules of the colony, which Lane's lack of tact only exacerbated. Soon this dissatisfaction took the form of single men packing their swag and walking away. Lane only made matters worse when he branded these seceders as scabs.

The leader of the rebels on this occasion was Gilbert Casey, an old associate of Lane but whose views on many matters was greatly at variance from those of Lane. He was a born stirrer who quickly gathered around him a band of malcontents.

Casey argued strongly for an elected Board of Management to run New Australia on democratic lines. He had strong support for this but Lane bitterly opposed any changes that he perceived would strip his authority.

At a mass meeting of colonists on April 1 1894 the vote for a Board of Management was carried by 106 votes to four (with most of Lane's supporters abstaining). Lane had been effectively sidelined, though he probably would have been voted in as chairman of the board had he agreed. He announced that he would secede with those of his followers who remained loyal and found a new colony This was an act of folly of the first order. While he remained on New Australia, even in a diminished role, he was effectively in control of the assets of the Association, assets which included the Royal Tar and considerable funds back in Australia. By walking out of the colony he had, in effect, handed all these assets over to the rebel group, though in fact considerable time and legal battles were to ensue before all this came to pass.

Lane seemed absolutely blind to his folly and to the pain and suffering that he was about to inflict on his loyal followers. The secession of Lane had not been expected by the rebels. They had merely been seeking some democratic control over their daily work routines. As a result there was open hostility between the rebels and Lane's supporters, causing personal feuds which were to last for generations.

The new controllers of New Australia permitted Lane and his followers to set up a temporary camp on land some 30 miles to the south-east while they searched for land for their own new colony. Lane moved here with 63 followers and some cattle and tools, purchasing 2 parcels of land totalling five square leagues (23,155 acres) in the fork of two tributaries of the Tebicuary River, about 45 miles south of New Australia. The land was purchased from a private owner for 305 pounds sterling, on terms of 100 pounds deposit with the balance to be paid over three years. The ever patient Paraguayan Government later came to the party by paying for the land.

Lane named his new settlement Cosme and he and his 55 followers (there had been a few defections) set about the task of carving a new colony out of the wilderness. They were short of cash and almost every type of equipment and suffered enormous hardships in the early months of the settlement. So desperate was their plight that they collected the wedding rings of the married women with the intention of pawning them to get needed food for the children. The men baulked at actually carrying through the plan and the rings were handed back to their owners.

Gradually the crops planted at Cosme came good and as time passed the colony almost became self-supporting, though it never prospered to the extent that it could pay dividends to its loyalist settlers. Over time the original numbers were bolstered by new arrivals from Australia, and later from Britain. The most notable of these new recruits arrived on January 2 1896; Mary Cameron, then aged 30, who had been persuaded to come to Cosme by Lane to take charge of the colony's school.

Back in Australia she had been engaged to Dave Stevenson, one of the original settlers on the first voyage of the Royal Tar.

But Stevenson had a roving eye, and by the time Mary Cameron came on the scene his attention was focussed elsewhere.

Mary Cameron did not appear to be unduly disturbed by this state of affairs and busied herself organising the Cosme school and later editing the colony's newsletter *Cosme Monthly*.

On May 29 1897 she married William Gilmore, a 31 year-old Victorian who had arrived in Paraguay with the second Royal Tar contingent. He was a quiet, reserved individual though well liked and respected by the other settlers. The match seemed to come as a surprise to many, prompting John Lane to rather unkindly remark that "Gilmore never smiled again".

The Cameron/Gilmore wedding took place while Will Lane was in England trying to recruit settlers for Cosme. This was not a great success as most of the English settlers recruited were unable to adapt to the harsh bush conditions on the Paraguayan pampas. By early 1897 departures outnumbered arrivals and Cosme was in deep trouble.

Over in the old original colony of New Australia the disintegration of the colony had begun almost from the exit of Lane and his followers. Lacking leadership or any firm goals, the only thing that held the remaining settlers together for a while was the thought that since they had inherited the assets of the old Association and they might benefit financially if they could find a way of translating these assets into cash . There was a steady stream of departures from New Australia throughout 1895 and the early part of 1896, and the only thing that held the remaining settlers there, was the belief there would be more dividends coming to ever-diminishing numbers.

By October 1896 they reached a decision to abandon New Australia as a colony and divide what land and assets remained amongst those that stayed on. In January 1897 the assets were sold and divided equally among members over the age of 18. After the big wash up, New Australia ceased to exist as a colony and the remaining families (comprising some seventy men, women and children) became individual landowners, with holdings and assets of varying size, within a village of New Australia, later Nueva Australie. It was the end of a chapter for that part of the Paraguayan experiment - a path that a few years later would also be adopted by Cosme.

The ups and downs of Cosme and its eventual disintegration can perhaps be best documented by a reading of *Cosme Monthly*. Initially produced in handwritten single sheet form in 1895, it graduated to a four page printed bulletin late in 1896 when it was printed in England. From early 1897 it was produced in Cosme when the colony acquired a small printing press.

Throughout its relatively short life it had no imprint of an editor, and it was only when the colony was nearing its end that some editorials were signed by Lane. Whilst it may have had an editorial committee, much of the writing bore the style of Mary Gilmore or William Lane. It was a newsy little magazine, recording the routines of the colony : births, deaths, marriages, and of course accidents, departures and arrivals. There was also the routines of the day, the weather, plantings and state of the crops, records of inward and outward mails, social functions and general village gossip. However, censorship over the growing tensions in the colony was complete. For these records it is necessary to look elsewhere, mainly to the letters from colonists to their friends and relatives in the outside world.

One sign that all was not well surfaced in 1898 when the first editorials signed by Lane began to appear in *Cosme Monthly*. These had a distinct religious tinge and resembled sermons, being strong on exhortations to the faithful, and little in the way of practical suggestions for tackling the many problems faced by the colony.

Matters came to a head in May 1898 when Joseph Sims

acquired a weaner pig and indulged in a feast with a few favoured friends, a clear breach of the share-all communist rules of the colony. A meeting of members voted to expel Sims and the chief beneficiary of the feast, John Pindar, in a vote of 19 to 6. These dissenting voters then all decided to leave the colony, and several others left in sympathy. In two months thirty eight people (including ten foundation members) had quit Cosme - some thirty per cent of its membership.

Cosme staggered on from one crisis to another for a further year, before William Lane acknowledged defeat on August 1 1899 leaving Cosme forever, handing the reigns of the colony over to his brother John Lane. His excuse for leaving was that he could best serve the interests of the colony by promoting it back in Australia.

Several other colonists decided to follow their leader into this new wilderness - including the Gilmores. Billy Gilmore went off to find outside work to raise the funds for their fares back to Australia, leaving Mary and her newborn child to spend a further nine frustrating months alone in the colony, at odds with many of those remaining. Her letters in this period are painful outpourings of frustration and bitterness of dreams gone wrong.

John Lane was popular with most of the remaining colonists but he was no leader of men. Under William Lane, the colony at least had some positive direction - it was his autocratic methods his followers found intolerable. Under the more easy-going John Lane, complaints about autocracy ceased, but the colony just drifted along in a rudderless fashion; from time to time considered winding up the affairs of Cosme and going the way of New Australia with the lands and assets being divided up amongst the remaining members.

By 1908 the colony had dwindled to nine men and five wives and it had become obvious that Cosme could no longer sustain itself. On August 12 1909 at Caazapa, the final documents were signed ending the Cosme Colony, creating the independent village of Cosme with its new capitalist owners of the village and surrounding lands. John Lane had resigned from Cosme back in 1904 so no Lanes were around for the final requiem to a lost cause.

Today Nueva Australie and Cosme survive only as dots on the map of Paraguay. Descendants of the original colonists survive in name but none speak any English, though some maintain irregular contact with relatives who migrated to Australia in the years following World War 1.

And what of the Lanes, William and John, those dreamers of a communistic Utopia of so long ago? When William Lane left Paraguay for good in August 1899 he returned briefly to Sydney where he became editor of the *Australian Worker* in 1900. He found little to hold his interest, and later that year migrated to New Zealand to take a job as leader writer on the *Auckland Herald*, where he remained for the rest of his life. He became Editor of the *Herald* in 1913, and died on August 18 1917, aged 55, after developing a severe bout of bronchitis. During the long years spent in New Zealand he did not take up his pen at any stage to speak of the colonies he led in distant Paraguay.

John Lane returned to Australia and became a school teacher with the Queensland Education Department, spending most of his career in schools on the Darling Downs. In all that time he had very little contact or communication with his older brother William. And he wrote very little in those years about the Paraguayan experiments. He died at his Coolangatta retirement home in 1947, aged 81.

Both New Australia and Cosme had relatively short lives as utopian colonies. While many of the colonists involved in these Paraguay experiments experienced great financial and personal hardships, many looked back on the Paraguay years with fondness and nostalgia, even as the "best years of their lives".

While most of the writings that have survived have been male-oriented, with strong political overtones and dealing in depth with farm management on the Paraguay pampas, the role of women in these very unusual social experiments should not be forgotten. While the women of both colonies encountered and largely overcame appalling physical conditions, the majority had already experienced tough times in the Australian outback.

These letters, articles and passing comments in the columns of *Cosme Monthly*, record the fact that one of the great advantages of the colonies was the prohibition of alcohol - viewpoints probably not shared by the males.

In the 1890's it was quite clear that alcohol posed an enormous problem for the average low income suburban family. In those days homes were rented with the dread rent collector coming around every week. If the male breadwinner proceeded to spend his wages on grog, as was so often the case, the family was left without funds for food or rent, leading to the inevitable eviction. At New Australia and Cosme the women were spared these painful experiences of the past and, on balance they felt that this was worth the shared kitchens and rough laundry facilities.

Mary Gilmore wrote a long articvle for the Sydney *Daily Telegraph* in 1902 after her return from her Paraguayan oddyssey, referring to the fact that she had just learned of the accidental death of the father of the largest family in Cosme. While nothing could ease the pain of his passing, she contrasted the financial circumstances of the widow at Cosme with what they might have been had she been back in Australia. In Cosme such a tragedy made no difference to the widow's material position. She had her house and her weekly allowance for food and clothing, exactly as before. Any medical expenses for herself and the children were fully absorbed by the Colony and she was not expected to pay for anything, or work harder, than before. Her children were not expected to work at an early age to keep the family afloat as would have been the case in Australia at the time. She makes a very good point.

Yet there always were deep divisions among the sisterhood at both colonies and in the dozen or so years the colonies survived as such, women never did get around to calling one another by their first names. Apart from cases of special friendships, it was always very formal, Miss Jones or Mrs Brown, even over the communal washtub!

As for the males, they were quickly on first name terms, as is the custom in the Australian bush, but there were other tenets of William Lane's utopia that sat uneasily on the shoulders of the participants.

Back in 1893 when preparations were afoot for the first sailing of the Royal Tar, a contributor to the *Bulletin* posed a very pertinent question. "In this Utopia", he asked, "Who gets to eat the salmon and who has to eat the haddock?"

William Lane did not deign to answer the question. If only he had paused a while to do so.

11

The Queensland Co-operatives

The final decade of the 19th Century saw the emergence of an entirely new communal movement in the form of Government sponsored (and partly funded) Co-operative communes, and the birth place of this concept was Queensland. There were good historical reasons why this was so.

The Gold Rush period, which commenced in the 1850's, had come to a halt in the eastern states as a result of the major alluvial deposits having been tracked down and exhausted by the 1890's.

Most of the tens of thousands of white gold seekers who had flooded the goldfields in the earliest days of the rush had departed Australian shores to seek their fortunes elsewhere, though significant numbers had stayed behind to take what paying work was on offer in the cities or had drifted to the bush as shearers or settlers.

This was a period when the population mix became seriously unbalanced, especially in the bush where males were in the overwhelming majority. This resulted in rougher and tougher social attitudes prevailing. The former miners were also an independent lot given to more radical ideas of socialism.

There was a strong movement afoot in both cities and the bush for better wages and conditions for the common man. Nowhere was this feeling being more forcibly expressed than in the pastoral areas of Queensland. The demands for better wages were being stoutly resisted by the pastoralists who brought in trainloads of non-union labour from the cities.

The use of "scab" labour has always been a tricky exercise on Australian soil. In this case it proved explosive with widespread violence and some deaths on station properties. The Queensland governments of the period backed the pastoralists and arrested the leaders of the militant workers. In most cases the strikes were broken by violent action and the pastoralists won the initial battles. Out of initial defeat there arose stronger, well organised unions and the birth of the Australian Labor Party which was able to give a political voice to their grievances.

Throughout this very violent period of industrial relations, change was in the air. This was cleverly exploited by William Lane, who unceasingly expounded his ideas for the establishment of Utopian Socialist Communes run by the workers. Lane's radical ideas and the initial success of his Paraguay adventure, sent shock waves through the Queensland government as Lane's Utopian movement had been born there and large numbers of his followers came from that state.

By 1893 the Queensland Government, then led by the Premier Samuel Walter Griffith, in a coalition with Thomas McIllwraith, had become so alarmed by Lane's apparent success that they decided on counter measures. If there were to be communal. settlements then they should take place in Queensland, not away in some far off country as Lane was planning.

Samuel Griffith was a forward looking person who favoured the idea of communes as a means of developing the outback and of absorbing the then very large numbers of city based unemployed. He believed that such settlements could only succeed if they were properly planned with strict legal guidelines and government backing, and some degree of government supervision.

He came up with the idea of communes governed by a new system of co-operative management and as an eminent lawyer, he personally supervised the drafting of the world's first such Act, the Queensland Co-operative Settlement Act. Griffith was not around to see it enacted as in March 1893 he resigned as Premier to become Chief Justice of Queensland.

He was succeeded as Premier by his coalition partner Thomas McIlwraith, who formed a coalition government in partnership with the then Leader of the Opposition Hugh Muir Nelson. McIlwraith was committed to the Queensland Co-operative Settlement Act and managed to steer it through parliament and have it proclaimed on October 13 1893. However, two week's later he was toppled by his coalition partner Hugh Nelson who became the new Premier.

This may well have sealed the fate of the proposed new movement because Nelson was decidedly lukewarm about the whole idea. When the whole scheme crashed in 1895 *The Queenslander* newspaper was able to quote Nelson as saying

…he has no faith whatever in the group doctrine , and sees no alternative but the dispersal of these misguided people, and their settlement upon individual homesteads.

Within the department responsible for the administration of the Act there was another strong opponent of the whole scheme, Francis Heeney, the Under Secretary for Public Lands. Just three weeks after the Act had been proclaimed, he issued confidential instructions to his staff which can only be interpreted as passive resistance to the idea of co-operative settlements:

You will understand that this form of settlement is not to be forced on, as it involves money demands on the government and must be kept within narrow limits… Information about land will not be given to men trying to set up Groups. They will levy blackmail on more decent men than themselves… Proper land is scarce: therefore they must take it or leave it quickly . Remember that we are not bound to recognise any Group or any man. We are doing them a favour in letting them have land so much easier than the ordinary selector.

So what was the government offering the new settlers under this Act? In summary the Act provided for the registration of co-operatives having thirty of more male members. But the government had to approve each member individually and ultimately decided to which co-operative such members were assigned. This prevented say a group of thirty men with similar political, religious or other interests from forming their own co-operative.

There was a distinct racial element to the legislation in that members of a co-operative had to be Australian-born or naturalised British subjects who had been resident in Queensland for at least twelve months. This effectively excluded the then very large Chinese population of Queensland and of course, Aborigines, although Australian-born, were not even considered suitable for such government sponsored experiments. This was despite the fact that they had some 10,000 years of successful communal experience to their credit. The Minister for Public Lands even had ultimate powers of rejecting any applicant for membership of a co-operative "without any cause assigned".

The Act provided for a management committee for each co-operative, with all disputes to be internally arbitrated and with expulsions from a co-operative to require a two thirds vote for the action by all members.

There were also some very tough provisions imposed on the proposed co-operatives, Within three months of registration more than half the registered members had to be in permanent residence and if membership dropped below thirty, or two thirds of the total membership, the co-operative was to be wound up.

On the plus side the Government pledged a perpetual

lease to each co-operative of up to 160 acres of land for each
member as well as a cash advance of twenty pounds for each
registered member as start-up funds for food, tools and stock.

Despite the restrictions and miserly nature of the cash
advance, the Government was swamped with applications from
678 males in the succeeding months and had to close off further
applications to enable them to process members and allocate
lands. Of the original applicants, 667 were accepted as suitable
for membership, but only 450 males were actually registered as
members of a co-operative.

Women were excluded from membership, in the custom
of the times, but when wives and children were taken into
account, the total number of individuals settled on the co-
operatives in the ensuing months exceeded 2000.

A total of fourteen co-operatives were actually registered
but two failed to get off the ground. The co-operatives which
were settled were:

- *Bon Accord* near Gayndah (60 members)
- *Byrne Town* near Gayndah (34 members).
- *Excel Pioneers* near Roma (45 members).
- *Industrial* near Chinchilla (38 members)
- *Mizpah* near Chinchilla (35 members)
- *Monmouth* near Chinchilla (35 members)
- *Nil Desperandum* near Roma (35 members)
- *Obertown Model* near Roma (45 members)
- *Protestant Unity* near Pomona (56 members)
- *Reliance* near Rolleston (41 members)
- *Resolute* near Gayndah (40 members)
- *Wollongabba Exemplars* near Noosa (59 members)

The two co-operatives which were registered but not
settled were "Barlowtown" (near Roma) and "Germania", near
Gayndah.

All the settled co-operatives experienced considerable

difficulties due to a variety of factors which included a long dry spell soon after settlement, poor soil, lack of experience and capital by the settlers and in a few notable cases, extreme clashes between management committees and members.

Initial crops and vegetable plantings failed, making it difficult for even competent management committees to produce a cash flow sufficient to sustain the members.

When things started to get desperate after the initial government grants ran out, many of the men breached the rules by temporarily leaving the communes to try and gain casual work outside, leaving their wives and children behind to survive as best they could, leading to some Management Committees withholding rations from them. On several occasions local police or the government had to step in to provide emergency rations to the wives and children threatened with starvation.

The biggest problems surfaced at the Byrnetown co-operative near Gayndah, a commune of 169 persons comprising 28 married couples, 6 single men and 107 children. From the start tensions arose because of heavy-handed actions of the management committee and incessant complaints about thefts of co-operative funds by the Secretary, Thomas Shannon who had a serious drinking problem. The government was slow to respond to the many complaints from members about Shannon. In April 1895 the Under Secretary for Agriculture stepped in and sacked the old committee at Byrnestown and appointed a new committee which eventually had the numbers to expel Shannon from the commune. But all this came too late and by June 1895 Byrnestown had exhausted all its resources and members were existing on emergency rations supplied by the government.

On June 29 1895 *The Queenslander* carried a lengthy report on the woes of the twelve co-operative communes and summed up the situation admirably thus:

...the average human nature is not the material for the millennium yet; and those who dream of Utopia must be content to live in dreamland ... jealousy, envy, strife, and all uncharitableness have sprouted like weeds among the wheat of good fellowship.

When the co-operatives were initially settled in the early months of 1894 the various regional newspapers gave them favourable coverage but as problems arose and became public concern, the tone of reporting and editorials became more critical.

In Brisbane, the Government faced an incessant barrage of criticism from the *Courier Mail*, normally one of its strongest supporters, but on the matter of the co-operative settlements a strident critic of the whole idea and losing no opportunity to report dissensions and problems as they arose.

The Government of Hugh Nelson was in an awkward position on several fronts as Australia was swept up in a very serious depression.

Nelson was a very able political leader who as both Premier and Treasurer steered Queensland through the worst of the financial crisis with a number of pioneering measures such as the Public Depositors' Relief Act, which saved the Queensland banks from crashing.

He had inherited the Queensland Co-operative Settlement Act which he had opposed as Leader of the Opposition, and now saw it coming apart at the seams. In a time when he was drastically engaged in slashing government expenditure, he saw the Co-operatives as a potential drain on the public purse.

He decided to jettison the whole scheme by withdrawing all government support and funding by introducing on December 23 1895 an amendment to the Queensland Co-operative Settlement Act extinguishing all communal land rights held by the co-operatives, with all lands reverting back to the Crown.

Some of these communes had already collapsed or been abandoned by the settlers. Those still attempting to struggle on found the ground taken away from them. The government took no action to evict them, but did provide free transport back to Brisbane for those who wished to do so.

Those who remained on the old co-operative lands were given the option to apply for leases on portions of the lands in the usual manner. Quite a number did so, and some even survived and prospered over the years. In most of the communities of the old co-operatives there are descendants of the original communal settlers farming district lands.

Hugh Muir Nelson was to go on to higher office and honours. In 1896 he was created KCMG and appointed to the Privy Council in 1897. In April 1898 as Sir Hugh Nelson he became President of the Legislative Council and in 1903 became Lieutenant Governor of Queensland. He died in Toowoomba on January 1 1906.

At the time Nelson was reviled by the settlers for his act in gutting the Queensland Co-operative Settlement Act and his actions remain controversial to this day.

In 1998 a history of three of the Gayndah district co-operatives was published, the first attempt to cover what really was a quite extraordinary Australian social experiment. This volume was *The Gayndah Communes* by Bill Metcalf of Griffith University and widely acknowledged as a leading expert on the history of communes in Australia. The book itself is controversial in that Metcalf seeks to establish a conspiracy of deception and secrecy on the part of the Nelson Government. While the author does provide a wealth of background material not previously published, much of it being disturbing reading, many will consider it falls far short of establishing a conspiracy.

Nowhere in the book does Metcalf ever address what should be the key question asked about experiments of this nature, namely: To what extent, if any, should a democratic government instigate, promote and finance from its taxpayers' funds, the Utopian dreams of a small segment of its electorate? That is, I suspect, a question to which there is no easy answer.

But what of the privately funded Utopian communes in Queensland in the 19th Century. There weren't all that many, but perhaps two are worthy of note. The Alice River Co-operative Commune, established near Barcaldine in 1891 without any government help or blessing. It arose out of the collapse of the great shearers' strike in 1891 and was founded by 72 ex-shearers They modelled their constitution on rules drawn up by William Lane and built huts, a kitchen, communal dining room, toolshed, library and piggery on their settlement as well as establishing vegetable gardens and a vineyard.

Despite the initial enthusiasm, it never really got off the ground through lack of finance and farming knowledge and after two years the initial 72 members had dwindled to a dozen. A few survivors struggled on until 1907 when it was officially abandoned.

A serious attempt by a group of socialists from Finland much later in the century met a similar fate. The leader of the Finns was a charismatic journalist named Matti Kurikka, who brought his followers to Australia as a result of reading articles and books by William Lane. He does not appear to have read of the disasters that beset Lane down in his two colonies in Paraguay.

Kurikka arrived in Australia in 1899 with 78 followers determined to establish a Co-operative Socialist Colony in Queensland based on social order and harmony.

Having in mind the disaster of the twelve official sponsored co-operatives of the 1893-5 period, the Queensland Government blocked Kurikka's move to register his colony as a co-operative because this would have automatically meant giving the new settlers a grant of twenty pounds each (that part of the old

Queensland Co-operative Settlement Act had not been amended back in 1895).

However, the Government was not entirely unsympathetic to the Finns and they did grant them free rail travel to enable them to seek out and buy suitable land for their commune.

Kurikka and 27 of the males in the group travelled north to Chillagoe, leaving the women and children behind in lodgings in Brisbane. At Chillagoe they set up a tent camp and got work cutting sleepers to finance their proposed land purchases.

Kurikka proved to be a poor leader and soon the group was in dire straits, not helped by the fact that they spoke very little English.

When they became stranded in Cooktown, Kurikka persuaded his small band of followers to trek up to the Gulf of Carpentaria where free land was on offer. Surprisingly the group did reach their destination and managed to set up a commune called Kalevan Kansa. Given the isolation of the commune, and their lack of farming experience, the experiment was a disaster and the Finnish paradise-seekers were forced to survive on a diet of honey and roots.

By July 1900 the Kalevan Kansa experiment had collapsed and Kurikka led most of his disciples back to Finland, blaming everyone but himself for the fiasco.

More than half a century was to pass before Paradise seekers again ventured up to Queensland to establish communes.

12

The Village Settlements

The scheme that the Premier Charles Cameron Kingston and his cabinet came up with was to settle groups of unemployed in village settlements (mainly along the Murray) with all members of each settlement sharing the land, workload and any income. The basics of the scheme as outlined to Parliament in August 1893 can be summarised as follows:

a) Twenty or more members could form a registered Association with all members having to sign an approved set of communal rules .

b) The Government would then provide at least 160 acres per member on a perpetual lease to the Association, rent free for the first year and thereafter at rents to be fixed, with the Association agreeing to spend two shillings per acre on improvements for the first ten years.

c) The Government agreed to advance up to fifty pounds to each member, with the maximum amount not exceeding half the value of the Association improvements. These advances had to be repaid over ten years and carried five per cent interest.

d) Management of each Association was to be in the hands of a Board of three Trustees who would elect their own Chairman.

e) At least half of the registered members of each Association had to live and work on the land, and all members were jointly and collectively liable for the repayments due by the Association and the observance of conditions, whether they lived in the village or not.

f) The division and distribution of the land was at the sole discretion of the Trustees.

There were also lengthy rules governing conduct of the villagers, their expulsion, the division of profits, control of trade and industries and for control of a common fund to which villagers had to contribute if they earned money outside the village, and for the settlement disputes.

The Bill attracted little comment when tabled but after members had had a chance to study this proposal, which gave communistic control over people in what was then an extremely conservative community, opposition started to mount to the whole idea. The Government had the numbers and ignored complaints that the proposal amounted to slavery and that it would attract only the dead beats of society.

One of the most novel objections came from an indignant member who claimed that unemployed eighteen year old youths would run off to the Murray with their girl friends and establish "highly undesirable communes".

The Bill became law on December 23 1893 and before the end of January 1894 two Associations had been formed for settlements at Lyrup and Mount Remarkable. In the period February 1894 to January 1895, thirteen Village Settlement Associations were formed and started operating (eleven of them along the Murray, two in other areas). In chronological sequence they were: Mount Remarkable, Lyrup, Waikerie, Holder, Nangkita, Wap, Kingston, Gillen, New Era, Moorook, Murtho, Ramco and New Residence.

Basic rules were drawn up in January 1894 and adopted

105

by most of the Associations (there were some minor variations). The rules stipulated that all villagers were to have equal shares, that no Asiatics were to be permitted, 'no foreigners could join unless they were conversant in English, that no man or woman could live together on a settlement except in lawful marriage, that every member should be obedient and respectful to the Trustees at all times, that a two third majority vote was required to expel a member, that Villagers were to be supplied with the necessities of life, including food and clothing for themselves and family from a common pool, that alcohol was totally banned from settlements, that members were to be allowed two weeks annual leave at a time to be determined by the Trustees, that Villagers could own some personal effects (such as furniture books, utensils etc), and that each Villager was entitled to occupy one acre of land on which to live and on which the Settlement would build him a home.

Some rather draconian rules were later drafted and adopted by most Settlements to deal with the specific problems of expelling members. Grounds for such action included (1) Being insubordinate or not respectful to Trustees (2) Disobeying instructions of the Board (3) Breaching Rules of the Association (4) Leaving the village for more than two days without permission of the Board (5) for conduct considered by the Board to be injurious to the Association.

Members who either resigned or were expelled from a village automatically forfeited all rights and interests in the Association and, in the case of expelled members, could be forcibly ejected from the Settlement.

At a later stage rules were introduced in most Associations to give power to Boards to determine how long a wife (and children) could remain in a Village after her husband had been suspended, prohibition on a Village accepting as a member a person who had been expelled from any other Village, and also barring from membership any person with a contagious disease or any unattached person under the age of eighteen.

It might be thought that rules and conditions such as these would frighten applicants off communism for life, but this wasn't the case, as the Associations were flooded with applications as soon as they were formed. The vast majority of the applicants were unemployed, had no money and most of them had no experience of farming. Perhaps they thought they had nothing to lose or the Irish in them reckoned that "rules were made to be broken."

The first Village Settlement on the Murray to get off the ground was Lyrup when a large contingent of settlers left Adelaide on February 20 1894, in a blaze of publicity, in a special train of fourteen carriages, five for the passengers, and nine for their baggage and equipment from Government stores. The group comprised 98 men, 40 married women and 212 children.

The train took them to Morgan where they embarked on a paddle steamer for a two day journey to the Lyrup settlement.

The first strains of communal living occurred on the boat when heated arguments developed over the allocation of cabins - some were better than others. Charges of favouritism were rife.

On arrival at their Lyrup destination the realities of communal living were brought home to them even more forcefully. What faced them was a bare riverbank on to which they and all their possessions were unceremoniously dumped. Most had to sleep in the open on the first night - in a few cases their menfolk had travelled overland in advance with cattle. The next few days saw furious activity with the erection of shanties of galvanised iron and hessian, after which the men turned their attention to clearing the land for cropping, building a crude wharf and establishing a pumping plant, and establishing fenced vegetable gardens guarded against the depredations of rabbits.

Lyrup was one of the luckier settlements, and one of the

few to survive (though under a different management system) as it had fertile soils and much of its acreage was low lying which meant it could irrigate a lot of its holding. Before the year was out the settlement had 200 acres planted with apricots, peaches, lemons, grapes, vegetables and fodder. They also had by then established a nursery of 90,000 vine cuttings and root stocks for 40,000 apricot, 25,000 peach and 3000 other trees.

Even so, their situation was precarious because of their inadequate pumping system, the long distance to markets and internal problems which beset all settlements.

Perhaps the best accounts of the problems facing the Village Settlements in their first full year of operation are to be found in reports of two ministers of religion who visited most of them in this period.

The first clerical visitor to record his impressions was a Catholic priest, Father Thomas Lee, who visited the Settlements in the month of November 1894 and who in December made a lengthy and quite harrowing report to Bishop Byrne.

Fr Lee said that never in his life had he been as tired as he was when he finished the trip and that he had taken six weeks to recover from the ordeal, commenting:

Had I only the slightest idea before starting that I would have to put up with what I did, I think somebody else would have to make the trip.

His problems mainly centred on lack of accommodation for visitors, clerical or otherwise. Father Lee's problems at the Village of Kingston (named after the Premier) are typical and should perhaps be left to him to describe in his own words:

Mr Neddan, who is a Frenchman … in a very offhand manner told me that arrangements had been made for me to sleep in the Camp with a Batchelor Scotchman whose mate, another Scotchman, had kindly given the use of his bunk to me for the night. I thanked him for his forethought but when I came to the Camp and had a good look at the bunk I nearly retracted all the kind expressions which I had only a few minutes before made use of. The bunk consisted of two bags of hay sewn together and placed on the floor without any pillow or clothes of any description. It was now 10.30 and the night was getting bitterly cold. I had nothing to do but divest myself of coat and boots and bring my big overcoat and valise once more into requisition. I had very little rest that night.

Most of Father Lee's letter is taken up with religious matters. He was the first priest to visit the Murray settlements and his methodical recording of the names of all the Catholics he unearthed in each village and their vastly varying degrees of religious fervour provide interesting reading. No doubt Bishop Byrne was not pleased with sections of the report which did not show a lot of his flock to be overly blessed in matters of Faith. Father Lee recommended that the Settlements should be visited at least twice a year noting: *If the Settlements are neglected, half the people will become perverts.*

He also had scant words of praise for the Murtho Settlement which was the only one of the Murray settlements to be set-up by middle class, educated Adelaide people. They were very selective in admitting members to their ranks and were the only Settlement to demand joining fees of forty pounds from single men, sixty pounds from married couples (plus ten pounds for each child). These were considerable sums in those days and were obviously designed to keep out the unemployed and "riff raff" accepted by the other Settlements. Murtho was also the only settlement to give full and equal membership to women.

Father Lee's report to his Bishop on this state of affairs is interesting:

There is a Village called Murtho opposite Renmark. This is run on the Communistic Principle and I am pleased to say you have no Catholics there.

If Father Lee's impressions of the Settlements tended towards pessimism, the report by another cleric of a different persuasion was simply brimming over with enthusiasm and optimism.

He was the Reverend Joseph Berry of Adelaide who visited eight of the Murray Settlements in late 1894 and early 1895 and whose comprehensive report was published in the *London Review of Reviews* of April 20 1895.

After giving a detailed history of the formation of the Settlements and the general day to day working routines, the Reverend Berry pointed out that after a full year all the Settlements were holding together, despite the many problems most of them had experienced. Those who had been unfit or unwilling to work had been weeded out, as well as some individuals he called "bush lawyers" who had taken off when they found they had no Capitalists to gird at! He said hardships were diminishing and comforts were increasing and nice stone cottages were beginning to replace the old shanty huts.

He singled out the Lyrup settlement for mention as being the most advanced with 72 married couples, 26 single men and 200 children. It had its own brick kiln capable of holding 32,000 bricks and a drying shed capable of holding 100,000 bricks. More than 500 acres had been grubbed and cleared and enclosed by an eleven mile long rabbit-proof fence. There were 1500 fruit trees and 15 acres under maize. He gave impressive details of the nursery which at the time of his visit had ready for planting 4100 apricot, 1300 peach, 270 plums, 50 quince, 1250 almond, 220 olive and 6000 strawberry plants. One hundred and fifty tons of hay had been produced in 1894 and stock on the settlement included 35 horses, 13 cows, 12 calves, 28 pigs and 1000 sheep as well as numerous poultry. Plant included the irrigation pumps, circular saw, horse chaffcutter, ten ploughs, three scarifiers, a mowing machine, a wagon, drays and carts and eight boats.

The Rev Berry provided a summary of daily work schedules on the settlement, commencing with a 7.30 am work muster and roll call when the men were assigned to their various jobs for the day in the brickyard, sawpit or work in the fields.

Like most of the settlements, Lyrup did not use currency but worked entirely on a voucher system with vouchers being handed out according to work performed. There was no shop on the settlement but stocks of all necessities were maintained at a communal store and once a week this was opened for settlers to exchange their vouchers for goods.

The clerical observer noted that one of the settlements had organised its own band, while several others had choirs. Steamers made frequent calls at the settlements to bring news and needed supplies and of course to take on board produce for the Adelaide and other down river markets.

Berry noted that two of the churches had what he called small yachts to carry ministers along the river to administer to their flock. One of these was kept by the Reverend W. C. Butler, of the Primitive Methodist Church, who was "an amateur doctor" able to render medical aid to the sick.

Berry noted that in addition to Government advances, the settlements had received a considerable amount of aid from public appeals. This included outright gifts of food, clothing, seeds, farm implements, and even horses and cattle. He estimated the value of these gifts (in 1894) to total four thousand pounds in value. The Rev Berry was extremely optimistic about the prospects of the settlements because they were able to produce an abundance of produce with cheap labour without any loss of dignity on the part of the worker. He estimated that within three years of the their formation the village settlements would be sufficiently established to be able to operate independent of government or other assistance.

Alas, the Reverend Berry's forecasts were not to be, and within his time schedule some of the settlements had ceased to exist and others were able to survive only under structures quite different to those of the original charters.

The reasons for the collapse of the Village Settlement schemes can perhaps be best summarised as follows:

1. For many it was because the land chosen was poor and not suited for irrigation.

2. In almost all cases the initial pumping systems financed by the government proved completely inadequate, Those villages that did survive did so only after installing more powerful and costly systems which imposed a financial burden on the settlements and added greatly to the cost of production of the farm produce.

3. All the village settlements were located a long distance from the only logical market (Adelaide) with a result that freight and other costs of getting produce to marked often exceeded the actual cost of production.

4. Very few settlers had any previous experience of farming or marketing and had to learn from costly trial and error experiments.

5. Human nature! In some settlements this was the biggest problem of all, as workers quarrelled with Trustees and their elected boards of management over various matters. Little dictators emerged in a number of settlements and proved difficult to dislodge from elected positions, but the majority of disputes centred around grievances over workloads and rewards for their labours.

Initial enthusiasm and optimism carried the settlements through the first year of 1894, aided by the fact that higher than average rainfalls brought good crop yields. The settlers in their ignorance of farming, thought this was normal. It wasn't and when 1895 brought lower normal rains the realisation at last dawned that their chosen land (mostly) was suitable only for dry-land farming, not irrigation, and the settlements started to fall apart.

The Lyrup Settlement, the first along the Murray, had land suitable for irrigation but quickly realised that the communal system was never going to yield enough revenue to sustain all the members. It converted to a co-operative system in 1897 and was one of the few which managed to survive in this new form into the 20th Century. Under this system each member was allocated his own acreage on a rental basis and was allowed to work it as he wished with a general manager overseeing such matters as water pumping, distribution and marketing arrangements.

But what of the Murtho Settlement - the pure communist settlement of the predominantly middle-class settlers? How did it fare? Not very well actually.

The Murtho Settlement was founded in July 1894 but got off to a shaky start when the wife of the first Chairman, Henry Cordeaux, refused point blank to go there. Instead he settled at Renmark as an agent of the settlement and a new chairman was appointed. They were well cashed up and the heavy rains of 1894 gave them good initial crops. Their land was well above practical pumping levels and so were quite unsuited to irrigation, a fact they only discovered when subsequent years brought near-drought conditions. The communistic ideals were put to the test and failed as individual members developed distinct capitalistic every-man-for-himself tendencies. Quarrels abounded and being well educated, they no doubt were in a position to air their grievances at some length.

The houses they had built in the early stages were well above the standard of housing in the other Village Settlements, but from mid-1895 they started to abandon them, cut their losses and trek back to the comforts of city life. Many families walked off the settlement destitute. In March 1899 the Murtho Village Settlement ceased to exist as an entity and the Government took back its land and appointed a manager.

Some settlements survived in a different form by adopting new co-operative systems and amalgamating with adjoining villages. Waikerie, Ramco and Holder amalgamated and became the Waikerie Irrigation Area, eventually developing into a prosperous district centred around Waikerie. Kingston and Lyrup also developed into thriving townships over time.

By 1903 the Government had decided to cut its losses - estimated at the time to have exceeded a hundred and thirty thousand pounds -by abandoning the communal experiment and gradually opening up its Crown Lands to sub division and sale to settlers under the capitalistic system.

Critics of the Village Settlement scheme have over the years been quick to write it off as a total disaster forgetting its redeeming features. Government agencies and prospective settlers gained much valuable knowledge of conditions along the Murray from the experiments carried out so hopefully by the Village pioneers, not least in the hazards and difficulties of irrigation. Out of the ashes of defeat, arose whole new ventures, new settlements, new villages and towns along the whole length of the river embraced by the initial Settlement Scheme.

Of course the human cost of acquiring this knowledge was considerable, and in many individual cases quite tragic. How many victims there were of the Village Settlement scheme is difficult to establish as figures compiled by the South Australian Surveyor General's Department differ from those maintained by the Village Select Commission. The peak figure in 1895 is given by the former was 1768 men, women and children for all thirteen settlements covered by the Act.

These figures provided by the Village Select Commission, are misleading because they denote total numbers at a given date or time span. They fail to take into account the very considerable monthly turnover of members for all the settlements (except Murtho) due to almost continual departures of disgruntled or expelled members, whose places were, at least in the first eighteen months, taken up by optimistic newcomers. No records of these departures and arrivals exist but it is clear that the number of men, women and children who passed through the settlements in the 1894-5 period must have been well in excess of two thousand. From mid-1895 the exodus was rapid from all settlements and by June 1905 when only four of the original settlements were surviving the total number of persons was down to 279.

Except for Murtho, the great majority of the members of the settlers were unskilled men drawn from the ranks of the unemployed. Most of them came to the settlements without money and very few possessions, so perhaps they did not see the failure of the ambitious settlement scheme in the same light as the minority who did come with possessions and lost everything. All left with knowledge gained and in most cases with friendships forged out of hardship and shared privations.

Many made a success of these ventures, owning their little piece of Paradise along the mighty Murray.

13

The Spiritual Factor

There is a general consensus that the settlements that have the best chance of success are those with a strong spiritual or ethnic base, for example the Israeli kibbutsim which is strongly based on both these factors. Since the great majority of Australian communes have lacked either of these factors, it might well explain the high failure rate of such enterprises.

Spiritually oriented communes of one kind or another have, of course, been around for many centuries in both Christian and Buddhist congregations, in abbeys, convents and monasteries. Most of these long-running communes form part of major religions, but in the 19th Century there were many attempts to form communes with a spiritual base, mostly departing from the orthodox theology of the major religions. These were mainly based on the philosophies and ideas of such 19th Centuries thinkers as Robert Owen and Charles Fourier.

The great majority of such communes sprang up in the United States of America and quickly sank without trace under the weight of the inevitable personality clashes and doctrinal differences of the members. In fact the United States continues to be a fertile breeding ground for the weirdest of the world's cults such as the Heaven's Gate Sect in San Diego, California, who in March 1997 departed from this planet in "vehicles" bound for the UFO then trailing the comet Hale-Bopp! Not all

American Communal experiments were so short-lived. Back in the last century one American commune based on an unusual mix of the Bible, Sex, Communism and some extraordinary capitalistic enterprises, lasted for more than three decades before its founder got sick of the whole thing, decamping in the middle of the night to Canada.

I refer to that quite remarkable social experiment known as the Oneida Community, located in up state New York and which attracted visitors from all parts of the world during its long operation. Although it was probably the most publicised and controversial social experiment of the 19th Century, no attempt was ever made to adapt its principles in Australia.

The Oneida Community was the brainchild of John Humphreys Noyes, born in 1811, who studied for the law, but at the age of 20 decided devote the rest of his life to God. The trouble was that his views on religious matters were at such variance with the Andover Theological College or the Yale Divinity School that he was expelled and forced into becoming a preacher with his own brand of Bible-based religion, which because he was so highly-sexed, had to embrace some unusual theological ideas. In an interview with a visiting English journalist, he attempt to explain his sex theories this way: *Religious love is a very near neighbour to sexual love, and they always get mixed in with the intimacies and social excitements of Revivals. The next thing a man wants, after he has found salvation of his soul, is to find his Eve and his Paradise.*

To take care of his excessive sexual needs, Noyes had married a woman, Harriet Holton, whom he admired but did not love, but who had some money which enabled him to carry out his preaching duties and publish his views. His real Eve, with whom he was passionately in love, was named Mary Cragin, but she was married.

He got around this problem by persuading his wife and

Mary's husband, to form a sexual foursome. He seemed to have been a very persuasive character , especially when sexual matters were concerned, so it is probably true to say that he did find his Eve and his Paradise!

In 1848 he took his philosophy which he called Bible Communism, and a number of followers to Oneida, where on an old Indian reservation he formed the Oneida Association and proceeded to transform it into the most unusual commune experiment the world has seen.

Noyes original idea had been to form a rural-based commune but the soil around Oneida was of such poor quality that the commune had no luck with any planting except strawberries which thrived where all else failed.

Fortunately amongst his disciples were several tradesmen who proved to be very adept at coming up with inventions and in no time at all the small Oneida community had a fully fledged manufacturing operation churning out such unusual products as the world's first lazy Susan, a mechanical mop-wringer, a mechanical potato peeler, a washing machine, travelling bags, and a wide ranging variety of animal traps.

All these ideas were sold throughout the eastern states of America and brought such wealth to the Oneida community that it was able to employ much outside labour, bonding itself to the wider district community. It also enabled it to build impressive modern factory buildings and buy machinery. Other funds were poured into very substantial three-storey buildings to house the ever growing Oneida community of 300 at its peak. Workers changed jobs frequently so they would not become bored by routines and generally enjoyed a standard of living considerably above that of their fellow Americans.

This side of the Oneida experiment was quite remarkable for its time, and often forgotten in the severe criticism over blatant sexual exploitation of women within the community.

While the men of Oneida certainly enjoyed a lifestyle they could not have matched in the outside world, both in the material sense and in sexual matters, this also applied to the women. At Oneida, all men were considered to be married to all the women.

Control of the sexual side of these multiple "marriages" was totally in the hands of the women. They could remain celibate if they wished and had the final say as to whom their sexual partners were to be at any time. Rape or assault of any woman was unknown in the history of Oneida. It was perhaps the first time in history that a large group of women had total control over their bodies and were treated as equal in all matters. Children were brought up in a separate nursery/juvenile building but were accessible to either parent any time, night or day.

Perhaps the most remarkable feature of the Oneida experiment was that there was no religious dogma or ceremonies of any kind, no church services or sermons. It is unlikely that membership would have been open to atheists or agnostics, but a belief in the general tenets of Christianity seemed to be the only criterion for admission to the establishment. The vetting process for prospective members concentrated far more on their sexual opinions than their theology.

The community was run on democratic lines with considerable emphasis on debates and discussions on current and social affairs and wide ranging exchanges of views. Only personal criticisms of Noyes himself appear to have been off limits.

When Noyes himself departed in 1879 for a quieter and less active life, the community started to disintegrate and soon became a place of squabbling and dissent - a very common pattern with religious communes when the key figure vanishes from the scene.

Why was the Oneida experiment never duplicated

anywhere else seeing that it existed for three decades and probably attracted a thousand followers? Probably it was the sexual side of the experiment that was the key to its success, and perhaps this was far too revolutionary in its time for other would-be pioneers in the communal field. Even in the 1960s!

The Australian spiritual experiments seem tame compared to the revolutionary events at Oneida and by and large followed orthodox social practices, usually being founded by breakaway elements of traditional religions.

Australia's very first experiments in this field resulted from events in faraway Prussia in 1817 when the Prussian King attempted to force unity between the warring Lutherans and Calvinists. This was followed in 1822 with restrictive laws governing the liturgy to be practised in Protestant Churches.

These laws were strongly opposed by the moderate Evangelical Lutheran Church whose followers and pastors were subjected to considerable persecution for their dissent.

In 1835 the congregation of the Evangelical Lutheran Church at Zullichau in Brandeburg decided to migrate to America where they might enjoy freedom to practice their religion. They sent their Pastor August Ludwig Christian Kavel (1798-1860) to Hamburg to arrange matters. In Hamburg Kavel heard of a remarkable English industrialist George Fife Angas (1789-1879) who was a Baptist with liberal religious views. A member of the Colonisation Committee formed in 1834 to open up and settle the newly proclaimed colony of South Australia, he was actively seeking settlers for this venture.

Pastor Kavel travelled to England to meet George Angas and found instant support for his plans. Angas advanced the group eight thousand pounds to enable them to get established in their new land and in the years 1838-9 he financed the passage of three shiploads totalling some 500 new Lutheran migrants.

Pastor Kavel led the first group of 200 settlers on the

Prince George and they settled on the banks of the Torrens near Adelaide, on land acquired from Angas on a 17 year lease paying five shillings per acre rental per annum.

They named the new settlement Klemzig and thanks to good soils and wise leadership from their Pastor the venture prospered. By 1841 the settlement could boast a population of 430 with 100 horses and 350 cattle. It was of course not a commune but a closely knit settlement bound together by ethnicity and religion.

Adelaide at this time had a small population of 5000 mainly English-speaking settlers. A later group of Lutherans who arrived in December 1838 on the Zebra from Altona (Denmark) had difficulty finding suitable land, being hampered by lack of English in dealing with the locals.

Captain DM Hahn, of the Zebra, became aware of their plight and negotiated very favourable terms with one of the few landholders, William Dutton, for 150 acres of land. Here 38 families from the Zebra founded their tiny village of Hahndorf in February 1839, the land was sub-divided into 53 sections and they set about the task of building huts and tilling the soil.

The first year was a difficult one for the newcomers who had little capital and no horses, carts or waggons to get their vegetables and produce by the circuitous rough tracks to Adelaide.

This problem was solved in a most unusual way by the teenage girls and young married women of the settlement who volunteered to carry the produce across the ranges. This undertaking, by what came to be known as the Hahndorf Walkers was not an easy one as they had to negotiate at night the Onkaparinga range, the Beaumont and Gleeson hills.

At that time there were two tracks across the hills to the tiny village of Crafters, one involving a six and a half mile trek, and another much steeper track which was a mile shorter.

The young women walked in convoys on each trek starting around midnight, carrying baskets of produce on their heads or strapped to their backs. Aboriginals in the area were considered hostile and there were bushrangers operating in the hills. As the women considered that the most dangerous places in the convoys were first and last, they drew straws to decide which walkers would occupy these vulnerable positions.

In darkness and with heavy loads, they had to proceed slowly with numerous resting stops. When they reached the bottom of the hills at Crafters there was a stream to wash and comb their hair before walking the seven mile road into the markets of Adelaide. As fresh produce was scarce, they were warmly welcomed and soon disposed of their basket loads.

On a weight-for-value basis, eggs were the most productive line fetching four shilling a dozen. Butter realised sixpence a pound and cheese three shillings a pound. Potatoes only yeilded fourpence a pound, the same price as a small cabbage, but it all added up.

The Hahndorf Walkers then spent the proceeds on goods needed back on the farm. Top priority was always given to flour which cost one and tuppence per pound and was of dubious quality. A pound of meat cost ninepence and a four pound loaf of bread cost four shillings. Candles were ninepence a pound and soap two shillings and sixpence.

With baskets refilled the Walkers rested until midday before returning to Hahndorf before sundown, although some of the younger walkers stayed overnight with friends.

One of these, Thelka Staude, has told of her experience as a fifteen year old, staying overnight with the family of a carpenter saying that "a couple of rugs on the shavings under the carpenter's bench made a fine bed."

Throughout the difficult years of 1839 and 1840, the women of Hahndorf made these remarkable night walks once a week, and when the produce was flowing at its peak they made twice weekly trips to the Adelaide markets.

From these efforts they prospered, purchasing horses, carts and waggons to take their produce to market in bulk, gradually phasing out this remarkable experiment in our history - the nightly treks of the Hahndorf Walkers.

Captain Hahn visited the valley in January 1839, in the company of William Dutton and was amazed at the beauty of the valley which later was named in his honour. As he wrote in his book *The Most Remarkable Events of My Life:*

I would never have believed such land to exist on the earth. If I had my family here with me, I would like to end my life in these peaceful valleys and never return to the world.

Sentiments shared by the settlers of Hahndorf.

A later wave of settlers to the Barossa was led by another noted Pastor, Gotthard Daniel Fritzsche (1797-1863). Initially the two groups worked together in harmony, founding the townships of Langmeil (Tanunda) and Bethany. The settlements were two widespread for one pastor to handle so Kavel serviced the northern districts and Fritzsche handled the southern areas.

There were clashes of personality and doctrine between the Pastors which quickly spread to the congregations resulting in the formation of two warring synods, the United Evangelical Lutheran Church of Australia and the Evangelical Lutheran Synod of Australia.

And that wasn't the only division among the new Lutheran s to Australia. Among the early settlers was the charismatic Johann Frederick Krumnow who had doctrinal views differing from both Pastors Kavel and Fritzsche. When he attempted to translate these into a Moravian commune near Hahndorf, the Lutheran community excommunicated him.

Krumnow then moved to Victoria where he successfully established the Herrnhut Commune , Australia's first commune in September 1853 on 640 hectares near Hamilton. This was a true commune. with members sharing in the property and profits, though Krumnow retained power of control.

In 1875 another Moravian commune was established in Victoria, This was called the Hills Plains Commune and was located near Tungamah by Maria Heller and a group of 75 followers from Germany. This experiment proved a disaster as they were unable to grow enough food to sustain themselves. After a number of the original members had died of malnutrition, the remnants made their way across Victoria to join Krumnow's Herrnhut Commune. When Krumnow died in 1880 only eight members remained and the lands in debt. The members struggled to maintain the commune for another 17 years but eventually it was sold up in 1897.

Nevertheless 44 years was a long time for a commune to survive, in Australia or anywhere else.

Victoria was also home to another well publicised 19th Century spiritually based commune when the Reverend George Brown established Community Home, a Christian Socialist commune near Drouin in 1889. Group members shared all property and profits and lived and dined together. The general aims of the society were in many ways, apart from the sexual arrangements, similar to the Oneida Community, aiming to be entirely self-sustaining and by starting various industries to provide employment. They failed dismally and by 1892 it had collapsed despite the funds poured into the project from a profitable cafe which the Reverend Brown owned in Melbourne.

Whilst Victoria seems to have had a monopoly on spiritually-based Utopian communes in the 19th Century, there was an interesting experiment in Western Australian which seems to have sprung out of the Victorian communal experiences.

This occurred in 1902 when James C Fisher, a Jew who had been converted to Christianity, led a group of Victorian farmers to the Yarling area, east of Narrogin in the Western Australian wheatbelt. There they established New Jerusalem, a "Jewish-Christian" community.

Despite its rather confusing, name it seems to have been a successful enterprise, at least in the early years. By 1903 the settlement occupied 4000 hectares of land of which 400 were under crops, and had a membership of 70. However, Fisher sustained a head injury in an accident and became unstable and hard to work with. He died in 1915 after which the commune was dissolved and the remaining members melded into the district community where many descendants still farm.

14

The Second Coming

The dawn of the 20th Century saw a change of direction for spiritually oriented communes with two such experiments venturing into new territory based on the Second Coming of the Messiah! Victoria was the venue for the first of these experiments when a Dr Dalziel, a retired physician from Edinburgh, led a group of breakaway Plymouth Brethren from England to Kyneton, where he established the Holy City Commune.

This prospered for a while but fell apart when Dr Dalziel had a "Divine Revelation" which instructed him to await the Second Coming of Christ in Jerusalem. There he died still awaiting this event.

The second experiment came from a most unlikely source, the Theosophical Society. Founded in New York in 1875, it transferred its headquarters to India in 1879. The original leader of the movement, Colonel Olcott, visited Australia in 1891 and established branches in Sydney and Adelaide. Subsequently lodges were established in all capital cities and most large regional centres throughout Australia.

The aim of the Society was the study of comparative religions, philosophy and science and the formation of a universal brotherhood of humanity without distinction of race, creed, caste or colour.

The Australian section of the movement took a completely new direction as a result of visits by Dr Annie Besant (1847-1933) a leading and very forceful member of the English movement.

Originally married to a clergyman, Annie Besant separated from him and became an active free-thinker, a proponent of socialism and (with Dr Marie Stopes) a leading advocate of birth control. In 1895 she became involved in the Theosophical movement and moved to India. There she identified as the New Messiah a young Indian, Jiddu Krishnamurti, who was born near Madras in 1897. Early in life he had been identified as a mystic and in 1911 Annie Besant succeeded in having him proclaimed as Leader of the Order of the Star of the East.

Dr Besant brought the young Krishnamurti to Australia and such was the impact on the Sydney community that they changed direction and adopted a Utopian stand, prepared for the "Second Coming".

The more serious members of this new revivalist movement lived in a 55-roomed commune called The Manor at Clifton Gardens. On the nearby Balmoral Beach they erected an enormous amphitheatre facing the Pacific Ocean, that could seat thousands. The idea was that supporters could be seated to watch Krishnamurti proclaim himself as the New Messiah.

Alas for the Theosophical planners, Krishnamurti decided in 1929 that he was not the Messiah and disbanded the Theosophical Society in India. The Amphitheatre was demolished in 1951 but The Manor still operates.

When the late Keith Wiley visited Cape Tribulation in the Daintree wilderness area north of Cairns in 1970 he found an interesting batch of beachcombers and dropouts which included Harry Moss, a Welshman who was a Greek scholar of some note; Walter Fireman, a Scotsman born in Russia, who worked in Asia as an engineer for many years before settling in the Cape area with his Malayan wife Teminah; and Barefoot Bert, a Canadian seaman who occasionally abandoned his beachcombing life for another brief spell at sea.

But the most unusual drop-outs encountered by Wiley were the Rykers ("a tribe rather than a family") all devoted followers of Krishnamurti.

The patriarch of this unusual clan was Hendrik Rykers, born in Holland in 1891 who had settled at Cape Tribulation around 1960 with his wife Agnes, their sons William and Robert, and the latter's wife and two children.

The Rykers acquired 140 acres of land on the north side of the Cape and cleared 10 acres for their two-storey house built of silky oak and black-bean timbers, and their extensive orchard, leaving the remainder a rainforest wilderness.

The Rykers were strict vegetarians, growing almost all their own food and eschewing all animal products, eggs, honey and fish. This was unusual for the area as fish was the staple diet of most of their reclusive neighbours.

The Ryker family were Utopians seeking True Communism and True Christianity bound by the Commandment "Thou shalt not kill" - this prohibition even extending to leeches!

They celebrated neither Christmas or birthdays, and avoided all contact with the Queensland education and health systems.

When Mrs Ryker senior had a fall climbing rocks and broke her leg, her sons trundled her home in their wheelbarrow and wrapped her in cold water bandages which healed perfectly. After a number of meetings with the Rykers, Keith Wiley later wrote:

Often I have wished I had the strength of character and the ability to live as they did, for they have chosen a beautiful place in which to work out their philosophies.

In the heady New Age era of the 1960's and 1970's

communes sprung up in all Australian states and among them were a few rural communes established by both older religions.

The Buddhists were the first in 1974 when two visiting Indian lamas, Yeshe and Zopa Rinoche came to Australia to conduct a retreat in the Diamond Valley, north of Brisbane, resulting in a permanent commune on a 65 hectare block outside Eudlo. This was named the Chenrezig Institute for Western Culture and over the years it expanded to include visitor accommodation, library, workshops, stupas and a nunnery. After a quarter of a century Chenrezig seems well established as part of the local scene and a major focus of Buddhism in Australia.

The Hare Krishnas have also gone bush in one of their three rural communes in New South Wales. There they practice their Vedic spiritual exercises and busy themselves growing crops and vegetables on their highly productive rural retreats. The members of these communes take all their meals together and unmarried members are celibate and sleep in sex-segregated dormitories. Married couples stay together but are forbidden to have intercourse except for procreation. Sometimes their ordered and secluded way of rural life is disturbed by the outside world in strange ways. Early in 1997 a bearded gentleman turned up on the doorstep of the 330 hectare Hare Krishna commune at Eungella, some 8 kilometres west of Murwillumbah. He was taken in to the commune, housed in the stables and in the months that followed showed great interest in Krishna literature. A keen participant in the commune's daily chanting sessions (though he had not got around to shaving his head) he also worked hard in the garden and was put in charge of a newly established permaculture section.

After three months the Hare Krishnas lost this honest toiler of the soil when police arrived and carted him off.

It was only then that the Hari Krishnas found that their "guest" was none other than Russell Goward, former high flying business tycoon, once touted as one of Australia's brightest and richest entrepreneurs; on the run, having skipped bail on various charges of perjury and concealing assets.

The stable accommodation on the Hare Krishna commune didn't enjoy a five star rating but Russell Goward probably found it preferable to his new quarters in prison. Whether he missed the music and the chanting in his new abode is not on public record. Probably the Hare Krishnas bore no ill feeling towards their departed guest, though their monk Lagudi, must have wondered whether he would ever get repaid the $100 he trustingly loaned to Goward to buy a bicycle and a pair of working boots.

15

The Israel of Oz!

Two well planned schemes for large scale Jewish settlements in the Kimberley region of north-west Australia both failed and to understand this it is necessary to know something of recent Jewish history.

Late in the 19th Century a Jewish journalist in Vienna named Theodore Herzl galvanised European Jews with a call to establish a Jewish homeland in Palestine, then controlled by Britain. Out of this sprang the powerful Zionist movement which sought to carry out Herzl's bold dream.

But the Zionist idea was by no means embraced by all Jews, even those who hankered after a homeland. For a start Palestine was occupied by Arabs who considered Palestine to be their homeland, and would stoutly resist being ousted from the lands they had held for several thousand years.

The Jewish community thus became sharply divided between two opposing ideas: The Zionists who held out for Palestine and the rest who might have preferred Palestine but were prepared to look at other locations for a Jewish homeland.

Both these Jewish movements flourished in Great Britain around the turn of the century. In Britain a Jew might expect discrimination, but seldom persecution and as Britain controlled Palestine it made sense to carry out lobbying for and against a Palestine homeland at the centre of power. The opponents of the Zionist ideal were also lobbying the British Government for a Jewish homeland in some part of the then far flung Empire.

This resulted in some unusual ideas being put forward. Perhaps the most bizarre of all such schemes was an offer in 1903 by the British Secretary of Colonies Joseph Chamberlain that Britain should hand over to the Jews for their homeland the entire colony of Uganda in East Africa. It was such an unusual offer that Zionist leader Theodore Herz supported it for a time! When Herz died in 1904 the Seventh Zionist Congress soundly rejected the Uganda plan.

The anti-Zionist forces then began to look around for alternate sites and various places were examined and rejected, including Argentine, Mexico, Brazil, Angola, Canada and Cyrenaica.

All were found wanting so it was inevitable that their eyes should turn to Australia's vast open spaces and small population, with particular attention being given to the Kimberley region.

Apart from the availability of land, Australia had a number of advantages. It was part of the British Empire, had a stable and prosperous economy, a long history of successful migration and no record of open anti-Semitism. It was true that discrimination against Jews existed at some levels, but not more so than in other parts of the civilised world.

The leader of the non-Zionist group was an influential English Jewish writer named Israel Zangwill, who expended quite a lot of energy pushing the Kimberley proposal. When the Australian Prime Minister Alfred Deakin visited London in 1907, Zangwill met with strong opposition to the idea. This was from a man who as Premier of Victoria had been responsible for bringing the Chaffey brothers from the USA to establish the vast Murray River irrigation schemes then being developed.

Deakin's objections were not to the Jews as immigrants

but to the fact that they wanted to set up their own state, with their own laws. A state within a state would not be tolerated by Australians he maintained.

Three years later Zangwill had extended talks with the Premier of Western Australia, Sir Newton Moore, but met the same response as he had received from Deakin.

In 1917 during World War I, Zangwill received a body blow to his cause when the British Foreign Secretary Lord Balfour officially announced British support for a Jewish homeland in Palestine. A few weeks later General Allenby's troops marched into Jerusalem.

Although it took a long time for Britain to honour its promise, the very fact that the pledge was there was a significant coup for the Zionist movement. In 1925 Zangwill admitted defeat and officially disbanded his organisation, thus putting an end forever to plan for a State of Israel in Australia.

A decade after he had called it quits it was taken off the shelf, dusted down and given a new lease of life in an amended form. There were two reasons for this. The first was the growing disenchantment of the Jews with the reluctance of Britain to honour the Balfour undertaking of 1917 on Palestine, a plan that seemed as far off and unattainable as ever; and secondly, there was the advent of the Nazis to power in Germany, with wholesale persecution of the German Jews. It seemed imperative that they find places to house the flood of Jews being driven out of their country.

An examination of the old Australian Kimberley plan made it obvious that it would never get off the ground as a proposal for a self-governing Jewish state. However, it could work as a Jewish farm settlement operating completely within the Australian laws, and the promoters of the idea had a model of such a system to draw upon. A model in the unlikely location of Siberia!

Given the long history of anti-Semitism by both the Czars and the Bolsheviks, Communist Russia would seem to be the last place to find a Jewish homeland system operating, let alone flourishing. Yet by 1935 one had been operating, apparently successfully for several years.

From the start of the Bolshevik revolution, Russian Jews had been agitating for the establishment of a separate autonomous Jewish state within the Soviet Union. Initially they wanted it located in the productive Crimea but there were no vacant lands and gradually their demands shifted to Siberia.

By the late 1920's the focus had settled on the relatively small region of Birobidzhan on the border between the USSR and Manchuria. The region had an area of 36,000 square kilometres, with its main town, also named Birobidzhan, being located on the trans-Siberian railway line.

The proposal to turn Birobidzhan into a Jewish region would not have got off the ground without the strong support given to it by Michael Ivanovich Kalinin, the President of the USSR (1923-1946), who probably took a personal interest in it because he had been exiled to Siberia by the Czars in 1904. Although his many titles within the USSR carried prestige rather than real power, his was a voice that still carried weight, especially on non-political issues as this one appeared to be.

In a speech at a congress of the Society for Jewish Agricultural Settlement at Ozet in 1926, he made this observation *The Jewish people now faces the great task of preserving its nationality. For this purpose a large segment of the Jewish population must transform itself into a compact farming population, numbering at least several hundred thousand souls.*

Two years later, on March 28 1928, the Presidium of the Central Executive Committee of the Soviet Union passed a resolution authorising the Committee for the Settlement of Jews (KOMZET) to supervise a Jewish settlement near Birobidzhan.

Jewish immigration to the region commenced in 1928 and continued for many years at varying rates, each family being given a land holding and considerable assistance in getting settled. In the early years the turnover rate was quite high - sometimes as much as 50%, as the new settlers struggled to cope with the farming practices and the harsh climate. Initially the migrants came only from the western zones of Russia but by the early 1930's more than 1400 immigrants had arrived from outside countries, mainly the United States of America, Europe and South America. A Yiddish newspaper was published, Yiddish schools were established, along with a State Jewish Theatre and a Regional Library. The purges of the mid 1930's resulted in a serious setback for the emerging colony, almost completely cutting off the flow of foreign migrants and donations.

At the outbreak of World War 11 the estimated Jewish population in Birobidzhan was around the 20,000 mark and this remained constant through the war years. It increased in the immediate post war years and reached a peak of around 30,000 in 1948.

In July 1935 the Freeland League for Jewish Territorial Colonisation was set up in London to investigate areas for settlement of Jewish refugees pouring out of central Europe, and decided to have another look at settlement in Australia.

They quickly realised that the Zangwill plan for a Jewish state had been impractical, but thought a settlement idea along the Birobidzhan lines might be more successful. Early in 1938 the Freeland League decided to send their Secretary, Dr Isaac Steinberg, to Australia to sound out the locals and actually check out possible sites in the Kimberleys .

Isaac Nachman Steinberg was an extraordinary individual, a charismatic figure who had made his mark in a number of fields as writer, orator, revolutionary politician and jurist. Born in Latvia in 1888 into a wealthy family of merchants, he enrolled in law at Moscow University in 1906 and soon became enmeshed in illegal student politics for which he received a sentence of three years exile in Siberia. On appeal this was reduced to two years and he was allowed to leave Russia for Germany, where he resumed his studies at Heidelberg University where he met Rosa Luxemburg, Victor Chernov, Vladimir Lenin and Leon Trotsky.

After his graduation in 1910 he returned to Moscow, gaining a reputation as a defender of the rights of Jews in the then very anti-Semitic Russian courts. when the Russian Revolution occurred in 1917 he joined the Bolsheviks and became the first Commissar for Justice in the new government.

Steinberg's zealousness and idealism soon put him on a collision course with some of the old Bolsheviks and his all too brief career as a revolutionary came to an end in protest over the signing of the Brest-Litovsk Treaty with Germany in February 1918. He was arrested then rescued by Lenin who exiled him on a one-way trip to an international socialist conference in Germany in 1923. In Germany he became active in the field of Jewish culture, a fairly dangerous field at the time.

While on a lecture tour of Britain in 1933, he received a message from his wife warning him not to return. Three months later she and their three children joined him in his life of exile in Britain where he founded a Yiddish journal and became one of founders of the Freeland League.

This was the rather extraordinary individual who set out for Australia in 1939 to try and persuade its leaders to allow him to set up Jewish settlements. Because of his political connections with the Bolsheviks, the Australian authorities were reluctant to grant him a visa, but after representations at a very high level, granted him a three months visa with an official warning that it was against Government policy for aliens to form colonies!

136

When Steinberg landed at Fremantle on May 23 1939 he had a fairly substantial ace up his sleeve - a very powerful and influential Australian ally awaiting him - Michael Patrick Durack, former member for Kimberley in the Legislative Assembly, and then owner of Argyle Station and other Kimberley properties. Durack's support for Steinberg's settlement scheme was partly self-serving because he wanted to sell the family's Kimberley holdings, and the Freeland League were anxious to buy them - if they could gain government approval for their plans.

Durack's support was critical because his influence opened many doors which might otherwise have remained closed.

One of the major hurdles that Steinberg faced was that the then Premier of Western Australia, John Willcock (1879-1956), had openly expressed opposition to the Freeland League scheme, mainly because a previous government had had its fingers badly burned as a result of supporting a scheme in the 1920's to settle British immigrants in the Albury-Bunbury area.

Within two days of his arrival, Steinberg arranged a meeting with Willcock and had managed to overcome many of his objections. The Premier said he would keep an open mind on the proposal and urged Steinberg to go up to the Kimberley and investigate the area and come back with detailed plans.

After an intensive few weeks in Perth lobbying influential people , Steinberg set off with Michael Durack for an inspection of the Kimberleys, flying to Wyndham and then embarking on a strenuous two week tour of the northern Kimberley area, in which they covered 1200 kilometres.

The trip was a revelation to Steinberg. He had expected to find desert and barren lands and instead found a paradise of grassy plains, extensive forests and rich soils. He was enchanted with the vibrancy of the whole area, an experience shared by many first time visitors to the Kimberleys and was to say he felt like Moses gazing upon the Promised Land, and had visions of great colonies spreading across the Top End.

Immediately he returned to Perth, Steinberg prepared an extensive and detailed plan for his proposed settlement, which involved the Freeland League taking over the lease of the Durack properties, plus a purchase of an additional half million acres freehold, so that the League could sell portions outright to the settlers, giving them a financial stake in the whole venture. The whole scheme was to be developed over fifteen years in stages, with rural economists, technicians and skilled workers being brought in for the initial stages. All the capital works of roads, dams and experimental farms would be funded by the League. The settlers would have complete religious freedom and run their internal affairs but would be subject to State and Federal laws on all matters governing taxation, defence, policing, justice and education.

This rather breathtaking proposal, which no doubt contained a certain element of hype, was presented to the Western Australian Government on July 28 1939. The proposal received a lot of solid parliamentary support from the major parties.

The Kimberley proposal had been receiving considerable press coverage in the eastern states and reaction there was very much along the lines to that in the west. Steinberg was particularly impressed with the widespread support he was receiving from church leaders throughout Australia.

This was a little surprising given the fact that at that time and for many years, Australia had been a nation deeply divided by bitter sectarian rivalries - usually on the basis of Protestant v Catholic antagonism. Yet Bishops and Archbishops in all states were joining forces in support of the Kimberely scheme. Some of this may have been dictated by a feeling of guilt over the role the churches had played in persecuting the

Jews of Europe, but there was also a nationwide sympathy for the. victims of the Nazi pogroms then being carried out in Germany, and the feeling of Australians for a "fair go". Having won the west, at least on a state level, he moved east as he found he could not get his scheme off the ground without the Federal Government granting entry to the large numbers of Jewish refugees to be settled in the Kimberleys.

Where his ideas fell on mainly fertile ground in the west, where development ideas were welcome, Steinberg ran into opposition in Melbourne, at that time home to a majority of Australian Jews, and a city where Zionist sentiment was overwhelmingly for a Jewish homeland in Palestine. They mounted a massive and long running propaganda campaign against Steinberg and his Kimberley scheme.

The ferocity of the Zionist campaign stunned Steinberg's non-Jewish supporters, many of whom were supportive of the Zionist cause and who saw no great conflict between the Kimberley plan and the more distant Palestine homeland goal. Bishop Pilcher summed up the matter when, in a letter to the *Zionist*, the Journal of the Australian Zionist movement, he implored the Zionists to cease their campaign against the Kimberley scheme:

Perhaps you can imagine what effect your attitude has upon the minds of Christian friends of Israel. The Western Australian Government has approved the Kimberley Scheme. As far as I know, with the exception of the Government of Soviet Russia, this is the only Government in the world which has declared its willingness to set apart a tract of territory for the homeless Jews who escape from the Nazi hell. It finds its efforts sabotaged by Jews. Some of us Christians have been doing all we can to secure the opening of the gates of Palestine. We find ourselves criticised by Jews. We endeavour to support a subsidiary scheme of rescue and again we find ourselves opposed - by Jews.

The Bishop's plea fell on deaf ears so far as the Zionists were concerned, but in Canberra the Federal Government had been taking note of the controversy over the Kimberley scheme.

Had there been a Prime Minister with the vision and courage of Alfred Deakin, the Kimberley Scheme might have got off the ground given the huge amount of support from churchmen, community leaders, the union movement and the general public. But the then Prime Minister, Robert Gordon Menzies was no Deakin, either in vision or political courage. He was an ultra cautious leader, well aware that he did not enjoy unanimous support of his party, well aware of the undercurrent of xenophobia and anti-Semitism lurking in every community, even the usually tolerant Australian one.

World War 11 had already broken out, which increased the difficulties of any action on such an ambitious scheme as that envisaged by Steinberg who was now resigned to getting plans in place for implementation in the post-war era. Senior Public Servants were hostile to the Kimberley scheme, believing it could prove to be a financial burden on the Commonwealth, and managed to stall the proposal until January 1941 when the Government announced that because of the war no decision would be made on the plan. When the Menzies Government was replaced by Labor, Steinberg re-submitted his plans, but received a frosty reception from the new Prime Minister John Curtin, who was deeply suspicious of Steinberg's old association with the Bolsheviks. After Curtin's death the new Prime Minister Ben Chifley was equally unresponsive.

Steinberg then tried to interest the Dutch Government in allowing a Jewish settlement in the Dutch Colony of Suriname off the South American coast. The Dutch showed initial interest but dropped negotiations after the establishment of Israel in 1948.

Steinberg died in New York in January 1957, without

realising his dream of a Jewish Paradise in the Kimberleys or anywhere else.

Writing long after the event, the former Labor Leader Arthur Calwell was to say that the Kimberley scheme never had a chance of getting off the ground. In 1978 Calwell raised an interesting issue which had never entered the pre-war debate on the scheme:

As for those Australians who supported the Kimberley Settlement, I do not suppose it ever occurred to them whether Australia had the right to take this land from the Aboriginals in the first place and give it to people from Europe or from Asia or Africa. If any people are homeless in Australia today, it is the Aboriginals. They are the only non-European descended people to whom we owe any debt.

The establishment of the State of Israel in 1948 probably meant the end to any idea of an Australian Jewish settlement, which meant that the Zionists had achieved their goal, so ensuring that the Middle East would be the world's main trouble spot for generations to come.

The event also posed problems for the far off province of Birobidzhan which immediately lost its flow of migrants from abroad. The Zionists had always bitterly opposed the idea of the Jewish settlements in Birobidzhan, now Israel threatened to extinguish them.

The tiny Siberian colony might have been down, but they weren't out and when the Soviet Union fell apart in 1992, the former province proclaimed themselves the new Jewish Republic of Birobidzhan. How they managed to do this is n't clear because at no time did the Jewish settlers account for more than a tenth of the total population of Birobidzhan.

Moscow may have been surprised by this move but there was positive shock and dismay in Tel Aviv. The last thing that the Zionists wanted was a rival Jewish state. The official reaction was to completely ignore the unwelcome news from Siberia.

News of the declaration does not seem to have made much impact on the international front as very little news appeared in the media but if the general republic remained in the dark about these developments in Siberia, the stamp collectors of the world were soon aware of the situation because the Birobidzhaners followed up their proclamation with the issue of a whole series of new postage stamps from the Republic, mostly carrying Jewish symbols. Such was the flood of these new stamp issues in the 1992-4 period that it seemed that the controllers of the new Republic were determined to make the philatelists of the world balance their local budget.

Trying to read a crystal ball into the future is always difficult, but I think we may assume that in the 21st Century there will be no revival of plans for a Jewish settlement in Australia. The future of Israel and Birobidzhan in that time span seems less certain, since the Zionist Goliath will have to continue to ward off Arab wrath while in far off Birobidzhan, the David of the Jewish world will have to cope with its own limitations of isolation and climate.

One thing is sure. It won't only be the stamp collectors of the world that will be watching developments in both places with more than a little interest.

16

Bob's Kibbutzim Plan.

When the State of Israel was created in 1948 it realised a dream of the Zionist movement of providing for the first time a home for the Jewish people of the world - the first case in modern times of a state being established on the basis of a religious faith instead of the usual norm of ethnicity.

The new structure of the old Holy Land also brought many physical changes to the cities and lands of Israel, and many innovations not found elsewhere around the globe.

Included in these changes was the establishment of great numbers of agricultural communes called Kibbutzim, thus adding a new word to the English language: Kibbutz (or plural Kibbutzim) from the Hebrew qibbutz, or Modern Hebrew qibbus.

Agricultural communes have been around in one form or another for millennia, comprising groupings of people with a purpose and beliefs, tilling the land and sharing tasks under ownership.

The Kibbutzim of Israel differed from other communes in several important respects. They were sponsored, and to a large degree financed by the State of Israel and they were mainly located along Israel's borders as strategic defence outposts. The young men and women of the kibbutzim were highly trained members of the Israel Army reserves and the kibbutzim were heavily fortified and armed against attack from across the borders. In effect they were part of the Israeli defence system.

The permanent members of the kibbutzim were expected to be of Jewish faith, as were the majority of the many thousands of younger people from the around the world who flocked to Israel to be part of the kibbutzim experiment, sometimes to spend months, or even a few years on these unusual communes. A few even married and settled permanently.

Over the years the kibbutzim attracted considerable publicity world wide, and eventually became magnets for visitors, Jewish and Gentile, to the State of Israel.

Included amongst the foreign admirers of the kibbutzim experiments, and of the State of Israel, was a very prominent Australian, Robert James Lee Hawke, Rhodes Scholar, and advocate and later President of the Australian Council of Trade Unions (1970-1980), and later still Prime Minister of Australia (1983-1991).

In his ACTU years Bob Hawke made many visits to Israel, in the process winning the confidence of the Israeli leaders. In 1971 he flew to Russia and had lengthy talks with Alexander Shelepin, the influential head of the Soviet trade union movement, which helped the easing of tensions then existing between Israel and the Soviet Union.

He was also successful in representations to have the Soviet Union ease restrictions on the migration of its Jewish citizens to Israel. In 1970 the Soviet Union had allowed only 1000 Jews to migrate. Following Hawke's talks with Shelepin the rates of Jewish migrated jumped dramatically : 13,000 in 1971, 32,000 in 1972 and 35,000 in 1973. On several visits to Israel Bob Hawke had briefly visited kibbutzim and had evidently been impressed by them. On his 1971 visit to Israel, which preceded his mission to the Soviet Union as an unofficial mediator, he had been accompanied by his fourteen year old daughter and had arranged for her to stay at a kibbutz for six weeks while he was jetting around the Middle East and Europe, so he had a chance to obtain a first hand family account. Twelve years on, as Prime Minister of Australia, he was to startle his party and the electorate, with a proposal that the Israeli kibbutzim idea was about to be brought to Australia - not as an experiment, but on a large scale to solve the youth unemployment problem.

To understand this extraordinary proposal, a little background is needed. In his ACTU years Bob Hawke had been a fierce critics of politicians in general and, even some of his own Labor Party members in particular. In 1973 he had made the sweeping declaration: *I understand what truth and democracy is, and I don't put my knees on the same altar as politicians.*

Times and opinions change and by 1980 Bob Hawke was ready to kneel down on altar in Canberra, as he sought and won, endorsement for the Victorian seat of Wills. And made it clear that he had Prime Ministerial ambitions.

Those were the Malcolm Fraser years and the leader of the Labor Opposition was the popular Bill Hayden, who came close to leading Labor to victory in the 1980 election. Hawke believed he could easily defeat Fraser at the polls but first he had to prise the ALP leadership from Bill Hayden.

His first attempt on July 16 1982, failed. The backroom boys in the Hawke camp then went to work and forced the resignation of Bill Hayden on the very day that Malcolm Fraser announced the February 1983 date of the next election. The very bitter Bill Hayden made the memorable remark that this was the election that "even a Drover's Dog could win".

Bob Hawke, in the new roll of Drover's Dog, in colloquial terms did Fraser like a dinner, forcing the latter's departure from the political scene.

So Bob Hawke became Prime Minister of Australia in controversial circumstances, leading a party that was riven with bitter discord over the manner of the Hawke coup.

To quell the dissenters in the party ranks, he must have felt the need to pull a few political rabbits out of the hat. There was also the need to do something drastic about the unacceptably high unemployment rate then prevailing that prompted him to make his extraordinary Kibbutzim announcement, not in Australia as might have been expected of such a radical proposal, but in his old ACTU hunting ground in Switzerland.

The venue he chose was the International Labor Organisation Conference in Geneva in June 1983 where he announced to a somewhat surprised audience that Australia was about to embark on an ambitious proposal to solve its unemployment problem by establishing rural communes based on kibbutzim lines.

The news of this proposal was received with incredulity back in Australia, both in and out of Labor circles. Before he departed for Israel Hawke had discussions with his Minister for Education Susan Ryan about the establishment of a pilot programme. He had even obtained a figure of 4000 settlements from officials of the Homeless Children's Association which had established a kibbutz-type village near Gosford in New South Wales, funded by several large corporations.

When the press sought information on the project from Labor sources in Australia they encountered a brick wall. No one wanted to be quoted, though opposition to the whole idea seemed to be strong from both factions.

Outside the Labor movement some authorities were willing to comment -all unfavourably - on the proposal.

Bob Santamaria, who had been closely involved with the failed Catholic Rural Movement of earlier years, pointed out that the only communes which had managed to survive for any length of time were those with a religious foundation and a strong ethnic or social solidarity.

Another strong critic of the whole idea was David Potts, of La Trobe University in Melbourne, who had studied the history of communes in Australia and overseas. He pointed to the many unsuccessful attempts by Governments from the late 19th Century onward to establish rural settlements. He thought the cost of providing suitable land, buildings, equipment and basic funding would be many times the cost of the existing dole payments to the participants. Furthermore, the idea of transferring large numbers of urban unemployed to the country was equivalent to sentencing them to a miserable future at a huge cost to the Australian taxpayer.

This was the conclusion that the hard-heads in the Labor Party seems to have reached as in the coming months they managed to quietly bury the ill-conceived scheme dreamed up by their Leader.

When the *Weekend Australian* of June 25-26 1983, devoted three quarters of a page to the plan and its many critics, it used a fairly telling headline across the page

KIBITZING HAWKE'S KIBBUTZIM

The funeral for the scheme was conducted late one moonless night well away from the public gaze and TV cameras, with little ceremony and minimum eulogies.

There was no period of mourning for the dearly departed and there was no subsequent resurrection from the grave of the idea of 4000 government sponsored and funded kibbutzim scattered across the Australian countryside.

Amen to that!

17

The Yeppoonese War

Despite the relatively short time span since white invasion and settlement of 1788, Australia has been involved in a considerable number of minor and major military conflicts.

From the start, it had a large military presence to keep the convicts in check and to exterminate troublesome indigenes as the need arose. Troops from Australia were extensively used in the Maori Wars over in New Zealand. New South Wales sent off a contingent to the Sudan War (only to arrive too late for any action), while a contingent to the Boxer Rebellion in China also arrived after cessation of hostilities. Troops from Down Under seeking action had more luck in the South African Boer War, though HH "Breaker" Morant and one of his mates, PJ Handcock, had the bad luck to fall to the bullets of a British firing squad after a pretty dodgy court martial.

There was plenty of action for Aussie youth in the two world wars that followed, and for their sons in the Korean and Vietnam Wars and the later unpleasantness in the Persian Gulf, as well as the Yeppoonese War of the 1970's, though this event doesn't figure in military histories of the day as no enlisted troops were involved in the hostilities.

Wars seldom happen by accident. Invariably there is some single event or underlying cause which prompts the outbreak of hostilities. Before we study the Yeppoonese War in detail let us consider the following scenario: Over a long period of time a small community, in a very scenic part of the Australian coastline has carved out a small segment of Paradise in a setting of magnificent golden beaches with a near perfect climate which enables its inhabitants to live very comfortably. One day along comes a developer who plans to dump on its doorstep a monstrous resort quite out of keeping with the environment.

Does this sound familiar? Unfortunately the answer must be yes, because in the post-war years this scenario has been played out on many parts of the coastline on both sides of the continent.

As history shows, there is not a great deal that the inhabitants of these little corners of Paradise can do about the situation since local councils and the State Governments can usually be counted upon to be pro-development, concerned more with the creation of jobs and the bottom line than with the environment. Litigation is too expensive and the various environmental groups are usually too busy squabbling among themselves to become interested in local disputes. It takes a big issue with lots of good photo opportunities to get any of them to volunteer to lay down in the path of the bulldozers.

All of which causes much heartburn in these small hardly done by pieces of Paradise. Add a touch of xenophobia to the equation in the shape of a foreign developer from a country recently at war with the folks Down Under, then the situation can become downright explosive. This is what happened in the case of the Yeppoonese War.

Most Australians would barely have heard of the small Queensland town of Yeppoon before the events of the 1970's. Yeppoon was then a seaside resort with a population of around 7000, located much too far up the coast to attract southern tourists, or even the Brisbane holiday crowd. It was a well known beach resort to the residents of Rockhampton ("Rocky" to the locals) and the nearby Mt Morgan from the turn of the century. Yeppoon had almost no passing traffic to contend with and that was the way they liked it, and planned to keep it that way.

These plans for tourist anonymity were shattered in 1970 when a Japanese Chamber of Commerce delegation led by billionaire Yohachiro Iwasaki, aged 80, visited the area.

The Japanese group were not interested in the town of Yeppoon, or its magnificent beach and bay, but they were vastly impressed with some 8000 hectares of beachfront land located north of the township.

The locals saw this vast tract as mainly scrub and untidy sand dunes which in colloquial terms "wouldn't run a sheep to the acre".

Iwasaki and his land-starved colleagues saw it in a different light entirely. Here was a huge stretch of flat virgin land with a superb beachfront 10 times longer and wider than Honolulu's famous Waikiki beach. All there for the taking and ridiculously cheap by Japanese standards.

Iwasaki returned to Japan and immediately started planning for the site an enormous development of quite breathtaking dimensions, to be built in several stages.

When completed the project would accommodate 18,000 Japanese tourists in 5 luxury hotels, 10 motels , 80 holiday units of varying sizes and 1250 villas. To entertain this vast horde there would be 18-hole golf courses, a marine park, botanical gardens, a wildlife reserve, a forest reserve, bird sanctuary, coconut plantation, and picnic, tennis and water sport recreational areas. The tourists would be ferried to and from Tokyo in a fleet of Jumbo Jets touching down in a new International Airport on the site.. It would seem that the ambitious Mr Iwasaki had plans to bring well in excess of half a million Japanese tourists a year into this one resort. As most Japanese have only single week long holidays, this meant that he would have needed to employ around fifty Jumbo jets every weekend to shuttle his holiday masses between Tokyo and Yeppoon!

Billionaires, wherever they are located, are a law unto themselves! After much detailed planning in Tokyo the proposal was submitted to a rather stunned Yeppoon local council and the State Government of Premier Joh Bjelke Petersen. After some negotiations between Tokyo and Brisbane, it was accepted enthusiastically by Sir Joh and his colleagues in 1978. The Local Council had more reservations because of community opposition, but eventually also gave it the green light.

One should consider here the motives of Yohachiro Iwasaki in this extraordinary venture. He was a very old man who saw it as an end of life dream, a project that would carry his name and fame into the next century. He also expressed the view that the project would cement relations between Australian and Japan after the disasters of World War II. The trouble was that he had no idea how his "Peace Offering" was thought of down in Australia.

Work on the first stage of the project, a multi-story motel and extensive landscaping, started in June 1979 and to mark the occasion Iwasaki staged a huge Opening Ceremony party on the site, attended by 260 guests flown in from Japan, plus a host of Australian personalities including most of the Bjelke Petersen Government. The entertainment included traditional Japanese drummers, dancing girls and fireworks.

The party didn't go down well at all with the locals and brought into open for the first time a latent racism originating from elements in the local RSL, and took the form of very blatant anti-Japanese posters and advertisements in the *Rockhampton Bulletin*. One of these advertised a protest meeting at which there would be "no free beer, no free food, no fireworks and no dancing girls"!

One advertisement inserted by the RSL was quite blunt

151

in its message:

ROLL OF HONOUR

In Memory of our fallen comrades who gave their lives in vain. When you go home, tell them of us, and say, for your Tomorrow, we gave our Today. President and Members of the Yeppoon sub-branch of the Returned Soldiers' League of Australia.

To emphasis their point the RSL placed outside their office, rows of small white crosses, one for each Yeppoon soldier who had died in World War 11. Feelings were running high...

On the evening of Saturday, November 29 1980, with the project motel nearing completion, some person or persons placed a huge bomb under the construction and blew up the motel - the first such act of terrorism against a project on the Australian mainland.

The event received considerable publicity in both the Australian press (where it was largely perceived to be a conservation protest) and in Japan where it was seen to be directed against the Japan as a nation, with wide publicity being given to the Launching Party in the previous year.

Mr Iwasaki, then very frail and his health failing, was quite devastated by the act. He died not long after the event and his family and companies showed no interest in carrying the ambitious project through to the end. They completed only the first stage, and that is what remains today.

The police selected as their main suspect a local who had been very vocal in the 1979 protests -Eric Geissmann, an elderly father of eight, always known locally as "Gunna" Geissmann (for his habit of saying he was *Gunna do this* and *Gunna do that.*) He earned his living in various ways, mainly by worm digging on the beaches and then supplying these as as bait to fisherman.

Police interviewed Gunna the day after the bombing, but without great result as their suspect was hung over from a night of heavy drinking. His story was that he had been working with a relative on a pineapple plantation the previous day and after work had had drinks at several pubs on his way home. At one of the pubs he had acquired a bottle of brown muscat wine which he had consumed after his evening meal, plus another half bottle of Muscat which he had at home. After this he had passed out and was in deep sleep or dead drunk when the bomb went off. Three relatives corroborated his story, and as the events he related seemed to be perfectly normal procedure for Gunna, they had to let him go.

Three months later, in February 1981, the police discovered suspect plants in possession of one of Gunna's best mates, Neville Wust, a former professional fisherman. Knowing Wust's connection with Gunna, the police applied a bit of pressure in questioning Wust and he mentioned that he had heard Gunna boasting in various pubs that he had done the Iwasaki motel bombing.

The police then coerced Wust into co-operating in an operation known in legal circles as entrapment. This is frowned upon in most police services, not the least because judges tend to throw out evidence garnered in this manner. In Queensland the wallopers have always done things their way and the operation proceeded.

Wust was instructed to invite Gunna out on his boat for a fishing trip in the bay, with lashings of grog of various kinds laid on. The likelihood of any fish being caught in these circumstances was remote, but Wust was instructed to keep Gunna drinking and talking, and when appropriate bring up the subject of the bombing in the hope that Gunna would repeat the boasts he was alleged to have made in pubs around town. To capture all this as evidence, the police took double precautions. They installed on the boat a tape recorder and as a backup a small radio transmitter which relayed all the conversations to a police team hidden on shore. This was also taped.

The operation went according to plan and allegedly Gunna did confess to the bombing (he claimed that he was aware of the taping and merely made things up). There were a few complications. The party aboard the boat had lasted 5 hours and only a tiny fraction of that time had been given over to the subject of the bombing. A very great deal of the time had been taken up by Wust and Gunna discussing at great length the various sexual proclivities, with assets and failings, real or imagined, of a great number of females in the Yeppoon and district community. The two old reprobates named "names". The tapes represented far more dynamite than had been used to blow up the motel in such a small close-knit community where everyone knew everyone else.

Initially ignoring the problem the police proceeded to charge Gunna Geissmann and his 23 year-old nephew Kerry Geissmann with the bombing. When the case came to court, the prosecutors regarded Wust as an unreliable witness and the case really rested on the tapes. If they presented only the portion carrying the alleged confession, the defence could claim they had doctored the tapes in some way and reached the painful conclusion that they had to produce in court the entire five hours of the tape or not use it at all.

News of this leaked out with a result that there were great queues of interested (mainly male) locals trying to get into the small court house when the case was brought on. The whole five hours of the tape was presented - an act that caused considerable repercussions out in the Yeppoon community for a long time afterwards.

It took the jury only ninety minutes to bring in a verdict of Not Guilty against Gunna and his nephew. The general feeling in the community was that Gunna probably did do the bombing, or had a hand in it somehow, but that the jury thought it was a dirty trick on the part of the police to trap him the way they did. Nor would the jury accuse Gunna and the relatives who had provided his alibi as liars. You don't do that in a small community. That is, if you want to continue living there.

After the case Neville Wust thought it would be wise to leave town, an action that was widely applauded.

If Gunna Geissmann did bomb the motel he didn't boast about it after the trial but he didn't let up in his campaign against the Iwasaki development. He had a significant victory when he spearheaded a campaign, which included a 50 day hunger strike, persuading the Queensland Government to resume for the Crown a 150 metre strip inland from the high water mark along the whole development frontage (thus ensuring that ordinary Australians would have permanent access to the beach along with the Japanese visitors to the resort). It was a major setback and embarrassment for the Iwasaki developers.

Gunna Geissmann died in 1991 after suffering a heart attack while walking along the beach he fought so strenuously to save for his fellow Australians.

In January 1993 I was travelling down the Bruce Highway after a visit to the Whitsundays area and decided to make a diversion to visit Yeppoon and the Iwasaki resort. My impressions of Yeppoon were all favourable - a really delightful hideaway from the rough and tumble of the outside world.

The Iwasaki Resort was quite a different matter.

Over the years I have visited all types of resorts in various parts of the world, and have found most differ only in their degrees of luxury and related charges. The majority welcome visitors providing they dress sensibly and behave themselves, though there are a minority who seek total exclusively for their guests and bar the casual visitor.

In the latter category is the Iwasaki Resort. Immediately inside the resort with its meticulously kept grounds the visitor is greeted with a number of very large, strategically placed signs proclaiming the fact that THIS IS PRIVATE PROPERTY.

I felt the urge to go back but decided to at least continue on up the long driveway to what can be classed as the village centre, a cluster of accommodation buildings erected in stage one of the project.

Apparently I was the only visitor that day since no other vehicles were parked in the square. In the short time I was there I did not sight another soul. Most resorts have a bar and coffee shop as well as a range shops, and my original intention had been to venture in for a coffee and a browse around in search of a suitable souvenir from a resort with such a fascinating history. There was no way of knowing whether any such amenities existed, let alone know whether or not a visitor might be welcome. The largest building had a door in the centre over which the word RECEPTION presided, but the door was closed.

I sat in the car for perhaps a quarter of an hour to see whether some sign of life might present itself to provide clues on the status of visitors then gave up, as the whole aura of the place was so unwelcoming.

I started the motor and headed back to the much friendlier atmosphere of Yeppoon where the residents were going about their daily routines in their leisurely fashion, apparently not paying much heed to the cyclone threat away up north.

Nobody ever really wins a war, as even the nominal victors emerge with scars, and this appears to have been the case in what I have termed the Yeppoonese wars.

In the beginning Yeppoon really was a little slice of Paradise. But one of the ingredients of Paradise is a sense of innocence, and that was certainly lost with the coming of the Iwasaki people, since the town quickly became divided into factions over the merits or otherwise of the development. And of course the Gunna and Wust tapes!

For the owners of the resort there can be no joy either.

The creator of the dream of a Japanese Shangri La, in faraway Australia has long gone to meet his maker, and his family and fellow investors are left with a financial millstone around their necks. By now they must have done their sums properly and have come to the realisation that the dream of old Yohachiro Iwasaki was just that - a dream.

18

The Weekender.

For centuries wealthy city-based families have indulged themselves in rural retreats to which they could repair for periods to recharge their batteries from the hurly burly of city life.

In Britain the country estate of the privileged is part of tradition, and these institutions have their counterparts in all parts of the world where there are families of wealth or prestige. During the last century some middle class families also indulged themselves in this manner. I have spent several idle weekends with such families in modest retreats in the beautiful Catskill Mountains just north of New York.

The power elites of Russia have long had their country dachas, but on a trip through Siberia and Russia in 1993 I found a revolutionary new trend in this sphere. The dense forests north of the Siberian capital of Irkutsk, close to the shores of the great Lake Baikal, the world's largest fresh water lake, were positively buzzing with the sound of chainsaws. In the new Russian Federation then taking shape, private citizens were allowed to take out a 50 year lease on land and the middle class citizens of Irkutsk were taking to this activity with considerable enthusiasm. The pattern appeared uniform. They would lease themselves a hectare piece of dense forest along some road, then get the chain saws in and saw down all the trees on their small patch. The logs were then used first of all to construct back and side fences, and then to build small but comfortable two room cabins with shingled roofs. Any timber left over was stacked at the back of the cabin for use as firewood.

Most of the cabins appeared to be built by the owners on a do-it-yourself principle. These cabins were all in isolated spots with no electricity, water or sewage. In other words the perfect getaway from it all retreat Russian-style.

A fair percentage of the good folk of Irkutsk, and no doubt of other places in the far flung Russian Federation, are experiencing the delights and drawbacks of the "Weekender", an institution that has been around in considerable numbers in Australia since the end of the 19th Century.

As no one has got around to writing up a history of Australian weekenders, we have no records of who started the trend. The artists of Sydney and Melbourne may have been in the forefront of the weekender enthusiasts - at least the members of the Heidelberg school were "going bush" on a fairly regular basis to do their rural sketches in the 1890's.

Much earlier than that the wealthy folk were indulging in the luxury of substantial retreats on the Mornington Peninsula in Melbourne and up to Palm Beach in Sydney, but these were a cut above the average plebeian weekender.

The middle and lower classes appear to have got into the weekender act in serious numbers in the early part of the 20th Century. The retreats ranged from crude one or two room shacks erected in isolated areas to cheap and nasty fibro cottages in more settled places. These were places to retreat in the school holidays and weekends, for a bit of fishing or mucking around in boats, or simply doing nothing much at all.

Some very interesting anomalies rose over the years. Every year tens of thousands of Australians (mostly city people) make the tropical city of Cairns in North Queensland their holiday destination. Cairns is an attractive city squashed between the sea and the Atherton range escarpment, with many tourist attractions. Yet along the coast, both north and south, are hundreds of weekenders owned by Cairns residents, all too anxious to get away from their own attractive city. Or perhaps they are just trying to get away from the out-of-town visitors!

While the majority of weekenders are acquired by city dwellers aiming to escape the rat race, if only briefly, there is a significant flip side of country people (at least in New South Wales) who have weekender units in Sydney, attracted to the bright lights of the city like moths to a flame. They don't want to get away from the rat race - they want to be part of it, to go shopping, take in the shows, and get of a whiff of the ocean breezes, all delights denied them in their varying home towns.

I have lost track of the number of Dubbo friends or acquaintances who have Sydney based pads (Manly is high on the priority list of such seekers after a city paradise) and who repair there on a regular basis.

While the number of genuine weekenders is quite enormous, there has been a slowing of growth in recent years as a result of the rising cost of acquiring and maintaining one of these havens to the standards demanded by councils. This trend has also been hastened by the counter trend of people buying caravans and taking to the roads to find paradise in the countryside. Or simply flying out for a week in Bali...

It seems that Paradise is not always easy to find, or to hold on to when you get it. At best weekenders might provide temporary glimpses of Shangri La, a kind of Clayton's Paradise, the one you have to have when you can't afford the real thing.

19

The Backyard Shed.

In England there is a long established practice of councils setting aside some land, often along canal and railway easements, known as Allotments. Residents can apply for plots in these Allotments where they can grow their own vegetables.

The system received quite a boost during World War II when growing vegetables on these Allotments became part of the war effort. Modern Brits seem to find other ways of using their spare time but the old Allotment system still survives in many parts of Britain in one form or another, because in many cases growing vegetables was secondary to the main attraction of having a plot.

Here the predominantly male owners could indulge in a bit of gossip and male bonding, getting away from home and the kids in the process. To have a plot was to have a little bolt hole and place of refuge, whether or not the seeds came up.

Most old long established British practices transferred themselves to Australia, but the Allotment system never did.

One reason is that Australians are not exactly noted for strict observance of the Seventh Commandment. From convict days, Australian attitudes towards other peoples' property has always been a bit flexible, resulting in them chalking up impressive reputations as souvenir hunters of anything not nailed down. And sometimes of things that ARE nailed down!

To give Australians access to Plots in Allotments would mean that no carrot would be safe from itchy fingers, and there would be mayhem and bloodshed over the cabbages and brussel sprouts.

The main reason for the absence of Allotments is the fact that Australians have become wedded to the idea of homes being built on the traditional quarter acre block. With that amount of space to play with even the Little Aussie Battlers if so inclined, produce vegetables galore in their own backyard, where they are comparatively safe from their thieving mates.

These holdings have proved useful for another Australian Icon - the Shed down the back; the ultimate retreat and refuge of the man-about-the house.

Sheds aren't an Australian invention, but nowhere else in the world have they sprouted in such vast numbers to become such passionate male possessions as they have here.

A typical Aussie shed is an old clapped-out structure of cast-off bits of timber, fibro and corrugated iron, tacked on to the back of a garage or erected in a far corner of the backyard in defiance and contravention of all local council bylaws. It probably has electricity (illegally) connected, but lacks any other visible amenity apart from a bench and some shelving.

Occupying every square inch of space is a mountain of dust or grease laden junk.

Into this den the male of the establishment will happily retreat for hours , especially on weekends, messing around with assorted tools, attending to his home brews of beer, or just listening to the races, the footy or the cricket on his tranny.

It is his little haven, his little bit of Paradise, and his escape from the rat race and his problems.

The Shed is a very blokey thing where no female dares to tread. Because of their blokiness, Sheds have attracted quite a lot of attention in recent years, and books have even been written about them and the general psychological condition of their owners.

Evidence points to a decline in the building and use of backyard sheds in favour of a new trend of the Newer Age Males of the nation seeking different types of refuges. These mainly take the form of him taking over a spare room in the house after one or more of the kids have flown from the family nest. In this new sanctuary the Bloke is wont to install a computer and modem spending most of his waking hours surfing the net.

Into the 21st Century, when the rest of the kids have flown the coop, the females of the nation may take over one of the other rooms thus made spare, and install a computer set up in rival fashion.

At least they will then be able to communicate with each other - on the Internet!. Two private Shangri Las under the same roof!

20

Make Love, Not War!

Most commentators date the Hippie Movement to the early swinging 1960's when Bob Dylan excited the youth of the world with his protest songs, *Blowin' In the Wind* and *The Times, They are a Changin'*, songs that led to the Hippie settlements in the San Francisco suburb of Haight Ashbury. Which in turn led to that remarkable 20th Century event, the Woodstock Carnival in Upper New York State in August 1969, when half a million excited, screaming and mainly stoned fans defied the rain and the mud to Rock Around the Clock.

And this in turn led to the Aquarius Festival in Nimbin in northern New South Wales in May 1973, often tagged as the start of the Hippie movement in Australia. Yet young Australians had been on the trail of the search for a personal paradise long before either of these organised events.

The first Hippie wave of the postwar years involved young men and women who had been born in the Depression Years and had come through the grinding poverty of that period and the problems of rationing and shortages of the war years.

The coming of peace in 1945 brought with it boom times as the nation set about the task of building a new society, aided by thousands of migrants from war-torn Europe who flooded into Australia. For once there was full employment arid plenty of jobs for those who wanted to work.

There were also great shifts of attitudes and questioning of past policies . The youth of Australia were disillusioned and tired of the old formulas which had proved such failures, both on the economic and diplomatic fronts. The times they were indeed a changing and they wanted "out" from the traditional regimes of schools, universities, jobs for life and the restraints imposed by the then prevailing social patterns of the cities.

Perhaps the majority were just determined to throw off the restraints of city life and put as much space as they could between themselves and family - at least until the money ran out.

This first wave of young protestors trekked out of the southern cities in considerable numbers and headed north. Always north, sometimes for the surf and the sunshine but mainly, one suspects, because the grapevine had it that was where the best and cheapest dope was to be had.

The majority of this first wave of freedom seekers came from well-heeled traditional families which enabled them to travel far and fast. Considerable numbers made their way up to far North Queensland where they made quite a nuisance of themselves, living in some squalor in groups in rented holiday cottages along the beaches north and south of Cairns. Their pot smoking and promiscuous habits arising from their much proclaimed slogan of "Make Love, Not War" aroused the ire of the locals and the constabulary, and the latter developed the task of "busting" these southern intruders into both a sport and an art form.

It was probably the tough stand of the police in all Australian states to the activities of the Hippies that forced the more adventurous and more affluent among them to go offshore in their search for a twentieth century paradise.

They soon established a well worn path up to Kathmandu and other exotic Asian destinations of the time, before reaching their ultimate destination - London. Once there, in the shabby digs and squats of Kangaroo Valley, as Kensington came to be known, they proceeded to get up the nose of the Brits, even to the extent of transplanting their Australian flagship, the *OZ* magazine in slightly amended form, to British shores. This enterprise that was to land some of the entrepreneurs in British gaols as a result of the English judges sadly failing to appreciate their editorial endeavours.

In his two books *Hippie, Hippie Shake* (1995) and *Out of My Mind* (1996), *Oz* editor Richard Neville has provided a brilliant first hand historical record of the adventures of the main players in the Australian Hippie invasion of England in the 1960's as well as events on the local Hippie scene.

Some of them left a firm imprint on their host country, especially in the fields of literature, arts and the law, with many a revolutionary Hippie of that turbulent period making it even into the upper echelons of the English scene. So the adventure was not always in vain, even if in the end the majority grew tired of English weather and cuisine and returned to the sunshine of their homeland, usually to cast off their revolutionary garments to blend themselves into culture and jobs which they had loudly denounced only a few years earlier in their Hippie phase.

A few remained true to the original cause and joined the Hippie communes up north, but the great majority of the young wanderers of the 50's and 60's decided to forsake dope and the dreadlocks for family, respectability and the 9 to 5 routines in the cities of their birth.

And that is where most of them are today, perhaps at times still dreaming of far off days at Trinity Beach, or Kathmandu or Kangaroo Valley, but these days more preoccupied with the problems of superannuation payouts than Free Love.

21

Going to Pot

The old English word "Pot", originally used to describe a cooking vessel or jar, has assumed all sorts of different connotations over the centuries and in Australia it has had some surprising appearances in both slang and colloquial usage. Some examples:

To Pot: To Get A Girl Pregnant (Now Obsolete)

To Pot: To Sink A Ball In Billiards Or Snooker (Probably Not Australian In Origin).

To Pot: For A Shooter To Take A Random Shot (Pot Shot) At A Bird, Animal Or Other Object.

To Pot: What Happens When A Gardener Places A Plant In A Container.

To Pot: To Inform On Someone, To Dob Him Or Her In For Some Real Or Alleged Misdeed (Probably Of Convict Origin).

A Pot: In Australian Terms A Middy Of Beer.

A Pot: A Trophy Or Prize In Some Sporting Event.

A Big Pot: Someone Important, Now Obsolete Being Replaced By Tall Poppy.

Pot Boiler: A Trashy Book (Not Australian In Origin).

Pot Luck: To Take Your Chances With A Meal If You Call In On Someone Unannounced Around Meal Time.

Go To Pot (Or Gone To Pot): To Deteriorate In Some Way.

The Last Example Is An Interesting One. Now Seldom Heard, It Was Used Extensively By Critics Of Governments of all political shades who would exclaim loudly that the country was fast going to pot (or down the drain) because of the incompetence or misdeeds of our leaders.

Such expressions went out of favour in the 1960's when a whole new meaning to "Going to Pot" was imported from America, Pot being an old slang expression for marijuana dating back to the pre-war years. It was almost certainly derived from the Mexican-Spanish name of POTIGUAYA applied to the marijuana leaf of the ancient hemp plant. Allied to the slang expression was the derisive term POT-HEAD used to describe a person addicted to the weed.

No doubt there were knowledgeable Australians around long before the 1960's who were more than a little familiar with the marijuana plant but given the laws and general attitudes of the times, they kept such information to themselves.

In the 1960's it might be said that marijuana came out of closet and into the public domain in Australia. The only really surprising thing about this is the fact that Australians had been kept in a cocoon of innocence about the drug for so long given the fact that the basic plant *Cannabis sativa*, had been brought to the country in the First Fleet in 1788 having been sent by no less a person than Sir Joseph Banks. He believed that hemp could be commercial grown for its oils in the new colony.

No records survive of the fate of the seeds sent by Banks, or of the earliest experiments, but from the 1820's onward there were spasmodic reports of hemp growing in the colony. Probably the first settlers to attempt to grow it commercially were the Bell Brothers, Archibald and William, who settled in the Singleton district of the upper Hunter Valley in 1823. Another early Hunter River settler to grow the plant was Dr Francis Campbell who had found the hemp plant growing wild on the

Hunter River bank near Singleton, and experimented with growing it on his property. He published his findings in a small book published in 1846 entitled *A Treatise on the Culture of Flax and Hemp*.

Almost a century was to pass before the plant came to the notice of the general public. In 1938 the USA introduced its Marijuana Tax Act, aimed at controlling the production and sale of marijuana, known colloquially in the US as the Loco weed (those who smoked the plant were known as Weed Wobblies).

As soon as the Act was passed the US Consul in Australia, Albert Doyle, wrote to the Prime Minister's Department explaining the purposes of the new American law and seeking copies of laws in Australian states relating to marijuana.

This seems to have resulted in some tardy action on our shores as the New South Wales Parliament shortly afterwards passed the Local Government (Noxious Plants) Amendment Act outlawing *Cannabis sativa* from our countryside. Queensland and other states quickly followed the example of New South Wales in supposedly making Australian youth safe from the dreadful affects of this poisonous and harmful weed.

After that nothing much happened until the 1960's with the coming of the Flower People, the Hippies and other assorted dropouts of the Alternative Lifestyle movement.

Parents of these young adventurers got quite a shock in November 1964 when they awoke to find their newspapers full of reports of extensive crops of marijuana found to growing on Crown Land along a huge stretch of the Hunter River in northern New South Wales. The Department of Customs, which had carried out a survey, estimated the crop to comprise about five hundred acres between Singleton and Maitland, all apparently descendants of crops originally sown more than a century earlier by the pioneer settlers along the river.

The New South Wales Department of Agriculture set about the task of destroying these crops but not before large numbers of enterprising citizens had made raids on the area bearing off considerable quantities of specimens to form the nucleus of numerous Cannabis plantations in other parts of the State.

In succeeding years the weed was to produce police corruption on a hitherto unknown scale in several states. Bob Dylan's plea to his followers to "get stoned", was to bring unintended social consequences in its wake as drugs became part of the counter culture.

Those who supported the use of marijuana, and advocated its legalisation, had long claimed that it was harmless and non-addictive drug. This apparently is not the case, as the Loco Weed seems to be just as addictive as heroin. A programme set up by the Australian Capital Territory Alcohol and Drug Service in the early 1990's aimed at helping drug addicts kick their habit has produced some startling results. Initially the programme was aimed at helping people addicted to alcohol and heroin but by the end of 1996 it found that almost 20% of the addicts enrolled in the programme were seeking ways of kicking the marijuana habit. In July 1997 the co-ordinator of the programme Dr Jillian Fleming predicted that in the not-too -distant future marijuana addicts would outnumber heroin addicts on the programme.

It would appear that those who go in search of paradise via the route of drugs, soft or hard, are more likely to encounter weed-wobbles at the end of the track rather than the expected Utopia.

22

Modern Communes.

The Aquarius Festival staged at Nimbin, in northern New South Wales in May 1973, attracted 10,000 visitors and considerable publicity, which in turn lead to the North Coast quickly becoming the Hippie capital of Australia.

The number of communes which started in this period certainly ran into the hundreds. Due to a variety of factors, communes that flourish in one year may well have disappeared off the map the following year. Perhaps the best record of what existed in the early 1970's is that covered in two very lengthy articles written by John E Lindblad, an American freelance writer and photographer, which appeared in the *Bulletin* magazine in March 27 1976 and April 3 1976. Lindblad had spent the three previous years travelling some 56,000 kilometres in all states, visiting and living in existing communes, so he was able to provide a very valuable record of the time, though by the end of that decade the changes would have been considerable due to the demise of many communes he recorded, and the rise of new ones.

Lindblad started his resume in the Iron Range of Far North Queensland, and then worked his way right around the coastline to Western Australia, with a side trip down to Tasmania. Along the way he visited and lived in many types of communes with interesting differences.

For instance he found the Cedar Bay communes to comprise very idealistic young people, with females greatly outnumbering the males, but even then being harassed by the Queensland police. This was long before the infamous police commando raid on one of the Cedar Bay communes in August 1976.

In that period while Lindblad found communes scattered along the coast from Cooktown down to the border, the main Queensland communal activity was on the Atherton Tablelands and particularly the famous Rosebud commune outside Kuranda at that time our largest and best known commune. Rosebud was an interesting experiment as it was established by drop out university students from the north-eastern states of America. Rich soil and climatic conditions made growing vegetables and fruits comparatively easy, so Rosebud came close to being self-sufficient, but was constantly bothered by hordes of freeloading "live on love" visitors from the south. In the end Rosebud adopted a firm policy of telling such visitors they could stay one night before showing them the gate. Paradise was only available for those willing to work for it in the commune gardens.

Lindblad found the north Queensland heat and humidity very trying and considered the New South Wales North Coast far more suitable for communal experiments. This is where the majority of Australian communes have eventually been established and sustained.From Bellingen up to the productive Tweed alternative life stylers are still to be found in considerable numbers as single experimenters or housed in the many and varied communes, both secular and Spiritual. This also has been the area where exclusive female communes have sprouted - and occasionally fallen apart.

Continuing his odyssey south, Lindblad found a large number of alternative lifestylers, some in communal groups, around the Eden area of southern New South Wales and across the border into Victoria's north east region, but most Victorian communes at that time were to be found to the north and north west of Melbourne.

Lindblad gave considerable details of the Round the Bend Conservation Co-operative Limited formed in 1971, under the new Victorian Co-Operative Act of 1968. This was over a 326 acre bushland property located in the Yarra Valley, of the Dandenong Ranges Leading figures in this move were Dr Moss Cass, former Federal Minister for the Environment and Conservation in the Whitlam Federal Government, and New Zealand born artist Neil Douglas.

This co-operative had 32 members who were bound by rules to follow a set of conservation guidelines to protect and develop the natural ecology of the property. These guidelines included the exclusion of cats and dogs and other predators from the area. Each shareholder was in turn entitled to a homesite and garden acreage, and houses had to be built in assigned clusters, but out of sight of each other (no over the fence back yard quarrels allowed in this paradise). The houses had to be "aesthetically compatible" and preferably made of mud bricks for their safety in case of bushfires.

Lindblad was much taken by this scheme, not realising that such projects with binding rules but little in the way of commonality of interest by the participants, are almost certain to fail after a few years as people drift away.

When he ventured down to Tasmania, Lindblad found in the early 1970's many small but flourishing communes. In fact more "back-to-the land" activity than in any other state he visited.

He found quite a few English, American and Canadian settlers among the Tasmanian communes, probably because they found the winters there far milder than in their homelands. He found amongst the Tasmanian communes a higher percentage

173

of both anarchists and doomsday cultists than on the mainland with settlements being located in the Huon Valley and in the north central area around Deloraine. Among the interesting groups he encountered was the much publicised twelve member Teapot Kibbutz in Jacky's Marsh at the base of Quamby Bluff, established by Jeff and Carol Williams in 1972. The pair met up at a Kibbutz in Israel and settled at Jacky's Marsh because they felt it was the most sheltered place on earth from nuclear fallout! Alas, the Teapot Kibbutz and most of the other communes that he visited at the time fell by the wayside, the main problems as usual being dissent within the groups and difficulties in making their enterprises self sufficient.

Lindblad found little communal activity in South Australia but was dazzled by the one-man communal show then in full swing in Western Australian under the banner of the mercurial and decidedly eccentric Fred Robinson, then aged 85 with his equally energetic ex-Scientologist partner Mary.

Fred Robinson at the time was probably Australia's oldest drop out. Born in England in 1891, he served in the British Navy but jumped ship in Perth shortly before World War I and "went bush". He ended up in Queensland with a sugar cane plantation but went broke in the Great Depression and from then on quit the rat race. He devoted the rest of his life to urging Australians to abandon the cities and towns and go back to the land and become self-sufficient.

He was a very charismatic character, an ex-Rosicrucian who peddled a weird philosophical mixture of religion and communism (he was a great admirer of Chairman Mao) together with a firm belief in Flying Saucers which one day would come and sweep him and all his lucky followers off to some great Paradise on a distant planet.

This Australian Moses had attracted thousands who settled with him on the various communes around Perth and in other parts of Western Australia.

His first commune, established in 1963 near Armadale, some 35 kilometres south of Perth, was named Shalam, but the group later changed their name to Universal Brotherhood and in the mid-1970's moved to a larger property at Balingup, 250 kilometres south of Perth where they built a large landing pad for expected Flying Saucers.

Robinson ran a tight ship on his communes insisting that his followers develop themselves into a "superior race" which called for hard work and a strict vegetarian diet, between marathon fruit and juice fasts of up to thirty days to cleanse their systems. Tea, coffee and other stimulants were strictly banned and members were asked to avoid sex so they could remain in a perpetually "purified state" for when the Flying Saucers came to carry them off to begin a new civilisation of light and purity. He believed that all the heathens who consumed alcohol, smoked tobacco, used drugs and ate meat would also be shuttled off the earth, but to a different planet to await their distant salvation when they had mended their ways.

Alas, Fred fell off the twig before the Flying Saucers came.

After his passing the movement fell apart despite a change of name to The Homestead. By 1994 only two families were still living on one of Fred's old communes and it was all over bar the shouting.

Three decades have passed since John Lindblad embarked on his great odyssey around the communes of Australia. If he went back on the old trail today he would find most of the old communes he had visited long gone. Some still survive and many others which have sprung up in the intervening years which still survive and even thrive - a hopeful sign for the great back to nature movement which sprang up in the 1960's.

To cover the whole commune movement of that period would require several stout volumes. Fortunately some of these have already been written and I know of others which are being researched, and readers wanting to pursue their studies of this interesting movement will find some references in the bibliographical section at the end of the book.

23

Anarchy Rules, O. K!

ANARCHY: A social theory which would do away with all authority except that sanctioned by conviction, and which is intended to secure individual liberty against the encroachments of the state.
Lloyd's Encyclopaedic Dictionary, London, l895

Let us consider the above definition and the history of anarchism as a theory. Its creator was William Godwin who in 1793 in his *Enquiry Concerning Political Justice* proposed the peaceful distribution of wealth among the needy, the ending of the state (in Great Britain) and the creation of a society of self-governing communities.

It didn't get off the ground, in Britain or elsewhere, though in the succeeding century the basic idea was taken up and advanced in varying formats by Pierre Proudhon, Bukunin and Prince Kropotkin, amongst other social reformers in the 19th Century. Their ideas even gained a certain amount of mass support in France and Spain, especially in rural Andalusia where its ideal of an earthly utopia had appeal in the peasant classes.

During the Spanish Civil War of the 1930's it had a brief resurgence when some industries in Barcelona where run along anarchic lines and rural communes were set up in Aragon and Andalusia. The victory by General France's forces brought a swift end to such experiments.

Anarchy is derived from the Greek word Anarchia -

meaning "without a ruler". How do you run a factory without a few foremen to tell the workers what to do? Considering this, it is amazing that one of Australia's largest and longest running, communal settlements is run on almost purely anarchic lines. More than two decades after its establishment, the settlement exists without a ruler, and appears to survive on minimal rules.

The settlement is the Tuntable Falls Land Co-operative Limited, near the small town of Nimbin in northern New South Wales. It rose out of the 1973 Aquarius Festival when the chief initiator Terry McGee and a few supporters negotiated the purchase of about 300 hectares of land (later expanded to around 700 hectares) with the aid of a distinctly un-anarchic mortgage of one hundred and ten thousand dollars (which was soon paid off, incidentally).

The land was in a beautiful setting at the head of the Tuntable Valley and comprised portions of dense bushland and tropical rainforest along with large segments of fertile farm and pasture lands.

The venture was financed by selling $200 shares in the co-operative (since raised to $1500 per share) to anyone, young or old who felt like participating.

Terry McGee made it clear from the start that he wasn't going to be the ruler of this new venture, that it was to be an experiment in an entirely new way of life:

The people who join us here have to be prepared to jump off the cliff with the certainty that when they get to the bottom they will be alright.

When John Lindlad visited Tuntable Falls shortly after its establishment he said the Nimbin co-operative was an anarchist's dream come true. He was later to record that in its initial stages the Co-operative had only three rules governing the actions of its members:

1. They were not to use soap when washing or bathing in

the creeks.

2. No cats or dogs were allowed on the property (to protect the fauna).

3. No one was allowed to drive vehicles on to the property. Cars had to be parked on the outskirts.

Over the years a few more rules have been added, but they are still fairly minimal such as a prohibition on using poisons or chemicals on the land, and the requirement that any new building erected must have the100% approval of all residents. Even after more than two decades of existence there is no central committee or body to supervise the Co-operative. Any decisions to be made are taken at monthly meetings of any members who may wish to attend.

The settlement comprises a number of mini-villages which may vary in size from 5 to 15 families, each group being responsible for organising its own affairs and amenities such a water supply.

The original members all lived in a large communal building (now used as the school) but later members built their own dwellings, in a huge variety of designs and sizes. A-frames and geodesic abound, but the majority are simple but comfortable 2 or 3 room abodes. Some individualistic types have shunned the communal village system and built homes in areas isolated from the groups, but these are exceptions.

Since the Co-operative members have no titles to their housing, all of which is owned outright by the Co-operative, most housing has over a period had various occupiers as the members tend to move out of the settlement for periods, as well as move around within the settlement. A member who finds a group not to his or her taste may look around for a more congenial village group.

In 1984 the members agreed on a fairly revolutionary new rule whereby a member who had employed an outside builder to erect a home, or who had expended a fairly large amount of money on a home he/she had erected, could recoup some of this outlay when moving on by "selling" the home through the Co-operative.

Although Tuntable Falls Land Co-operative Limited had about 500 members in the early years, not all chose to live on the site permanently, and some members never did take up residence. Over the years the number of families in residence at any one time ranged from 40 to a 100. A survey in the mid-1990's turned up 160 adults and over a 100 children living at Tuntable Falls.

What sort of people are prepared to pay up to the present $1500 a share to joint anarchist co-operative? Its earliest share register showed members in a wide range of occupations, from a 14 year-old schoolboy to a 70 year old pensioner. A reporter who visited the settlement in 1982 found it comprised a wide range of professional types, philosophers, gurus, freaks, misfits, craftsmen, bushies, nihilists, adventurers, feminists, environmentalists, peaceniks, save-the-planet missionaries, numerous single parents, political. identities and a bunch of mixed-up kids from wealthy families! That such a heady mix could not only survive, but apparently thrive without any apparent leadership or rigid organisational structure for a quarter of a century, is something of a minor mystery.

Perhaps Thomas Henry Huxley (1825-1895) the great English biologist, was right when he observed:

... in this sense strict anarchy may be the highest conceivable grade of perfection of social justice; for, if all men spontaneously did justice and loved mercy, it is plain that all swords might be advantageously turned into plowshares, and that the occupation of judges and police would be gone.

24

Pitt Street Farmers.

Running in tandem with the minor exodus from the cities to rural communes and co-operatives in the 1960's and 1970's was the equally interesting trend of well-heeled city people buying up small acreages in the country as leisure time retreats.

These acreages in the country were well away from the coast, usually located inland within a few hours drive from the city home base. Far from being places to relax in the sun, these were enterprises that required considerable effort on the part of the adults while the kids raced around the sole paddock on their ponies.

This was a back to the bush on a mini scale, and the owners of these minuscule enterprises were labelled Pitt Street farmers or Collins Street Farmers, depending on which state was involved, since it was assumed that these adventurers were stockbrokers or professionals indulging in their rural whims as a tax dodge. This may have been true in some cases, but the majority seemed to have engaged in these endeavours to escape city life for a while and give the kids a whole new experience.

One of the first destinations to gain popularity with this new breed of city farmer, was the old gold mining town of Gulgong near Mudgee in the Central West of New South Wales. In the 1960's Gulgong was going through one of those crises that country towns often experience, with a result that its main street had many boarded up empty shops, some historic old stone bank buildings up for sale at ridiculously cheap prices (the old Opera House at one time was on the market for a modest $3000), and there were numerous small farm holdings, some with 19th Century stone cottages, near the town.

In no time at all some Hippies had moved in to a couple of key sites to the great dismay of most of the locals. Empty shops became trendy shops for their new Flower People owners, and the small farms and oldly worldly stone cottages were snapped up by the Pitt Street farmers. All of which brought considerable and unexpected prosperity to the small town and prompted local entrepreneurs to subdivide large farms into small 25 acre (10 hectare) holdings to meet this new demand.

Other districts within easy driving distance of Sydney such as the Hunter region and the Southern Highlands quickly followed in what can only be described as 25 acre bush mania.

My home town of Dubbo also got into the act by sub-dividing more than 600 of these 10 hectare blocks, plus another 100 or so smaller blocks.

Now Dubbo is far too distant from Sydney to attract the Pitt Street farmers to these newly created mini farms. They were created for, and still substantially used by Dubbo families seeking more than the traditional quarter acre urban block while being only 10 or 15 minutes from the city. The blocks have also proved popular with retirees from western farms wanting a little more space than offered by a town house or unit. The Dubbo blocks, and those created around all the other Australian regional cities, were occupied full time by their owners, so their purpose was an entirely different one to that of the Pitt (or Collins) Street Farmer, who commuted to his little patch on (some) weekends or holiday periods.

As long term farmers have learned, land can be a hard taskmaster. It can yield up great bounty, but must be treated with respect and cared for in a loving fashion, which cannot be done if the owner is absent most of the time. Fences get broken or fall over and weeds like blackberries, lantana, crofton weed, bracken fern and other pests get out of hand very quickly if not supervised and cut back regularly. All this leads to sometimes heated clashes with neighbours who don't like such invasions from next door properties and from Councils and various Government agencies who have strict laws about such matters.

In short, there is a considerable down side to ownership of a 25 acre holding which is not being farmed intensively and many a Pitt or Collins Street farmer has found his hobby farm a millstone around his neck rather than the delightful rural retreat it was supposed to be. Especially when the kids get bored out of their minds riding around the paddock a few times and resolutely refuse to go bush.

Despite all the setbacks, the numbers of the hobby farm brigade haven't significantly decreased in recent years though there has been no great expansion as was the case in the 1970's.

The interest in hobby farming can perhaps be best gauged by the annual Small Farm Field Days held at Mudgee each year. These events usually attract around 30,000 visitors over the days they are held, indicating that in a lot of city breasts there still lurks the primeval urge to "go bush" — preferably on your own bit of dirt.

Australia must be one of the most urbanised countries on the planet but deep down the city-bound dweller seems to understand that the real soul of the continent is only to be found in the bush.

25

Sydney or the Bush.

The first wave of the Australian Hippie movement was essentially a youthful one which started in the 1950's, and which had lost most of its momentum by the early 1970's when the focus of the youth of the nation was more on Vietnam War protests than heading north or overseas in search of adventure.

The 1970s saw an entirely different movement away from the capital cities by a more mature generation of Paradise seekers, and this second wave was itself split into two distinctive segments.

The first grouping mainly sprang from the staging of the Nimbin Aquarius Festival in May 1973, and led directly to the establishment of a wide range of various types of communes and settlements in all Australian states.

There was however a little publicised movement out of the capital cities of large numbers of mature single men and women and families seeking alternate life styles in rural settings, sometimes on small farms but often to new less stressful jobs in smaller towns and villages right around the continent.

This "Sydney or the Bush" syndrome had some unusual aspects in that very considerable numbers of men and women sacrificed quite large portions of their income and even their careers in their search for environmentally friendly surroundings.

Almost three decades on there are indications that although the momentum of this Back to the Bush movement may have slowed, there is still a considerable yearning amongst city dwellers for a more fulfilling lifestyle. This was clearly demonstrated in 1999 when a fairly low key ABC Soapie drama called *SeaChange* soared to the top of the national ratings to the surprise of everyone -including ABC programmers.

SeaChange was all about a highly-paid Melbourne female lawyer who, after a marriage breakdown, fled with her two children to a much lower paid position as a magistrate in a sleepy but scenic coastal town -to find peace of mind, job satisfaction and, of course in the best soapie tradition, true love! It probably helped the credibility of the programme that its creator Deb Cox had taken a similar route and was living in that Hippie Haven of Byron Bay when she put it all together.

This Back to the Bush movement seems to have been unique to Australia in the period - at least in its scope and spread of time and this was probably due to geographical factors as much as economic forces. One of the leaders of the Green movement, Ian Cohen, a Member of the New South Wales Legislative Council, observed in 1996 that Australia led the world in the alternative lifestyle movement because it was the only advanced technological nation with a climate like that found in the Third World: *So you don't need that much. You can wear a sarong and the land is very bountiful. It creates every opportunity for self-sufficiency.*

These alternate lifestylers ranged in age from the young to the very old, both male and female, came from all sorts of classes and backgrounds and with widely varying financial resources. Their goals varied widely, with many participants having no aim other than to escape the stress of city life, not realising that rural life has its fair share of stress, though of a different kind.

Perhaps the majority would have shared the philosophy that a pay packet may prevent you dying but it doesn't show

185

you how to live, or as that wise old American sage Henry Mencken expressed it so eloquently many years ago:

One daffodil is worth ten shares in Bethlehem Steel.

If there was a common aim of all these new Utopians it was the pursuit of personal happiness which novelist Nathaniel Hawthorne admirably summed up thus:

Happiness is as a butterfly which when pursued, is always beyond our grasp, but which if you sit down quietly, may alight on you.

The problem with these new seekers of happiness, of course, was they were so attuned to the hectic rush of city life, that they found it almost impossible to sit down quietly when they did go Bush. The drop out rate was considerable as a result of them not being able to cope with the isolation, the lack of beloved amenities (such as electricity, running water and TV), and brushes with creepy crawlies of the bush and unfriendly locals.

However the success rate was also high and surprisingly large numbers of these escapees from the cities did find rural life to their liking. Most quickly adapted to Drizabones, Blunderstone boots and Swiss Army knives and settled down amicably in their new environmentally friendly communities.

One of the interesting trends of this migration from the cities was that where couples ventured out into new rural pastures friction soon developed with one partner loving the new lifestyle, the other loathing it. And it wasn't always the female partner who was the disaffected one. This led to many broken relationships, often with one of the partners returning to city life. Surveys taken of longstanding alternate lifers consistently show them to have different partners to the ones they started out with, sometimes resulting in considerable local confusion where numbers of children are involved. This has led to the widely circulated joke giving a definition of total chaos as Father's

Day in Bellingen!

As the success stories outnumber the failures in the Back to the Bush movement, we should not overlook the importance of some of the early pioneers in the movement who were able to provide later pilgrims with guidelines for what really was a venture into uncharted territory.

High on our list of these pioneering free spirits were Abbie Heathcote and Neil Douglas, not only for succeeding against seemingly impossible odds to achieve self-sufficiency in middle life but to live to tell the story of their venture in a delightful book *The Book of Earthly Delights* published in 1976 which provided so much practical information and guidance.

Tired of life in Melbourne in 1964, Abbie and Neil, with a young child Biddy, sought out a rural retreat with no capital and no regular income - Neil was an artist relying on occasional sales of his paintings.

They eventually found a ten acre block of degraded red box land, steep and scraggy in nature, with terrible soil, located in the Greensborough area, some 25 miles from Melbourne. The price of the block was $3000 offered on terms of $200 deposit and repayments of $10 a week. There was no water and no electricity.

They lacked the deposit but by some stroke of luck Neil sold a painting for $200 the week they first inspected the block. They were in business.

On this very unpromising turf they set about carving out their very own little Garden of Eden, living in a tent while they designed and built their mud brick house and established their own garden. With some poultry and goats, eventually they were self-sufficient, and over time they resolved the degradation of the soil by using environmentally sound methods.

This remarkable couple did succeed in their pursuit of health and happiness and provided a beacon through their best selling book for countless others.

An equally inspiring story of pioneering against the odds is that of Olive Cotton, the noted photographer.

Olive came from a family with an unusual background. Her father was Professor Leo Cotton, a noted geologist who accompanied Sir Ernest Shackleton on his 1911 expedition to Antarctica. Professor Cotton was also a keen photographer whose photos of that expedition are still ranked among the best of the great white continent.

He taught his daughter Olive the basic techniques of photography and when she graduated in arts from Sydney University in 1934, she went to work for Max Dupain, then one of Sydney's leading photographers, whom she had known since childhood. In 1939 they married but it was a disaster and they divorced in 1941. They remained on amicable terms and when he enlisted in the army she returned and kept the studio going in the war years.

In that period her life changed direction when she met and married the great love of her life Ross McInerney.

After McInerney's discharge from the army, the talented city born and bred Olive, abandoned her flourishing photographic career to go bush with her new husband to an undeveloped property of 200 hectares , all uncleared bushland, a few miles out of Cowra, in central western New South Wales. There was no running water or electricity on this piece of scrubland which they called Spring Forest. While a house was being built they lived in a tent, using army grey coats for blankets and in the 2 years that followed Olive bore 2 children.

Spring Forest was not large enough for practical farming purposes so McInerney preserved the existing trees and added more natives to turn the holding into a conservation area.

To keep the home fires burning Olive went to work in Cowra, teaching maths at the local High School. McInerney gained a small cash flow bee keeping and supplemented this working around the district on fencing and other jobs.

Photography had to be forgotten in the tough struggle for survival in the early years, but in later life Olive turned to her old profession again, opening a commercial studio in Cowra in 1964 and in the succeeding years gaining wide national acclaim for her exhibitions, All McInerney's environmental work on Spring Forest also paid off in his later years when in the 1990's the property became one of the first to be registered under a New South Wales Government Voluntary Conservation Agreement, aimed at protecting private land of environmental significance. Spring Forest now has a permanent covenant on it, protecting all its bushland, flora and fauna through all future ownerships of the property, making it in effect a tiny privately owned national park.

Another interesting example of a couple Going Bush for environmental purposes, rather than self-sufficiency, is that of the Forest of Tranquillity rainforest sanctuary, near Ourimbah in northern New South Wales.

This came about more or less by accident as a result of Ed Manners noticing an unusual patch of lush rainforest while on a flight from Sydney to Maitland in 1980. Intrigued, he and his wife drove up to inspect the area the following weekend. They were so impressed by what they found that they bought the secluded property of 135 acres of beautiful pristine rainforest set in a valley with a crest of hills on both sides.

With the assistance of a senior botanist of the Royal Botanic Gardens in Sydney they set about creating a rainforest sanctuary with 5 kilometres of walking trails for visitors to view the forest and its abundant animal and bird life from different perspectives. In December 1985 the property was opened to the public and the following year it won a New South Wales Tourism excellence award.

An interesting example of a Sydneysider going bush to nurture the environment and ending up with a nice little tourism earner in the process, a kind of Sydney AND the Bush co-operative venture.

And I must end this chapter with the story of a noted Australian city-dweller who did not go bush, but who managed to create a tiny slice of Paradise on his very own city patch.

I'm referring here to the noted artist Ken Done who since 1954 has lived at Balmoral, above Chinamans Beach, in the fairly upmarket North Shore municipality of Mosman. Ken Done leads a very busy life both creating and marketing his very colourful and popular art forms for an international market.

He may have had an urge to "Go Bush", as so many of his fellow Sydneysiders have done over the years, but such a move might in his case be impractical for purely business reasons, so, being a creative person, he managed to organise his own piece of bush oriented paradise in his own backyard. He was able to do this because he not only owned four adjoining blocks of land at Balmoral, but had the necessary talents and the financial resources to create on one of the blocks a quite magnificent cave-studio (with water views, of course) to which he can retreat in beautiful, peaceful surroundings to work on his colourful masterpieces.

Now that is what I call Paradise-seeking with style!.

26

Island Hideways

Most Australians at some time in their lives would have had the occasional day dream about an Island Paradise to which they could retreat when the daily grind got too tough. And such musings no doubt would have dwelt upon well publicised islands away out in the Pacific somewhere or at least far distant up the Queensland coast.

But some island hideaways are to be found lurking under one's nose at it were, at least in the case of Sydneysiders, who have such retreats on their doorstep, unknown to the majority of nearby city dwellers.

Back in 1950 a well known Dubbo public servant told me that he was about to retire and with his wife take up permanent residence in a place I had never heard of, namely Dangar Island, near the mouth of the Hawkesbury River.

As this seemed an unusual retirement destination I sought some details and was astounded to find that this island paradise lacked (at that time) all the basic amenities : no electricity, water supply, sewage, made roads, telephone , mail service etc. Not even a shop, though there was an infrequent and none too reliable passenger ferry service to Brooklyn, which did have a few shops and where they could get a train to Sydney.

The difficulties and expense of getting one's goods and chattels to such a place seemed to me to be a daunting task in itself for an elderly couple. Taking into account the lack of medical and other essential services I thought the decision of the former civil servant to be an act of lunacy. I was wrong and over the years letters came back from the couple to old Dubbo friends expressing great contentment, teaching me the valuable lesson that amenities we take for granted may not be necessary in a true slice of Paradise.

The isolation of Dangar Island is such that commuting to Sydney (or Gosford in the other direction) might not be a practical option for a resident, so it has remained a little haven for retirees and weekenders.

But much closer to central Sydney is another, much larger, island retreat from which daily commuting to work in the city is possible, though perhaps tiring over a period. This retreat is Scotland Island located off Church Point in Pittwater. So popular has it become that it now has over 1000 permanent residents and seems in danger of losing its paradisiacal status, though it will always remain an island with a very interesting and unusual history.

Its original owner was the extraordinary Scottish ex-convict Andrew Thompson (1773-1810) who was transported with a fourteen year sentence for his involvement in the theft of cloth worth ten pounds. He arrived in the colony in 1792, but after a year he was allowed to join the police force. He served with such distinction that he quickly climbed up the ladder to chief constable, then grain assessor (1799) and eventually magistrate (1810), the first emancipist to achieve that honour.

His police work seems to have been the least of his interests as along the way he became a very successful farmer at Windsor and in time accumulated so much property either on lease or by grants, and had so many industrial endeavours, including ship building, that by 1806 he was considered to be the wealthiest man in the colony. Not bad for an ex-con.

One of Thompson's enterprises was the establishment in 1804 of a salt manufacturing plant on Mullet Island in Broken Bay, but this location proved unsuitable and he later transferred this to Scotland Island (which he named) and which had been given to him on lease by Governor King. This was converted to an outright grant by Governor Macquarie who much admired Thompson's abilities.

There is no evidence that Thompson ever lived on Scotland Island. Thompson never married and when he died in 1810 he left a quarter of his estimated twenty thousand pounds estate to Governor Macquarie, a bequest that was to cause Macquarie some problems when it was investigated by Commissioner Bigge.

In the succeeding years Scotland Island changed hands a number of times before being subdivided in 1920 into 365 blocks most of which have now been built on with a range of houses from the modest to mansions valued at a million dollars or more.

Paradise it seems can accommodate all classes in the Land of Oz.

In the pre-war years, and even in the early post-war years, life on Scotland Island apparently was pretty basic, but the island now has electricity and telephone connections, though the roads are basic and quickly become quagmires after heavy downpours. The islanders still have no basic water supply, sewage or the convenience of a shop, but have a good ferry service to Church Point on the "Mainland", count themselves blessed that crime is non existent , that community spirit is extraordinarily high (just like a village in the bush) and they are spared many of the distractions and nuisances of suburban dwellers, such as salesmen and Mormons knocking on their doors. Nor do tourists or stickybeaks use the ferry to explore the island, because there are no public toilet facilities. And that's just the way the "Islanders" like it and want to keep it.

A few brave or monetary driven souls commute into the city daily (they park their cars in secure parking areas at Church Point) while others have careers lending themselves to work from home activities with only occasional ventures on shore. And of course there is large population of retirees.

In such an isolated place one would expect that the inhabitants would mainly be elderly retirees or at least well to do middle age couples able to self-fund themselves this way, but this is not so. In recent years more and more young couples have moved to the island to raise families with the result that it has a surprisingly large number of children in its community.

There is a pre-school on the island to take care of the little ones, but the rest go to school by a special ferry service to school at Newport.

When Deborah McIntosh visited the island in 1998 for a feature article for the *Sun-Herald* she found the pre-school vibrating with noise from the 20 very active toddlers and found a distinct difference between the island pre-school and those on the mainland. In the latter the carers have to spend a lot of time encouraging kids to socialise. On the island the kids already know each other well before they start and tend to act more like siblings than ordinary friends. Which is as it should be.

In a twist on that old saying about the Jesuits, perhaps if you get the little ones used to paradise from the start they might seek it out throughout later life.

27

Third Age Nomads

Around 1970 a university in France conceived the idea of sponsoring a new educational organisation for retirees based on the concept of learning in the original universities of the Middle Ages, when people gathered to share knowledge and ideas.

They called this new movement the University of the Third Age - meaning the Third Age of Life - and set the enrolment benchmark of retirees or semi-retired people 55 years or over.

The idea moved across the English Channel where several universities sponsored U3A groups and added the Third Age to the English language.

In 1981 a Melbourne University took up the idea and the U3A was soon off and running at breathtaking speed, whereas on its home turf of Europe growth has been quite slow.

Although some Australian U3A chapters maintain affiliations with universities or other tertiary education bodies, the majority have not bothered with academic ties but have simply gone their own way, though in most states and regions networking of U3A Chapters is common, for the sake of sharing knowledge among themselves.

By 1998 the U3A in Australia had grown to 135 chapters with a total membership exceeding 35,000. The Australian Oldies were really flexing their muscles and brains and taking to learning in all types of classes in that magic Third Age of their chronologically enhanced lives.

A Chapter of the U3A was formed in my home town of Dubbo in 1991 and our members range from the active 50's to the rather slower-reflexed 90's. I note that in the winter months there is a fall- off in class numbers across the board as members head north for the sunshine like flocks of migratory birds. During the gentler months of Spring, with an odd exception, they come back in their old nesting and learning ground.

My U3A contacts in cities in the colder southern climates tell me that this is not a general pattern. Each year they report they are losing members on a permanent basis as their members sell up or lease out their homes and go on a perenial walkout, mostly in the northern half of Australia.

Nobody knows for sure exactly how many of these Golden Oldies - not all ex-U3A members of course - are on this nomadic prowl around the Continent since they don't stay long enough in any one spot to be counted on a statistical basis. Tourist bodies have not, until recently, considered them part of the tourist statistical picture but now believe these Third Age nomads must certainly number many thousands at any given time..

A fascinating glimpse of this aspect of Australian life was provided on September 23 1997 when the ABC screened an hour long documentary on the 'Grey Nomads'.

It concentrated its footage on half a dozen different individuals, couples or groups, but in following them around provided interesting glimpses of hundreds of others. The focus was on both loners and couples, including the story of the lone Victorian woman, widowed at 32, who raised six children, then in her sixties sold up her house and belongings and set out on her big adventure in life in a rather dodgy old panel van. The ABC cameras tracked her over 12 months from her start in Victoria to Broome - about as far off as you could get on our vast continent.

Then there was the aged and bearded psychiatrist who, when his marriage broke up, took his motorbike on an endless trek around the outback. The camera also provided interesting glimpses of 3 elderly widows travelling in a 3 vehicle convoy, obviously on the "safety in numbers" principle.

The couples featured in the documentary were an extremely diverse lot, differing as much in their personalities as the vehicles they used for their trek. These ranged from very modest vans or station wagons to the most lavishly equipped caravans.

The cameras also dwelt on some of the many caravan parks which these nomads of the outback used to rest up on their seemingly endless movement around Australia - usually in an anti-clock direction incidentally, because they had all worked out, or been told, that by doing it this way they would be driving around on the left lane all the way and would thus save themselves several hundred kilometres of travel!

For many years tens of thousands of Australians have spent their holidays caravanning , in the early years with the kids, and in retirement usually only in the winter months spent "up north" to get away from the frosts "down south". This new breed of "Grey Nomads" (as the ABC called them) or the more descriptive Third Age Nomads are a different breed altogether to the traditional caravanner of yesterday. - These people are on the road forever!

Most of them are retirees who are financially independent as a result of their superannuation payments and sale of their city homes. With the kids all married and off their hands, and no other ties they are off to cross and criss-cross our vast inland exploring as they go, and in many cases looking for that very magic spot , that little slice of Paradise, which might tempt them to stay put for a while - or permanently. The camera c crew of the ABC documentary came across several of these one time wanderers who had settled more or less permanently in some very remote corner of the continent-For them it was a case of "done roving" - at least for the time being.

While there must inevitably be a fairly high drop out rate amongst these Third Age Nomads, as either their cash ran out or health problems surfaced, thousands more seem to enter the field each year to keep the nomadic merry-go-round active. How many of them find along the way a Garden of Eden in which they tarry or even settle is a matter of conjecture.

We stay-at-homes can only marvel at their energy and tenacity and wish them all the best of luck in their quest for their own Holy Grail along the dusty roads of the outback.

28

The Drop-out Spin-offs

The Back-to-the-Bush movements of the 1960's and 1970's had a number of interesting spin-offs, of a direct or indirect nature such as the growth of books, magazines and merchandise to meet the needs of the these new alternate life-stylers taking up residence outside the capital cities.

Perhaps the best examples of these were the two main alternate magazines *Grass Roots* and *Earth Garden* which in their first two decades of publication, carried an enormous range of informative articles and helpful hints about living off the land. These two large mainstay publications were backed up by a whole host of smaller, localised publications and information bulletins of a more transitory nature.

Book publishers were quick to see new opportunities out of the Back-to-Nature trend in this period by producing a wide range of Do-it-yourself and How-to books on almost every aspect of alternative life-styles.

Back in 1983 with my daughter Lindy I launched The Book Connection which was an entirely mail order operation devoted to non-fiction books. Right from the start our biggest sections were in the Self-sufficiency and How-to-Do it fields. Throughout the 1980's our best selling title remained a rather weird volume produced by Angus and Robertson comprising pasteups of articles from an old long defunct journal entitled

HANDY HOME AND FARM DEVICES AND HOW TO MAKE THEM. Other sellers included books on keeping cows, goats and various exotic animals, on bee-keeping and worm farming and lucerne growing So great was our turnover of these books since we did not seem to have a huge base of rural customers that we started to keep tabs on where these volumes were going. To our surprise we found the majority were being purchased by customers in the capital cities -especially Sydney and Melbourne. We came to the conclusion that most of our buyers were not (yet) "doers" but dreamers - city folk trying to prepare for the day when they could quit the rat race and go bush! Perhaps some actually did achieve such gaols, in which case their newly acquired How-to-do-it libraries would have been of some practical use.

In this period there developed new enterprises, outside the so-called Hippie movement, which were embraced by the alternate lifestylers to such an extent that they thrived in a manner not experienced anywhere else in the world.

Since most of the Hippie communes, and many of the houses or properties of the individual alternate lifestylers, lacked amenities such as electricity or refrigeration, of necessity they had to adopt part or full vegetarian diets to survive.

The quite revolutionary methods of organic farming and Permaculture developed independently of the Back to the Bush movement but both were quickly embraced by the alternate lifestylers, to such extent that some of the larger and more stable communes, including spiritually-based groups, now have experimental Permaculture sections.

In the early colonial years pise construction housing (buildings of rammed earth or mud bricks) was very much part of the rural scene in most parts of Australia. By the early years of the 20th century this old European method of house construction had virtually disappeared from the Australian scene giving way to the more practical timber, fibro or standard fired brick methods.

Since many of the alternate lifestylers of the 1960's could not afford bricks, timber or even the lowly fibro, they turned to the older methods of mud bricks, made and laid by themselves, where rural councils permitted - and in many cases in defiance of council bans on such structures.

Home birthing was another 19th Century practice that was given a revival by the rural alternative lifestylers and by many of their city-based cousins.

Rejection of orthodox religions was also a feature of the New Age movement resulting in the rapid rise of the often non-religious Marriage Celebrant.

And to complete the cycle of Hatched, Matched and Dispatched changes, burial practices also got a working over in this period with a number of innovative industries producing el-cheapo papermache coffins, and a whole range of individualistic made-to-measure coffins to the needs of the clients' whims, painted up in colours seldom seen since the days of the Pharoahs.

The greatest revolution of all in the alternative lifestyle movement in the last three decades of the twentieth century has been the explosion of growth in both the arts and crafts markets, and in Australia there are some unique features.

Crafts have always played a prominent role in the Bush - less so in the cities. The annual bazaars and fetes of bush towns and villages were always crammed with an amazing array of very individual crafts displayed alongside the jams, pickles, cakes and other culinary delights.

Such displays reached their pinnacle in the annual Shows in major regional cities and the capital cities such as Sydney's Royal Easter Show. That the men and women of the Bush could produce fine crafts - and also to a lesser extent fine arts - was never in question - but these creations were almost exclusively produced for the love of creating, not of necessity.

For the Hippies in their communes and for the individual alternative lifestylers in their varying abodes, the realisation soon came that it was almost impossible to survive by growing some vegetables and keeping a few chooks. They needed some cash flow for goods and services they could not provide themselves.

For some the dole or a pension was the answer, but most of the New Age Bushies sought independence from Government handouts and turned like generations before them to trying their hands at producing arts and crafts. Many of them proved to be quite a dab hand at the task.

Creating items to sell was one thing. Actually disposing of them was quite a different proposition, and in time these new breed of crafts persons developed into entrepreneurs in markets where they already existed, or in the creation of new markets to meet the specific needs of their particular communities.

Markets such as the famous Paddy's Market in Sydney have been around for thousands of years in all parts of the world, but the new markets which sprang up in since the 1970s were different in character to the older and usually larger city-based markets, being mainly craft oriented. And the majority of the art and craft offerings were produced by alternative lifestylers who previously toiled away at uninteresting jobs in the cities.

In places were there were large indigenous populations - such as northern New South Wales, north Queensland, Darwin and the Kimberleys, there was an interesting development with aborigines taking advantage of these new sales outlets to sell their very creative pieces of aboriginal art developed over thousands of years.

In the vast markets of Kuranda, on the Atherton Tablelands, there is to be found on market days an incredible range of both indigenous and non-indigenous arts and crafts of a scope and character not equalled anywhere in the world, enabling their creators to live comfortably in their chosen lifestyle away from the rush and bustle of the capital cities.

There is even a flourishing bi-monthly magazine devoted to these enterprises , *The Australian Markets & Fairs*, running to over a 100 pages per issue packed with information about the current markets and fairs held on a regular or casual basis in every part of Australia. The publishers, Rick and Lynette Rayner, estimated in late 1998 that they had files on some 1300 regular markets around Australia, plus another 600 or 700 run on an annual or irregular basis. And they were aware that there must be many smaller markets out there which have not managed to get their events recorded.

Who can guess the annual turnover of sales in these widely scattered fairs! Obviously many thousands of alternate lifestylers are happy with the results they are achieving with the products of their creative talents.

29

Paradise for Sale!

The advertisement is now several years old, but it will probably never go out of date, continually dragging the eyes back to those glaring black headlines staring out of the magazine page: DISCOVER THE SECRETS OF OWNING YOUR OWN PIECE OF PARADISE IN THE BARRIER REEF...

Priced at only $105,000 with a guaranteed 7% net return.

There it is. I can actually own my very own slice of Paradise by buying for a modest outlay (considering house prices these days) a unit in a block of flats on one of the larger developed islands on Queensland's north coast. And I can either live in this paradise and struggle to pay off the mortgage, or I can rent this Shangri La to some stranger while working some negative gearing tax fiddle that will only cost me ten dollars a week. All set out in tempting detail.

Paradise for sale indeed! Yet this is one of many such promotions thought up in the dream factories of the developers and the Real Estate agents of the nation.

You can't take it with you, they assert, so buy your little bit of Paradise NOW... and enjoy! Paradise must be the most overworked word in the English language these days, a constant challenge to the cartographers attempting to cope with the ever increasing numbers of sub-divisions, suburbs, streets, lakes, man-made canals, islands and destinations featuring the magic word so that advertisements like the one quoted above can persuade the populace to part with good money for distant dreams.

And these modern dream peddlers cast their net very wide in their search for the elusive dollar. They are just as adept at producing structures for the masses as they are at crafting expensive retreats for the well-heeled in the community, the main difference being that the latter projects are these days geared more around security than comfort which is taken for granted in such ventures.

When Sanctuary Cove was developed on the Queensland Gold Coast in the 1980's the emphasis was entirely on its exclusivity and high tech security - to "keep the cockroaches out" as one candid advertisement put it. The cockroaches were mightily upset by this terminology, but the so-called White Shoe Brigade for whom the project was developed just loved it.

In cities right around Australia, developers are busily copying the American pattern of urban living by producing no-through road enclaves with fortress walls and the tightest security for their inhabitants - mostly DINKS (Double Income No Kids) of the Baby Boomer generation. For them it is back to past living in medieval fortress style with the cockroaches well out.

These comparatively new experiments on the Australian scene are for the middle class workers in the cities, and for the more affluent retirees in the more scenic areas of the continent. For the majority outside these havens, there are more fleeting glimpses of Paradise on offer by the bands of Travel Agents - the second cousins to the Real Estate agent brigade.

These enterprising folk are even more energetic and resourceful in selling their dream destinations! Some of the colourful brochures produced by these dream merchants are indeed works of art in the creation of images of paradise using a combination of highly selective photographs and seductive (if not wholly truthful) descriptions. They never mention the sandflies or leeches or other nasties infesting their Shangri La destinations. The Travel Agents cater to all tastes and to all pockets and have plenty of package deals for the "cockroaches" seeking a 5 or 7 day paradise, as well as steering their well heeled clients I towards magic island boltholes where the tariff per person per night edges towards four figures.

Not all these destinations are overpriced or described in outrageously exaggerated terms. Right around Australia there are a huge number of holiday destinations that are honestly promoted and give value for money. The competition for the dollar sees to that and word of mouth recommendations means repeat business, ensuring such operations have long and productive lives.

One unusual tourist destination was constructed in 1996 on a small portion of what was once the Rosebud Commune near Kuranda, up the range from Cairns, called the Tentative Nests. Described as a co-educational overnight rainforest experience, the visitors sleep in tents erected on tree top platforms while the eating and recreational areas are down in the floor of the rainforest and devoid of walls. Open-air living with a vengeance! While nightly trips down a ladder to a jungle-based composting toilet even with the aid of a powerful torch (provided) struck me as being slightly on the wrong side of the road to Paradise. I was intrigued enough to write away for some details of this unusual destination and its creator.

The latter turned out to be one Joell Bacon (and his partner Teena), an ex-American, now naturalised Aussie, with a quite remarkable background.

Joell was born in 1945 and raised in New York, his mother a judge and father in the rag trade. His grandfather was a gangster and a night club owner partly responsible for the well known Cotton Club in Harlem.

Growing up, Joell was into drugs for 20 years before

shaking off the demon and coming to Australia in the 1980's to run a restaurant in Fremantle during the America's Cup days.

After the magic of the Cup had passed he set out to travel around Australia until discovering, as many had done before him, the magic of the Kuranda area. This eventually led to Tentative Nests which seems to be an experiment in introducing ordinary people to the magic of a rainforest by having them live in and explore it all first hand, always with a strong preservation theme running through his talks with his clients: *An idea isn't worth the paper it is written on if you have to cut down a tree to remember it.*

Joell's brochures are full of humour, philosophy and information, and unlike most other establishments they don't shirk at mentioning the problems of rainforest living. He even has a whole page devoted to Things That Suck And Sting And Bite (and make strange sounds at night). While maintaining that his rainforest is safer than any street, he provides precise and colourful information on how to deal with leeches, ants, bees, wasps, scorpions and spiders, snakes and stinging and hostile plants. Such refreshing candour is all too rare these days and should be applauded - and rewarded.

So far I have mentioned only the land-based pieces of paradise on offer by the dream merchants but also on offer are a host of destinations with cruise ships anxious to take you all around the globe.

In the post-war period cruise ship operations have been one of the great growth industries and Australia, and especially Sydney, has been a major departure point for cruises to various tropical islands of the South Seas. This large, and hugely exploitative trade, has cashed in on the mainly mythical allure of the Pacific islands and their (female) inhabitants. Floating hotels, called cruise ships, now convey paradise seekers around endlessly cruised specks of land bobbing up around the Pacific.

The fact that most of the islands turn out to be somewhat tatty and tarnished from centuries of being transformed from their natural heathen idyll to a "civilised" status, is ignored or glossed over in the colourful brochures of the travel agents.

Still, hope does seem to spring eternal in the human breast and passengers on these cruise ships seem to enjoy the experience with many returning for repeat journey into balmy tropical zones.

The South Pacific cruise trade had its origins back in the 19th Century when the various steamship lines plying South Pacific trade routes occasionally took time out to run cruises out of Sydney to the major islands.

An interesting example even rated a small feature by an unknown contributor to the sporting section of the July 9 1898 issue of the *Bulletin*. The correspondent made mention that there had been over the years a number of successful cruises to the Pacific Islands, the latest being that of the Union Steamship Company's Waikare which had just departed from Sydney on a six week cruise to Tahiti and other islands along the way.

It was noted that despite the very low cost of only 30 pounds per ticket for the cruise, sales had initially been very slow. He attributed this to the fact that while there were plenty of people around who could afford the fare, there were relatively small numbers in Sydney who could afford to be away from their daily endeavours for 6 weeks of swanning around the South Seas, despite the many attractions on offer for the cruise. These included the fact that the ship carried 7 tons of ice, 2 tons of game, copious stocks of selected wines and a substantial selection of buttonhole flowers preserved in wadding for the festivities when the ship reached Tahiti. Other advertised attractions included a dark room for the photographers among the passengers and (wait for it) a spacious deck for flirting! All this for 30 quid.

The price of cruise tickets may seem a very low sum on a straight conversion to today's currency (ie $60) but allowance has to be made for the actual spending power of the pound in Sydney at the time. The pages of the *Bulletin* provide quite a lot of clues on this subject.

This was a period when a labourer or a clerk would have considered himself well paid if he earned a pound a week. An advertisement in the *Bulletin* for a Town Clerk for the New South Wales town of Junee carried a salary of 156 pounds an annum. Had the successful applicant for this job taken leave to sail on the Waikare, he would have had to outlay 10 weeks of salary to find out what delights awaited in Tahiti.

For the price of a ticket on the cruise one could have purchased the very latest luxury imported bicycle (ladies or gents) and got a fiver change. Or for a mere 6 pounds he could have purchased a brand new sulky or for 21 pounds he could have acquired a smart Ladies Park phaeton for his wife. A return ticket to London was being advertised by the rival P & O Steamship Co from 65 pounds to 110 pounds first class.

Coming down the scale a bit both the Hotel Brighton at Kogarah and the Coffee Palace Hotel in the Lower Domain were offering full board for 25 shillings a week. Tickets at 'The French Maid', the then hit show at Her Majesty's Theatre, ranged from 1 shilling (in the Gods) to 5 shillings front stalls. A serviceable men's three piece suit was available for 2 pounds, a subscription to the *Bulletin* cost a pound a year or sixpence per copy (incidentally the price of a pack of four cigars). Several pages of the *Bulletin* were given over each week to advertisements from quacks claiming to be able to cure any complaint with various nostrums they peddled from a shilling upwards. And for a shilling the lucky Sydneyite could procure and wash with a bar of Dr Mackenzie's magical Arsenical Soap!

Maybe a 6 weeks trip to Paradise on the Waikere at 30 quid wasn't the bargain of the year after all.

30

The Beachcomber

BEACHCOMBER, 1. one who lives by gathering articles along the beaches, as from wreckage. 2. a vagrant of the beach or coast, esp. a white man in South Pacific.

THE MACQUARIE DICTIONARY.

Is there an Australian adult male, past or present, who has not at some time had idle thoughts of taking off to some distant Pacific Island to indulge in that most pleasurable of occupations - beachcombing - especially if in the company of some shapely island wahine?

Back in the last century there was a man who did more than daydream about such an idyll; he carried out his beachcombing activities for more than a quarter of a century, though admittedly he only went a few miles offshore to do this accompanied by his lawful wedded wife, (not a wahine) and for most of the time a servant to help with domestic chores! That man was Edmund James Banfield, Australia's best known self-proclaimed beachcomber because of the many articles and books he wrote over the years about his experiences on his little piece of Paradise - Dunk Island.

Banfield was born at Liverpool England, on September 4 1852, the son of a printer who migrated to Australia when Edmund was a child. Banfield senior eventually became the proprietor of a newspaper at Ararat in Victoria and it was here that his son gained his basic training as a journalist.

After stints on metropolitan newspapers in Melbourne and Sydney, Banfield went to North Queensland in 1882 to become sub editor of the *Townsville Bulletin*, then and now one of Australia's foremost regional daily newspapers.

In 1884 he experienced great problems with an injured eye and took leave of the *Bulletin* to go to England for specialist treatment - resulting in the removal of the eye. While there he met up with old friends of the family and renewed acquaintance with a childhood friend, Bertha Golding. He returned to Australia and two years later Bertha, who had also triumphed over a physical disability - deafness - joined him. They were married in Townsville in 1886. In 1889 Essie, a little Irish family retainer, came out from England to join them and was to be part of their great island venture for many years.

Banfield was a man full of nervous energy and in 1897 he suffered a breakdown from overwork and quit the hectic pace of journalism. He decided to go beachcombing on one of the many offshore islands. This was not the idle day dreaming of a city executive. The 15 years that he had spent on the *Bulletin* had made him familiar with all the pitfalls and problems associated with his proposed venture. He was well acquainted with the hazards of the north, including the fury of cyclones in the wet season.

He also gave very careful thought to a choice of island for the venture. He was familiar with most of the islands along the coast as a result of his journalistic work, and finally settled on Dunk Island as the most suitable for the family needs.

Dunk is only a small island located in Rockingham Bay, some 20 miles north of the better known Hinchinbrook Island, and some 30 miles from the port of Geraldton to the north. It has a good beach on Brammo Bay on the northern side of the

211

island and in 1897 was heavily timbered. The native name for the island was Coonanglebah, but when Captain Cook sighted it on June 8 1770, he named it Dunk Island after his patron, George Montagu Dunk, First Lord of the Admiralty.

Cook named the vast bay in which Dunk Island was located Rockingham Bay after the Marquis Rockingham, who as Whig Prime Minister, opposed the notorious Stamp Act tax on the American Colonies, saying that while the Parliament had the legal right to impose the tax, it was unjust and impolitic, "sterile of revenue and fertile of discontent". How right he was, and it is ironic to note that had his advice been heeded, there would not have been an American Revolution of 1776 - and no great need to establish a convict colony in Australia!

One of the main reasons that Banfield favoured Dunk ahead of other islands in the vicinity was its location. Brammo Bay was directly on the track of several steam vessels which made weekly runs up and down the coast. Banfield was able to make an arrangement with one of the companies to make a weekly drop of newspapers and food and other supplies.

Banfield didn't rush into his venture, but took the precaution of leasing a small portion of the island at a modest rental of 2 shillings and sixpence per acre per annum. This gave the applicant a priority to more permanent lease arrangements for most of the island under the very liberal land laws operating in Queensland at the time. Later, when he had determined his experiment would work, he applied and obtained a deed of grant of the land in fee-simple on terms that would make today's island seekers green with envy. Payment of a mere 2 and sixpence per acre for 10 years, after which the land became freehold!.

Banfield also planned the whole operation in some detail, arranging for a mainland builder to construct a pre-fabricated cedar hut and take it to the island and assemble it there.

He decided they would give the island adventure a 6

months trial and if it did not work out, the hut could be dismantled and taken back to the mainland. This hut was gradually expanded into a house by Banfield over the years, using driftwood and timbers imported from the mainland.

On September 18 1897 Banfield and his wife Bertha took up residence in their small hut on Brammo Bay and he described their coming as follows:

"I landed feebly… and crawled upon the beach beyond the datum of the most recent high tide to throw myself prone on the consoling sand. I was worn, world-weary, and pale , and weighed 8st 4lbs.

At the time Banfield must have had thoughts that he had left it all too late, that he had come to the island to die but in the coming months he was to undertake physical activity of the like he had not before experienced.

The top priority of the Banfields was the establishment and cultivation of their garden, because they were counting on it to provide them with most of the food on their table. With the help of an ancient aboriginal then living on the island, they managed to clear, cultivate and sow some 4 and a half acres of plants - bananas (a staple of their diet), oranges, pineapples, pawpaws, custard apples, coffee, jackfruit, pomegranates, lychees, mangoes, sweet potatoes, pumpkins, melons, a variety of herbs and occasionally maize. They dispensed with meat from their diet but made exceptions of an occasional chicken from their poultry run, and of course fish was plentiful and easy to catch. Despite all the physical exertions this involved, or because of them, Banfield's health rapidly improved and he threw off his depressions.

With the garden taking shape, he was able to turn his attention to what had brought him to the island in the first place - a new pursuit of beachcombing. He took to it with zest and in his book *Confessions of a Beachcomber*, he was able to hint at some of the benefits of the pastime:

> *And when the sea casts up its gifts on these radiant shores, I boldly and with glee give way to my beachcombing instincts and pick and chose. Never up to the present have I found anything of real value; but am I not buoyed up by pious hopes and sanguine expectations? Is not the game as diverting and as innocent as many others that are played to greater profit? It is a game, too, that cannot be forced, and therefore cannot become demoralising: and having no nice feelings nor fine shades, I rejoice in it.*

He speculated on what he should do if a particularly valuable piece of flotsam should come his way from some distant shipwreck, and decided he be would of the same mind as the Pastor on the Shetland Isles who included in his prayers, the plea: *"Lord, if it be Thy holy will to send shipwrecks, do not forget our island"*. Over the years much flotsam came to Dunk Island from shipwrecks, including valuable timbers which were very useful in making additions to the small original living quarters.

In time Banfield turned his attention to the flora and fauna of the island, particularly the bird life. Although he had no scientific training, he loved nature and was a meticulous observer through his journalistic training. This lead him to start writing articles on his observations for the *Townsville Bulletin*, and for various journals. This writing led on to his books which not only brought fame and provided some useful income for the little luxuries of life, but between them held a remarkable record of the minutia of a Barrier Reef Island.

Essie, the little Irish retainer, had not accompanied them to the island in 1897, but rejoined them in 1904 and became a valuable member of the island team.

Banfield always believed that he had found his own personal Garden of Eden, and after fifteen years on Dunk, was able to write of it:

> *This delicious Isle, this unkempt, unrestrained garden where*

the centuries gaze upon perpetual summer! Small it is and of various charms - set in the fountain of a time-defying youth... it typifies all that is tranquil, quiet, easeful, dreamlike, for it is the Isle of Dreams.

Edmund James Banfield became ill in May 1923 and died on June 2, aged 71 years, of which 25 had been spent on the island.

Essie, their companion, was away on holiday at the time and it was 2 days before Bertha could attract the attention of a passing ship, the Innisfail. The sailors made a coffin and the captain read the burial service before burying him in his own tropical garden in Brammo Bay, the bay of butterflies.

Bertha Banfield left the island of so many happy memories and died in southern Queensland in 1933. Her body was taken back to Dunk Island to be buried alongside her beloved husband; two bodies resting in the little piece of paradise they had jointly helped to create in a quarter of a century of tender loving care...

31

Cedar Bay Bill

Some people like Edmund Banfield can select and carefully plan their personal Garden of Eden; others stumble across their Paradise by accident or a sudden twist of fate. Nowhere is the latter more in evidence than in the quite remarkable story of Cedar Bay Bill.

William Yale Evans was born into a Welsh mining family on April 17 1893. He migrated to Australia in 1912 and like his forbears became a coal-miner.

He toiled at this task for more than twenty years whereby coal dust entered his lungs causing phthisis. The prognosis of his doctor was that he probably had three months to live.

"Bugger that", said Bill, who bought a horse and cart and headed north in search of eternal sunshine. His trek was a long one and didn't end until he was well past Cairns and into the mountains behind Cedar Bay. That would be in the early 1930's when the Great Depression was biting really hard.

Evans began tin scratching, an occupation requiring lots of labour and patience for little financial return. However, his needs were not great and he managed to earn a living while his health came back as a result of all the exercise and mountain air.

While carrying out his tin scratching activities, he came down from the hills and discovered the then uninhabited Cedar Bay, a place of great tranquillity and beauty. Here he established a base and built a hut, which over the years he expanded into a comfortable house.

Being a prudent individual, he took out a perpetual Miners' Homestead Lease on 80 acres of land on the northern end of Cedar in 1933. This act gave him security of tenure but involved him in a running battle with the Queensland Government a long way down the track.

When he reached the age of 65 in 1958 he qualified for the Old Age Pension. Life became much easier for him as the pension provided for most of his basic needs, plus the occasional luxury.

Evans was a very private individual and for many years was known as the Hermit of Cedar Bay, but with the passing of time he was usually referred to simply as Cedar Bay Bill. For more than four decades he was the sole resident of Cedar Bay, which is an extremely isolated spot. There was only two practical ways in and out of the area - a roundabout up-river journey by boat, or a fairly strenuous hike up a rough fifteen mile track to the Bloomfield area - a journey usually taking four or five hours depending on the fitness of the traveller.

Because of its isolation there were few visitors and that is the way Bill Evans preferred it as he cherished his solitude - but Gardens of Eden tend to attract serpents, sometimes of the human variety.

One such individual emerged from the woodwork in the late 1950's when Cedar Bay Bill began to receive visits from a German called Georg von Konrat. This pudgy, fast talking adventurer, then in his mid-thirties, was destined to have a considerable impact on the life of Cedar Bay's original settler.

Georg von Konrat was born on February 16 1924, at Tilsit, East Prussia, and came to Australia around 1950, probably as an illegal immigrant. He eventually settled in hippie style in a rented cottage at Holloway Beach, north of Cairns, with two compliant young women in a *menage a trois* arrangement. Here he wrote a quasi-biographical book *Escape to Adventure*, which was eventually published early in 1963 by Davies of London.

By the late 1950's Kurat was getting restless, not having discovered in Australia the Garden of Eden he had sought. Having heard stories of Cedar Bay and its sole inhabitant he decided to gain possession of this Paradise by taking over Old Bill's lease. However, Old Bill was having none of that and in 1964 he was to testify in court that in the previous five years Konrat had made at least half a dozen visits to him trying to persuade him to rent or sell his holding. Konrat was not to be shaken off so easily and sought other ways of dislodging the sole tenant of Cedar Bay.

Shortly after midnight on July 18 1963, Bill Evans awoke to find two assailants in their late teens at his bedside with guns and every intent to do him harm. They tied his hands together with fishing lines and proceeded to beat him up, torturing him with lighted cigarettes, all the time demanding to know where he had hidden his money and gold. As no such hoard existed, Bill was not able to assist them, which only lead to more torture. Bill Evans knew they had some connection with Georg von Konrat because the youths mentioned a forthcoming operation he was shortly to have. The only person who knew of this operation, other than his doctor, was Konrat who had been told on a recent visit.

The punishment and torture continued all night and well into the morning before the youths came to the conclusion that Bill might be telling the truth, and that there was no gold.

In daylight they had turned everything upside down in the house and had discovered seventy five pounds in cash (from Bill's pension payments), two rifles and ammunition, an outboard motor, a transistor radio, binoculars, compass, and various items of food and clothing. They decided to decamp with this slender haul.

It was early afternoon before they made this decision and in all this time they had refused Old Bill's requests for food, but had given him a glass of water with cigarette ash stubbed in it.

Their boat was moored almost two miles from Bill's house so they marched him down to the landing spot and tied him up with fencing wire to a log, telling him they intended to kill him before they left. It may have been an idle boast, but Bill was not to know that. After all, if they had left him tied to the log he would have perished anyway, so seldom did he receive any visitors.

They proceeded to transfer their loot from his house to the boat and Bill struggled mightily with his wire restraints and managed to flee into the dense bush. Here he was on familiar ground and there was no way they would find him.

Returning from the house with a load of loot, the youths found Bill had escaped, and panicked. They must have realised that the game was up with their victim free to report the attack and identify them. They took off in a hurry, leaving behind a vital piece of evidence, a mud map of Cedar Bay and a full drawing of the rooms in Bill's house - supplied to them by Georg von Konrat.

Bill Evans lay low in his hideout until midnight, not knowing whether or not their departure had been a ruse. When they had gone, he made his way back to the house and managed to cut himself free of the fishing line cords cutting into his hands.

Next morning he found the dropped map, but he was too shaken by his ordeal to attempt the arduous trip up the track to Bloomfield immediately. It was twelve days before he made it to the small town to get medical aid and to report the hold-up.

The police were quickly on the trail of the culprits and tracked them down at Townsville. Each readily admitted the crime, saying they had been urged to do it by Georg von Konrat.

The culprits turned out to be two Sydney salesmen, Jaroslav Tarkovich , aged 20, and Warren Keith O'Neill, aged 19. They had travelled north looking for drugs and adventure as so many other Sydneysiders had done of that age. They had been befriended by Konrat who had driven them down toMission Beach, a large resort south of Cairns, and had pointed out to them a number of unoccupied holiday houses. The pair had broken into several houses over the next few days and had returned with a boat and some stolen goods that they gave to Konrat. They claimed that Konrat believed Cedar Bay Bill had a lot of money and possibly gold stacked away, and he had given them the map. After the raid they had thrown all the guns away in a creek (they were subsequently recovered) and had given the rest of the Cedar Bay loot to Konrat, before fleeing to Townsville.

Tarkovich and O'Neill appeared in Townsville Court on August 30 1963 and pleaded guilty to various charges of stealing and assault, and were initially sentenced to nine months gaol. The Crown successfully appealed against the leniency of this sentence and the youths received four year gaol terms.

The police then turned their attention to Georg von Konrat. As the two youths were extremely reluctant to give evidence against him, the Crown proceeded only with minor charges of stealing and selling stolen property. Konrat appeared in Cairns Court in March 1964 and pleaded not guilty to all charges. He was found guilty by the jury on three of the four counts. Despite having a previous conviction at Cooktown for theft, the Judge let him off with a suspended sentence on a bond of fifty pounds on each count.

After the court case Konrat left the Cairns area and for a time settled on the Queensland Gold Coast. In 1967 he kidnapped his four year old daughter Weronika, who he had sired with a Brisbane woman, and fled with her to New Zealand, where for a period he worked on a major hydro development scheme in the south island.

In 1969 he travelled to South Africa with Weronika and for a while settled on a small holding outside Cape Town, where he had published to some local acclaim his second book *Assault from Within*. This account of his James Bond style wartime activities with a top secret German commando unit, was like his first book, more fiction than fact, even contradicting many of the accounts of his life given in the original *Escape to Adventure*.

In January 1971 he secured a job working on a major engineering project in what was then South West Africa (now Namibia) at Ovamboland, on the northern border with Angola.

His anti-apartheid activities soon brought him to the notice of the infamous South African security police, and when they managed to seize the manuscript of another book he had written called *Strangers in Paradise*, severely criticising the South African government apartheid policies, his position became perilous. Realising his predicament, he fled with Weronika across the border at Calueque into Angola to its capital Luanda, where German embassy officials arranged safe passage to England, where they arrived on August 23 1971, and were given political asylum.

Safe in England, Konrat wrote his final book *Passport to Truth: Faces of Apartheid*, published by WH Allen in 1972. This was an account of his South African experiences and, unlike his earlier works, has a certain ring of truth about it - despite its many obvious embellishments.

Georg von Konrat (the "von" almost certainly was a self-bestowed title) lived the rest of his life in the United Kingdom, with only minor problems with the law. His final years were spent at Haverfordwest, a very picturesque part of Wales, where he died in 1990, so perhaps he did at last find and savor for a while his own piece of paradise.

Back in Cedar Bay, Bill Evans knew nothing of the

remarkable life and adventures of his nemesis, Georg von Konrat. As Evans was a generous soul, he probably would have forgiven the German adventurer for the distress that he had inflicted on him, as in some respects they had much in common. Both had sought their own Gardens of Eden. Whereas Bill Evans had found his and hung on to it grimly for most of his life, Konrat had usually managed to foul his own nest each time he had wandered into a piece of paradise in various parts of the world.

It took Bill Evans a long while to recover from the injuries he had received in his 1963 ordeal, but a few years later he had to come to terms with a different kind of invasion of his treasured turf. This came in the shape of mostly young Hippies seeking a new life style of self-sufficiency and a place, well away from prying police eyes, where they could grow and partake of illegal substances!

What Cedar Bay Bill thought about this invasion of his patch is not known as his diaries have been lost to posterity, but he must have had mixed feelings about the sudden arrival of numbers of people with rather weird dress and unorthodox lifestyle into his tranquil bay.

Perhaps there was the consoling thought of safety in numbers. The Hippies were a peaceful lot, even if wont to ignore the drug laws of the day. At least their presence would be a strong deterrent to misguided youths intent on robbery with violence.

As it turned out, the arrival of the Hippies resulted in considerable changes to Old Bill's lifestyle and despite the great differences in age and outlook, harmony prevailed.

For their part the Hippies were immensely impressed with the fact that Old Bill had managed to survive for so long in the alternate lifestyle they were seeking. He was able to give them practical survival advice in all sorts of areas, such as what was edible in the surrounding forest, what vegetables to grow in their gardens, and where the best fishing spots were to be found. In no time at all he became a Guru to the Hippie tribes of Cedar Bay.

Bill was a great favourite of the kids, teaching them the ins and outs of his favourite pastime of beachcombing. Like Edmund Banfield on Dunk Island, away to the south and many decades earlier, Old Bill had managed quite a harvest from the flotsam and jetsam washed up on the Cedar Bay beach. These treasures included thongs, not just an occasional specimen, but thongs by the score, and in time by the hundred!

Now open foot sandals have been around for thousands of years, but the modern plastic thong is an Australian invention so beloved and faithfully worn by the inhabitants of Terra Australis that it has almost achieved Icon status. Thongs are manufactured and sold in such vast quantities, that the turnover rate in lost or discarded specimens must reach impressive proportions for such numbers to have ended up on a small and very isolated beach as Cedar Bay.

Where do they come from? It is unlikely they would be thrown overboard from passing ships. Perhaps they were left behind by careless owners on southern beaches, scooped up by the high tide, and gently carried north by the currents and deposited gently on the Thong Nirvana of Cedar Bay.

As no thong-count was undertaken at the time, it is difficult to assign numbers to Old Bill's hoard, but it was a very sizeable pile stacked up outside his modest home; a pile frequently called upon by the Hippies on their regular forays up the track to Bloomfield in their quest for the dole and supplies. Before departure they would come around to Old Bill's place and search through the thong pile until they found a pair to fit. Then off each would go on his or her journey up the track, to deposit the borrowed thongs back on the heap on their return. And the thong pile also provided an important role at the end of Old Bill's life.

When Old Bill's 80th birthday rolled around, the Hippies decided that this was an occasion deserving a special celebration. After all, it is not often that a person given a few months to live by some medico, can still be found living in a piece of paradise more than four decades later.

They decided to stage a big party in his honour, but had some difficulty determining a suitable birthday present to bestow on him. His needs were simple and he appeared to have all the routine creature comforts of the time.

It was a vivacious redhead who went by the name of Feathers who came up with an answer. "I'll stay with him tonight and give him a real good time," she volunteered.

Everyone thought this a splendid idea and the suggestion was approved with acclaim. What Old Bill thought of this rather unique birthday present is not recorded, but the Hippies are unanimous in averring that he didn't say no.

Councillor Colin Burns, of the Bloomfield Shire Council, was a good friend of Old Bill in has latter years and has vivid memories of going down to Cedar Bay on one occasion, to find Old Bill under a big mango tree with a group of young female Hippies indulging in a mango feast. All, including Bill, in their birthday suits. Not a stitch of clothing in sight.

When you come to think of it, that is really the only sensible way of consuming a number of ripe mangoes!

While the Hippies brought security and great changes into the life of Cedar Bay Bill, they also brought problems for him - most of them centred on his 80 acre lease.

The Queensland Lands Department had plans to convert Cedar Bay into a national park, but both Bill Evans with his lease and the Hippies with their lifestyle and lack of clothing posed obvious problems to these plans.

It now seems clear that one of the aims of the infamous

police raid on Cedar Bay of August 28 1976 (see Chapter 34), was to frighten the Hippies away from Cedar Bay. The fact that the raid concentrated only on the Hippie group living on Old Bill's lease land, ignoring the two other Hippie groups on the centre and southern parts of the bay, probably was no accident.

While Cedar Bay Bill himself was not targeted in the raid, he was then well into his 80's and not in robust health. Perhaps the bureaucrats in charge of the operation figured that if his Hippie friends could be driven away, Bill Evans would feel so exposed that he too would quit the area.

The plan did not succeed. Although a majority of the Hippies drifted away from Cedar Bay after the raid, some did stay on, and Bill Evans resisted all suggestions that he should leave.

The bureaucrats then floated a plan whereby the government would pass a law extinguishing Evans' lease so the whole area could be proclaimed a National Park. When Old Bill heard of this he went down to Cairns seeking legal advice. His advisers publicised the proposal and community support was so strong for Bill Evans that the Government quickly backed off.

The Lands Department, which was handling the matter, had a problem here that they could not very well reveal. Their private fear was that Old Bill might marry one of the young Hippie women and even begat offspring in traditional Biblical manner, thus complicating the position on the lease no end. They could even envisage court actions by Old Bill's new family dragging on well into the next century.

Faced with these possibilities they came up with a compromise plan. This was that Bill Evans would surrender his lease to enable the proclamation of the National Park to go ahead but that he would be, given in writing an agreement that he could remain on the land for the rest of his life. As Old Bill was in favour of the National Park and had all along only sought tenure for himself, he readily agreed to this arrangement, to the vast relief of the bureaucrats involved.

The proclamation of the new National Park gave the Government the power to evict the few remaining Hippies so Old Bill lost his young friends, though many of them continued to visit him on a regular basis. The newly appointed National Park rangers kept an eye on Bill and even built him a new water tank. When Old Bill aged 93 became too ill to look after himself, the Rangers conveyed him down to Cairns and had him taken into a nursing home, where he remained for the next eighteen months. He died in the Cairns Base Hospital on September 7 1987.

Bill's money had run out and there was nothing left for a funeral and it seemed that Old Bill might be destined for a burial in a pauper's grave in Cairns. When news of this leaked out, friends of his rallied around from all parts of the Cairns district. Funds were donated and a committee quickly set up to ensure that the old fellow received a proper send-off at Cedar Bay where he had spent more than half a century. A Helijet was hired, its doors were removed, and the coffin carrying Old Bill's body was loaded in sideways, a portion hanging out both sides of the tiny craft. Piloted by Bernie Fisher, the small helicopter took off from Cairns airport on the morning of Sunday October 4 1987 and headed for Cedar Bay, where a large group of friends of Old Bill had gathered for the occasion, coming from all around the district and including many of his former Hippie friends and their children.

Remember that hoard of old thongs, salvaged by Old Bill in his beachcombing days and stacked near his house? Well, as the helicopter headed north that morning, the children gathered at Cedar Bay, transported all the thongs from Old Bill's hoard down to the beach and carefully arranged them in a large circle on the sand, where the tiny helicopter came to rest with its precious cargo.

That afternoon they buried Old Bill on a slope bordering on the rainforest of Cedar Bay, facing out to the wide blue Pacific Ocean. Old Bill had specifically requested that there be no religious ceremonies to his passing so the event was marked simply by a song specially written for the occasion, some recollections of his many friends and the sprinkling over the grave of flowers gathered from the nearby forest. And the whiff of smoke from a forbidden weed hung heavily in the atmosphere.

There was a sequel to this unusual funeral that has not previously appeared in print.

A burial of this sort, away from a designated burial ground, and in a National Park, required a mountain of paperwork and guarantees of all sorts - all of which was carried on the helicopter by the chief organiser of the event, who must remain nameless. Everything went to plan on the outward trip, but on the return flight late in the afternoon the helicopter encountered some extreme cross winds and turbulence. With the doors removed, all the signed and sealed papers were plucked out of the hands of the person carrying them and dispersed to the winds.

When this information was conveyed to the bureaucracy concerned in Cairns the next day there was a wailing and gnashing of teeth never before experienced in the proud city of the north. It took weeks to sort out the mess. Old Bill, no lover of officialdom, would have been delighted.

After the funeral his friends quietly dispersed, but a few months later many of them returned to the spot for another ceremony, this time to erect an impressive memorial over his grave, with a message that said it all:

WILLIAM YALE EVANS
(Cedar Bay Bill)
Born 17th April 1893

Died 7th September 1987
Strange to the World,
He wore a bashful look,
The sea and the shore his study,
Nature his Book.

32

Shooting up in Paradise

It has often been proclaimed that the only two certainties of life are death and taxes. However history indicates another truism is that whenever someone discovers or creates a Garden of Eden there is a near certainty that someone else will emerge to destroy it. Usually the serpent of destruction emerges from within, human nature being what it is, but there are occasions when the destroyers come from outside with envy being a major motive for their actions.

And this was the case with the communes hidden away in their remote little Gardens of Eden in the Cedar Bay area.

If ever there was a place destined to be a human Garden of Eden it was Cedar Bay. Wild and beautiful with a two mile long golden beach, leading into dense tropical rainforest areas backed by a high mountain range.

By 1976 there were three hippie settlements in Cedar Bay usually numbering about a hundred persons. Down the southern end of the beach, near Sailors Rest and Ayton Rocks, was one of the vegetarian communes. In the centre of the beach there was another smaller vegetarian group, while up on the northern end near Fritz Creek, and just south of Obree Point, there was the original meat eating group on Cedar Bay Bill Evans 80 acre lease. It was also the most developed area of Cedar Bay, as it had coconut palms and mango and other fruit trees planted by Old Bill. All three settlements had extensive vegetable gardens while the northern group supplemented their diet with pork from hunting wild pigs.

Apart from activity associated with erecting shelters and tending their gardens, the hippies enjoyed a relaxed lifestyle given over to music, free love and a fairly regular smoking of marijuana. Clothing was often dispensed with in these little mini Gardens of Eden but this sort of lifestyle was by no means exclusive to Cedar Bay - it was fairly general in the more secluded areas of the far north Coast of Queensland in that period. A tour guide who worked in the area in the 1960's told me: "If you walked along a beach and encountered someone wearing clothes, you wondered what was wrong with them!"

The tranquillity of Cedar Bay was rudely disturbed on Sunday, August 29 1976, when police mounted a massive dawn raid on the northern group, coming ashore by boat and helicopter with guns blazing in quite extraordinary Rambo style. This raid that was to have far reaching political consequences for Queensland for years to come.

The raiding party was led by Inspector RC Gray, the newly appointed officer in charge of Cairns Police, with his second-in-command on the raid being Detective Sergeant HH Doull, then officer in charge of the Cairns CIB. The attack force was a strong one comprising twenty four police officers (including two women), four Customs Department agents and three Federal Police Narcotics Bureau Investigators. The raiding party was armed with machetes (for hacking their way through the jungle in search of the expected marijuana plantations), riot guns, rifles and revolvers. Also used was a police spotter aircraft, Army helicopter, the Customs launch Jabiru, and the Royal Australian Navy patrol vessel HMAS Bayonet. Also taken along for the ride were two Aboriginal blacktrackers.

When the force arrived off shore shortly before dawn there

were several fishing luggers in the vicinity. Sighting the patrol boat they departed the scene, but the HMAS Bayonet caught and searched each of them in turn as they were suspected of being involved in the drug scene with the Cedar Bay hippies. To the intense disappointment of the raiding team no drugs were found on any of the luggers.

What happened on shore that morning filled the columns of newspapers for weeks to come and involved the Queensland Parliament and Federal Parliament in many hours of debate. Accusations flew thick and fast for many weeks, mainly that the raid was a "search and destroy" operation with the police being over-zealous, loutish and using storm trooper tactics.

The Police, of course, at every level denied this, but the evidence is very strong to support the claims by the hippies that the raiders went far beyond normal tactics in the raid. They went in with guns blazing and shot holes in water tanks, chopped down fruit trees, shot coconuts and other fruits out of trees, destroyed and burnt all the huts and bush shelters and the communal kitchen. Perhaps worst of all, they gathered all the possessions, bedding and clothing of the hippies into a big pile, poured kerosene over it and destroyed all by fire.

The raiders ignored the screaming and crying children and concentrated on arresting the men who had not fled into the surrounding jungle. In all they arrested twelve men, handcuffed them in pairs or to trees and in two instances tied their hands with wire before transporting them in relays by the Army helicopter to Cooktown. One of the hippies arrested for vagrancy produced a bank passbook showing he had a balance of several hundred dollars. When he showed this to the arresting officer, the latter simply tore it in half and threw the book on the ground, proceeding with the arrest anyway.

With all their food destroyed, along with their gardens, the remaining women and children were left without shelter or sustenance after the raiders departed.

In the Senate on September 7, Senator Keeffe (Labor) summed up the situation very well with the remark: "A lot of things happened on that morning that should not have happened in a so-called civilised country".

The raid itself also turned out to be a bit of a fiasco so far as drug hauls were concerned. Despite an extensive search of the surrounding bush, the raiding party only managed to find a hundred marijuana plants (plus a small bottle of seeds).

A very curious aspect of the raid was that it was directed only against the northern (non-vegetarian) group who were settled by old Cedar Bay Bill on his leased land. This in itself was to cause the Crown problems and throw into doubt the charges of vagrancy laid, since those charged were all on private property by invitation at the time and all had means of sustenance by way of food and shelter.

Police never subsequently explained why the other two Cedar Bay groups were not touched by the raid. In fact shortly after the raid commenced a senior police officer visited the central group and assured them that they would not be disturbed. The southern group were not bothered, though they were aware of what was going on from the shooting and smoke rising from the northern beach site. They did have some unexpected visitors later in the morning when five weary and footsore police turned up. Sent in by the only track over the mountain saddle, probably to intercept any hippies attempting to flee back up the track, these police had not made contact with any hippies during their arduous trek but had had a number of painful encounters with ticks and barbed vines. They were totally exhausted by the time they reached the south camp where the hippies welcomed them in traditional fashion with coffee and banana cake.

The twelve male hippies who had been arrested in the raid appeared in Cooktown Magistrate's Court the morning of

August 30 before Mr MA Arrowsmith, Acting Stipendiary Magistrate. Four of them appeared on drug charges and received gaol sentences of four or three months, plus fines of $500 and $400. The other eight defendants appeared on vagrancy charges and each received fines of $40 or $30, but were not allowed time to pay, so were gaoled along with the others as they had no money with them to pay their fines.

The court cases proved to be a bigger farce than the raid. It was subsequently discovered that Mr Arrowsmith, who was the acting Clerk of Court at Cooktown, had not been appointed an Acting Stipendiary Magistrate (the regular magistrate was away on leave at the time) and therefore was without jurisdiction to hear the cases. With further egg all over its face the Queensland Government was forced to release the prisoners, though it played it tough by re-arresting several of them on other matters.

The Cedar Bay raid was seldom off the front pages of newspapers throughout Australia in the weeks that followed, as condemnation of the heavy handed police tactics caused public outrage from all quarters - particularly in the southern states where civil libertarians welcomed the opportunity to rub salt into the wounds of the bleeding Government.

The Premier, Joh Bjelke Petersen, sniffed the wind and left the task of defending the police and government to the newly appointed Police Minister Newberry. In turn Newberry made a very poor fist of fending off the attacks in Queensland Parliament and the media, claiming that accounts of police brutality in the raid were untrue and that those who opposed this view were acting in the interest of the drug trade.

Newberry consistently warded off calls for a public inquiry, first from the Queensland Labor Party and even from the Nationals' Coalition partners the Liberals. He rejected similar calls from Labor members in the Senate and House of Representatives. A letter of protest against police actions in the raid signed on September 14 by the entire Residents and Registrar Medical Staff of the Cairns Base Hospital was simply ignored.

In the Senate, Senator Keeffe managed to winkle out of the government the fact that the raid cost somewhere between fifty and seventy five thousand dollars, but he could not extract from the government who actually sanctioned the use of the Army Helicopter and the Federally-owned launch and patrol boat. The Minister for Administrative Services, Senator Reg "Toecutter" Withers, flatly rejected a request for an inquiry into Commonwealth Involvement in the raid. He tried to offload some of the blame on the shoulders of a colleague, stating that the responsibility for Federal agents fell within the jurisdiction of the Minister for Business and Consumer Affairs – one John Winston Howard MHR - later to become Prime Minister.

A very interesting sidelight to the issue occurred when the Australian Broadcasting Commission evening programme *This Day Tonight* aired two lengthy segments on the Cedar Bay raid on the evenings of September 7 and 8. The initial programme was devoted to interviews with hippies involved in the event and drew a heated attack on the ABC in the Queensland Parliament by Police Minister Newberry claiming extreme bias against him and the police.

The presenter of the programme, the late Andrew Olle, immediately responded by pointing out that he had extended an invitation to appear on the programme to Mr Newberry, to the Police Commissioner (Ray Whitrod) to Mr Hodges (the former Police Minister), and to Inspector Bob Gray who led the raid. All declined to appear.

Subsequently Sergeant Raymond George Marchant took out a writ in the Queensland Supreme Court against Andrew Olle, John Douglas McLean and Damien Ryan, claiming damages for defamation. However, Sergeant Marchant does not appear to have proceeded with the action, as in 1998 the Legal and Copyright Division of the ABC could not find any material relating to the action and Damien Ryan, still then an ABC employee, had no recollection of it ever going to court.

The ABC still has tapes of the two *This Day Tonight* programmes though they refused to allow me to view them on the grounds that the contents "were too sensitive". Hopefully they will be aired again on some programme dealing with the history of the ABC.

Initially the Police Commissioner Ray Whitrod, who had not been consulted about the raid, declined to comment, but mounting public concern over the affair forced his hand and on October 6 1976, he directed an internal police inquiry into the affair. Following this inquiry he announced that charges would be laid against four of the police involved. Shortly afterwards he tended his resignation as Commissioner, and subsequently cited the way he had been by-passed on the raid itself as one of the reasons for his leaving the job.

This had dramatic and painful consequences for Queensland. Whitrod was a straight shooter who was trying, with moderate success, to root out corruption in the Queensland force. His sudden departure left the way open for the unexpected appointment as the new commissioner - the corrupt Terry (later Sir Terry) Lewis, who some years down the track was to be exposed and gaoled (and stripped of his knighthood) as a result of the findings of the Fitzgerald inquiry.

The state of Queensland paid a very heavy price for the bungled raid on a bunch of harmless pot smoking hippies on Cedar Bay.

In February 1977 three police officers were committed for trial on charges of arson and wilful destruction of property. After a seventeen day trial in July that year two of the officers were discharged during the hearing and Inspector Gray was found not guilty by the jury.

After the abortive police trials of 1977, no doubt the Queensland Government considered that was the end of the matter, but the trials really proved nothing, and in fact raised far more questions than they answered. To this day no satisfactory evidence has been forthcoming to the following questions:

A.   Who ordered the raid on Cedar Bay?

B.   Why was the raid considered necessary?

C.   What was the actual purpose of the raid?

To all these questions both the Police and Government of the day gave contradictory and evasive answers which concealed rather than revealed the truth about the raid.

Who ordered the raid? We know it wasn't the Police Commissioner, Ray Whitrod. We know it wasn't instigated by the Cairns Police Headquarters, although they were responsible for the on-ground operational organisation. The raid was so large and involving so many Federal agencies that the initiative had to come from a high level of government. But which level and which arm? A senior retired police officer provided me with a name, but the laws of libel being what they are I can't commit it to print without supporting evidence.

On question B there are a number of conflicting theories. One theory that had considerable circulation in the Cairns area at the time was that the highly moralistic National Party was collectively outraged by the "Goings on" at Cedar Bay (by this they meant the nudity, free love and the pot smoking) and by the publicity given to it by sections of the media; and that Cabinet as a whole simply ordered the police to stop this piece of localised Sodom and Gomorrah. There may have been an element of truth in this, but the employment of such a large complement of State and Federal forces against such a small group of hippies up one end of the Cedar Bay beach, entirely ignoring the other two Cedar Bay hippie groups, doesn't add up. There simply had to be a larger agenda, and this is where the hippies themselves split into differing camps.

Well to the fore in one group is the theory that the raid was part of a plot to develop Cedar Bay by a well known northern developer with close connections to the National Party - the theory being that the Government stood to gain mightily in a financial sense from the operation. This particular conspiracy theory rather falls flat on its face by the fact that plans were at the time well advanced for the declaration of the whole of Cedar Bay as a National Park.

If there was a hidden agenda to the raid it may well have involved the National Park plans. The whole stumbling block to the plan at the time was old Cedar Bay Bill's perpetual lease on a key eighty acres of land at the northern end of Cedar Bay. Efforts to have the lease overturned were getting nowhere at the time and the department responsible may well have been prodding the Government down in Brisbane to do something about it.

Question C: What was the actual purpose of the raid? The Police themselves were closely questioned after the event and came up with conflicting answers.

Initially they claimed it was a drug raid based on "information received" and apparently they had high hopes of seizing vast plantations of marijuana. Had their information been more accurate they would have been aware that far from being exporters of drugs, most of the marijuana smoked at the three Cedar Bay groups was bought from outside (usually from Cooktown). The few plants they grew themselves were considered very second grade and for emergency use only.

A Police spokesmen even said that the purpose of the raid was partly to seek out a very dangerous American criminal who had escaped from the Cairns lock up some weeks earlier, and who was being sought by Interpol. With straight faces the spokesmen said they had information this dangerous criminal might be hiding at Cedar Bay, a laughable idea as the escape had been well publicised. Any stranger of his description would have immediately been sent on his way by any of the Cedar Bay or other hippie groups. They last thing they would have wanted was to fall foul of the law in such a matter.

Although both the Police and Government strenuously denied it, the REAL purpose of the raid was to not to discover drugs but to terrorise the hippies into leaving Cedar Bay. Not all the hippies either, only the ones camped on Cedar Bay Bill's lease at his invitation.

More than two decades after the event the raid still arouses deep passions both among surviving hippies and police. On August 30 1998, the Brisbane based *Sunday Mail* ran a special three page feature marking the twenty second anniversary of the raid. The feature included interviews with many of the survivors of the raid and a long interview with former Inspector Robert Gray, who led the raid and who now lives in retirement at Gympie. If the *Sunday Mail* was hoping for any contrition or apology from Gray for his part in the event, they were to be disappointed. His attitude was quite openly defiant. He claimed that Cedar Bay was far from the beautiful place as it had been described. In his view it was a depressing dump and that all he had done was to set fire to disease-ridden hovels.

The housing of the hippies may well have been sub-standard by normal suburban reckoning but housing in a tropical climate like Cedar Bay was very low on their priority list.

Perhaps the last word on this should be given over to one of the young women hippies present nursing a baby at the time of the raid, looking back at the experience more than two decades on:

Cedar Bay (before the raid) was the closest thing to a Garden of Eden that Queensland will ever have. It was the most wonderful period of my life. The freedom and all that. I would love to go back and experience it again, but you can't, can you? You can't turn the clock back..

33

The Noble Savage

While Cedar Bay Bill stumbled upon his Paradise almost by accident and then contentedly stayed put there for the next half century, one of his much younger friends and proteges, Michael Fomenko, roamed much the same territory for decades without finding his Shangri La.

Young Michael marched to the beat of a different drum in his quest, seeking a territory peopled by Noble Savages which had long disappeared from the Queensland landscape. Perhaps part of Michael's problem was that he was not born on these shores and therefore was not fully attuned to the harshness of the Australian landscape or its history.

Michael Fomenko was born in 1930 in Tiflis, the capital of the Republic of Georgia in the old Soviet Union. His father was a lecturer at Tiflis University and his mother was said to have once been Princess Machibelli, a distant relative of the long gone Czars. It is certain that the family was caught up in one of Stalin's purges and fled Russia, reaching Australia via Manchuria and Japan in 1939 when Michael was 9 years old.

His father, Peter Fomenko obtained employment as a teacher at the prestigious Sydney school Shore, which Michael attended as a pupil. Michael was a good student and a brilliant athlete, becoming shot putt and high jump school champion in 1947. He competed in the national championships and was considered a likely contender for the Melbourne Olympics of 1956, but this was not to be.

After leaving school he gained employment as a shipping clerk then on attaining his majority in 1951, he gave up his job and headed north to Queensland.

But Michael Fomenko was not on any pot-smoking adventures like so many other youngsters of the period. His was a quest for a lifestyle which had long vanished, seeking to find tribes of the Noble Savages of fiction and to emulate them by adopting their lifestyles.

The problem was that the Queensland Government had long put paid to any activities of Noble Savages, and had been busy rounding up all black coloured individuals it could locate and confining them to compounds like Palm Island. Under a crude paternalistic system of apartheid, compounds from which they could only emerge with special permission of their white administrators. The last thing the Government wanted was for their coloured charges to mix with white skinned intruders like Michael. There was no way of knowing what dangerous infectious and rebellious ideas they might pick up by such contacts! Michael Fomenko found his jungle without difficulty, up in the ranges behind Cedar Bay but the rainforests there were totally devoid of dark skinned inhabitants.

However, Michael must have made some contact with aborigines in one or more of the missions, because he appears to have acquired some indigenous skills. A former resident of the area told me how he had once come across Michael on the river flats near Bloomfield, practising spear throwing with some of his home made spears, first with the left arm and then with the right.

He also learned the art of hollowing out a log to make a canoe and in 1959 he managed to make himself a serviceable outrigger which he paddled right up the coast to Thursday

Island, which was no mean feat. On Thursday Island he was befriended by the natives who bestowed on him the nickname of "Tarzan of the North", a name that was to stay with him for the rest of his days.

He then set out for and eventually reached Irian Jaya where the natives started to match up to his idea of Noble Savages. However, his joy was cut short when the Indonesian controllers of Irian Jaya arrested him and deported him back to Australia. Making his way back to the heavily forested hill country behind Cedar Bay, Michael built a number of shelters and did his best to exist in what he believed to be the original state, surviving on fish, the occasional bird or wild pig and bush plants such as palm hearts. Occasionally he paid visits to Old Bill down at Cedar Bay, and he was also sometimes sighted in the Bloomfield area.

Life in the jungle can be tough, even for a Tarzan and there were occasions when hunger drove him out of the bush to isolated homesteads seeking handouts. Women and kids sometimes were alarmed at the sudden emergence of the ill-clad straggler, and complaints were made. It was not that Michael committed any offences, it was just that his appearance out of nowhere tended to frighten the good folk of the district.

The police decided to take action and managed to catch Michael on one of his rare outings from the bush. They charged him with vagrancy and then (probably illegally) shipped him off to the care of his parents in Sydney. Within a few years he was back in his old jungle haunts and a later expulsion southward had the same results.

In July 1996 a TV station ran a programme on alternative lifestyle with a feature on Michael and a newspaper associated with the same channel did a feature on the programme, skirting around the rather inconvenient fact that Michael had long given up his life of living in the jungle, stalking his food with bow and arrow, and was then living a more comfortable life in Cairns on the old age pension.

Never spoil a good story with an inconvenient fact! Some folk might view Michael Fomenko as a failure, a drop-out. They would be wrong. While the vast majority Australian males stayed tightly glued to their chairs in couch potato positions, seeking their thrills on the Telly or in wild day dreams, Michael was out there actually doing something - seeking out an ever elusive Garden of Eden. He at least tried and failed in his quest, while the majority of his fellow Australia never got past their front doors in their quest for anything.

34

On the Beach

Since occupation of the land in 1788 the new white skinned settlers of Australia have been obsessed with the country's seemingly endless parade of golden beaches and pounding surf - because from where they originally came such attractions were in extremely short supply.

They have continued these pursuits on the coast in spite of the risk of skin cancer and some pretty stout efforts, at least in the early years, of prudish authorities to stamp out such unseemly pleasures as sunbaking and sea bathing. They managed to overcome or ignore such prohibitions as were proclaimed in the New South Wales Prohibition of Bathing Act of 1838:

It shall be unlawful for any person to bathe near or within view of any public wharf, quay , bridge, street, road *or other place of public resort within the limits of any of the towns between six o'clock in the morning and eight in the evening.*

And the wowsers of the nation were still out in full cry against mixed bathing and sunbathing well into the twentieth century. On March 8 1912 the Melbourne *Argus* devoted a whole leading article to the fact that men and women were indulging in this pastime of the gradual browning of the skin under the sun's rays:

... in their blind enthusiasm for the sun, they are prepared to neglect such necessary formalities as the earning of a livelihood. ...

Lolling on the sand, either for individuals or for mixed groups should be regarded as strictly forbidden, not only by law, but by etiquette, which is more effective than law.

Of course these and other strictures from the moralists were completely ignored by many generations of ordinary Australians who took off for the beach and never lost an opportunity to build or buy a weekender as near as possible to the high-tide mark.

The average bloke (and Sheila) managed to balance this taste for hedonism with the Protestant work ethic they had inherited from their forbears. Work was work which paid the rent and the grocery bills. The sand and the surf was for the leisure hours.

This formula held good up until the years following the end of World War 11 when the cult of the surfie developed and hordes of young individuals deserted jobs and a life in the cities for the dole and days on the deserted beaches of our coastline.

The term 'surfie' had up to then been an honourable badge, but even dedicated members of the craft of riding the waves were shocked by the trend. Surfie became a pejorative term to be linked by to other epithets hurled at these taxpayer funded sun lovers -Hippie, Dropout, Layabout, Dole Bludger. Such terms did not seem to fit the bill for this new breed of sun/surfie (male and female) and it was left to the *Macquarie Dictionary* to come up with an alternative term (probably borrowed from America):

BEACH BUM. One who spends most of his or her life lazing on a beach.

All of which doesn't seem to bother in the slightest the myriad of so-called Beach Bums who believe they have found their little piece of government-funded paradise.

In a different category entirely is the Beachcomber which most dictionaries define as a "person who lives by gathering articles along the beaches, as from wreckage."

This definition belongs to a former time and place, in the era of shipwrecks when indeed people along the coasts of the British Isles and Europe could gain revenue and even a living at times, from the bounty washed up by the sea. Only the *Macquarie Dictionary* provides an additional , and more relevant, note to the term :

a vagrant of the beach or coast, especially a white man in South Pacific regions.

A vagrant… on a beach. Quite a descriptive term. Almost a larrikin element to it which suits the Australian character. With our immense coastline and beaches one would expect to find beachcombers everywhere, but this isn't the case.

After fairly extensive searches of our literature I can find reference to only 2 individuals who might be classified as Australian beachcombers. The best known of this pair is a bit suspect, at least in dictionary definition terms.

He was, of course, Ernest Banfield of Dunk Island.

The other noted Australian beachcomber was William Yale Evans, better known as the Hermit of Cedar Bay, or in his latter years, simply Cedar Bay Bill. But Banfield and Evans make a pretty meagre haul of noted beachcombers given our vast coastline.

When the first European navigators ventured into the South Pacific in the late 16th and early 17th centuries they thought they had discovered a paradise. Hundreds of islands, many of rare beauty, with plentiful supplies of food, a warm climate, inhabitants who led a leisurely, relaxed lifestyle and beautiful women, wahines, anxious to satisfy their every whim and sexual need. They couldn't believe their luck and the early arrivals on the scene such as Louis Antoine de Bougainville returned with such stories of South Seas wonder and licentiousness that Europe was inflamed. At least the males of the time were. Most of these stories were somewhat exaggerated but basically true. However, another side to this picture did not emerge until sometime later: the habit of the Polynesians in souveniring anything that wasn't fastly battened down, the well established class system which produced infanticide when infants were produced outside the guidelines, and of course the religion that called for human sacrifices and occasional cannibalism.

The minds of European males from then on were so concentrated on the sexual delights said to be on offer in the South Pacific that they chose to ignore the darker side of the coin. In the ensuing centuries considerable numbers of white males found their way into the South Seas in search of Paradise and sexual adventure. A few succeeded in the quest, the majority didn't and ended up alcoholic messes, a burden on their Polynesian hosts. They became such a pest in the early part of the 20th century that almost all the islands introduced laws or regulations either prohibiting or making it extremely difficult for would-be beachcombers to gain residency.

A few of these latter day Lotharios slipped through the net and some even sent back frequently ignored messages that their island paradise was not what it was supposed to be - not on the sex front anyway. Apparently the Polynesian wahines had changed a bit since Bougainville's day, having picked up an unpleasant trick or two from their contact with the white civilisation.

One of these more or less modern beachcombing casanovas was Robert Julian Dashwood (1898-1966), son of an English Anglican clergyman, a drifter and adventurer who arrived on Australian shores in the late 1920's. In 1930 he found his landlord and assorted creditors breathing down his neck so decided to abandon his wife and head for a beachcombing life in the islands. He managed to gain entry by means of false documentation into the Cook Islands, where he remained for the rest of his life, first as a beachcomber, storekeeper, trader, politician and government minister and finally a criminal convicted on bribery and corruption charges.

In his early years in the islands he bedded down many a willing wahine and wrote of many of these adventures in a very candid manner in a book he wrote *South Seas Paradise* under the nom-de-plume of Julian Hillas (Robert Hale, London 1965).

In brief he found beachcombing was not all that it was cracked up to be, and that the wahines left much to be desired as bed partners - a subject on which he was able to speak with some authority. He soon found that "grand passion" was entirely absent in island affairs and that when it came to love making the average Polynesian girl "had as much soul as a breadfruit".

He then went on to make the following interesting observation which should be required reading for all would-be Island beachcombers:

… in spite of everything, from Bali to Bora Bora, the white man continues to seek out the brown woman. Like moths to a candle or unhappy spiders in the grip of a suicidal passion, the European male is inexorably drawn into a contradictory and conflicting relationship, during which he not infrequently tosses away marriage ties, social position and even his income.

But it wasn't sex that brought Dashwood undone in the end but politics and the inborn greed of the adventurer of old.

When the Cook Islands obtained their independence from New Zealand in 1966, Dashwood abandoned his semi-beachcombing lifestyle on the island of Mauke to become a member of the first Cook Island Government led by the very corrupt Sir Albert Henry.

And such was the shortage of talent in this new island state that Robert Julian Dashwood found himself Minister for Social Development and Police and Assistant Minister for the Post Office and Printing Office.

The minor post provided ample opportunities for corrupt activities, which initially yielded him handsome dividends but which became so blatant that in no time at all he was up on a bribery charge over a proposed coin issue. He pleaded guilty, was fined 50 pounds and given a 3 year suspended sentence. He died soon afterwards.

When the scandal first erupted, Sir Albert Henry threw him to the wolves by forcing his resignation, but this only postponed the reckoning as a couple of years later Sir Henry himself was engulfed in an even greater scandal which resulted in the sacking of his government. Sir Albert was stripped of his knighthood after he too was fined and given a suspended sentence for theft of $350,000 of Philatelic Bureau funds to finance his party's election!

There is, of course, another type of desert island or isolated beach dweller not covered by the definitions of Beach Bum or Beachcomber - the castaway. A relatively rare bird these days though common enough in former centuries when shipwrecks were frequent along isolated coastlines, including Australia. The most celebrated castaway in the latter category was Alexander Selkirk (1676-1721) the Scottish seaman who was marooned in 1704 by William Dampier on Juan Fernandez Island. The 4 years that Selkirk spent there inspired Daniel Defoe's great adventure story *Robinson Crusoe*.

Castaways whether they be victims of a shipwreck or a displeased captain, can hardly be said to be seekers after paradise. They are victims and in earlier times were either lucky enough to be rescued or died after much suffering.

The voluntary castaways who deliberately strand themselves on a deserted island or remote beach is another matter. Such experiments are rare in this commercialised age but one such venture was undertaken by an English couple on an uninhabited island in Australia's far north in the 1980's and lasted year before one of them packed it in and left.

The initiator of this enterprise was GW Kingsland, a farm boy who became a small time publisher, a venture which failed. He had married twice and raised 2 families before travelling the world in search of an island paradise. For a period he had even lived on the same Juan de Fernandez island as Selkirk (only to find it too crowded). Back in England in the early 1980's and then in his early 50's he still had ideas of finding an island paradise, this time on one of the islands of the Torres Straits.

He placed a small classified advertisement in a magazine stating *Writer seeks 'Wife' for year on tropical Island.*

He received a response from 25 year old Lucy Irvine who had left school at 13, had worked in a variety of low paid jobs including cleaning lady and waitress and had been married.

She too had dreams of an island paradise but the venture faced some formidable hurdles right from the start. Neither had any real survival skills and their pooled funds were meagre, just enough for one way tickets to Australia and for some basic supplies. Then there was the matter of sex.

After spending a few nights with Kingsland in London, Lucy lost all sexual interest in her partner and proclaimed the venture would have to be on a "no-sex thanks, we're British" basis. Kingsland apparently went along with this, thinking he could make her change her mind once they were on the island.

The Australian Government also threw a spanner in the works by objecting to an unmarried couple being allowed to live together on one of their uninhabited islands and insisted on a marriage of convenience before approving the venture.

The paradise eventually chosen was the uninhabited island of Tuin, in the western islands group of the Torres Strait, and located near the two larger inhabited islands of Moa and Badu.

Torres Straits islanders ferried them to Tuin in a small aluminium dingy with their meagre possessions and food supplies comprising a box of tea, some oat flakes, dried fruits, noodles, rice, dried beans, salt, pepper and some cooking oil. They also had some water bottles, a machete, fishing lines and hooks, some knives and kitchen utensils and a two person tent. They had no radio or any means of communicating with the outside world if they ran into difficulties and they did not take the elementary precaution of arranging with the islanders to visit them at intervals to check on their safety or survival.

On the island they found a small fresh water spring and a some fruit bearing trees and even coconut trees but lacked the basic skills of the islanders of being able to climb up the trees to reach the nuts.

Their limited food supplies and unbalanced diet caused them to be malnourished and infections on their legs broke out into ulcers, exhausting their stock of medical supplies.

Tensions also arose from the start as a result of Kingsland bringing incessant pressure on Lucy to perform her "wifely duties" on the sexual front, pressure which Lucy stoutly resisted throughout the whole experiment.

The islanders on Badu had become worried about the safety of the pair and after several months elapsed visited them to see how they were getting on. They were able to give the couple some invaluable survival advice and built them a permanent shelter and kept them supplied with food and water. They were also worried about the deteriorating health of the pair and ferried across 2 white nurses to attend to their medical needs. Without this help the pair would have had to abandon the experiment as they had soon realised that the resources of the island would not enable them to be self-sufficient.

They became completely dependent on the islanders but it was not a completely one way deal. The only industry of the islanders was lobster fishing and for this they used dinghies powered by outboard motors. When these broke down they had trouble because the nearest mechanic was on Thursday Island far to the south and sending a motor there for repairs could take months.

Kingsland may have lacked survival skills but somewhere along the way he had learned something about motors and was able to overhaul and repair most of the broken motors of the islanders. In no time at all he became an indispensable member of the island community in that part of the Torres Strait.

He had finally found his niche in the scheme of things in his island paradise but for Lucy the experiment was over and she returned to England.

Of the two Kingsland was supposed to be the writer - or that is what he claimed in his advertisement - but it was Lucy Irvine who eventually had the skills in this department. On returning to England she wrote a best selling book *Castaway* which was made into a major movie.

In the end she was able to express some very positive thoughts about her island paradise:

The island had me *like a lover. I* was *totally captivated by the very indifference of its charm, aware always that my soft body was the alien, but as it toughened and moved more naturally to the rhythm of Tuin time I felt that I was beginning to blend…the more I simply existed, obeying the few rules that made existence possible. the more 'at home' I became.*

When she did return to the United Kingdom in June 1982 to write her book she really only swapped one island for another, since she took shelter with her father Robert Irvine, proprietor of the Summer Isle Hotel at Achiltibuie on tiny Summer Island off the coast of the Scotland.

35

Overlanding to Paradise

The north-west corner of Australia generally known as the Kimberleys was one of the last places on the continent to be settled because of its isolation, daunting terrain and the fact that colonisation and self-government came late to the state of Western Australia.

The Kimberleys area was not even explored until an expedition led by Alexander Forrest penetrated its vast ranges in 1879.

When John Forrest (later Sir John) entered the newly-formed Western Australian Legislative Council in 1883 as Surveyor General and Commissioner for Crown Lands, he acted on the 1879 report by his younger brother Alexander by offering long term leases of large tracts of East Kimberleys on favourable terms.

The response was not overwhelming and many of the leases were taken out by eastern state speculators who failed to follow up with settlement.

Yet some genuine starters overlanded cattle across to the top end of the Kimberleys from Queensland, the best known being the Duracks whose story is so brilliantly outlined by Mary Durack in her *Kings in Grass Castles*. The award for sheer guts and stamina in their quest for a Kimberley Paradise must surely go to the MacDonald family who made what was probably the

253

world's longest cattle trek in the face of almost insurmountable odds. The driving force behind this venture was Donald MacDonald, who was born in the Isle of Skye, Scotland in 1820 and whose parents Archibald and Sarah, migrated to Australia in 1838 under one of the free settler schemes then operating. Archibald took up a lease on a block at Cliffords Creek near Goulburn, New South Wales and immediately sent for Donald.

On his arrival Donald married Ann McCallum, daughter of a local Scottish family, and they raised a family of six boys and two girls. Only three of these concern our overland story: Charles (born 1851), Donald (known as "Dan" - born 1857) and William Neil (called Will or Willie, born 1859).

By the 1880's Donald MacDonald's cattle venture at Cliffords Creek was prospering, but with a growing family he looked to wider horizons. He had been much impressed with the 1879 report by Alexander Forrest on the Kimberleys. His eldest son Dan had caught the gold prospecting fever and was in Western Australia at the time so Donald MacDonald asked him to go up to the Kimberleys and check out the situation.

Dan carried out this survey in 1881 and was tremendously impressed by what he found. He seems to have been particularly infected by the enthusiasm of one his contacts, a Bavarian Jew called Leopold Hirschon, one of the first settlers in the Kimberleys, who had a trading store at Derby and later at Halls Creek in the gold rush period. Hirschon was later to become Chairman of the Kimberley Road Board and one of the greatest promoters of the Kimberleys in its pioneering period. In his later years he built and operated the well known Leopold Hotel in the Perth suburb of Bicton.

Dan's reports were so enthusiastic that Donald MacDonald called a meeting of the immediate MacDonald clan and William, Kenneth and Alexander McKenzie, of Tuena, who were related by marriage to the MacDonalds.

The result was a decision to undertake a joint venture into the Kimberleys with the McKenzies putting up most of the funds and the MacDonalds providing the labour of getting the cattle across to the Kimberleys and running the station to be established there.

On Dan's advice they applied for a lease of a holding of 100 square miles on the junction of the Margaret and Fitzroy Rivers, with the McKenzies putting up the 25 pounds holding deposit. A condition of these leases was that the property had to be stocked and occupied, so the next major task was to get some cattle across to the site by sea or land.

No one had attempted overlanding cattle across Australia before, though the Duracks and others had overlanded some herds from Queensland to the northern Kimberleys. The MacDonalds decided on the overlanding option and believed this would take close to two years.

This meant that they would have to carry considerable amounts of food and other provisions. For the journey they prepared two specially reinforced four-wheel supply wagons, backed up with a team of a hundred horses. Their plan was to herd 1000 head of cattle across 6000 kilometres of wild country, lands that had taken considerable toll of lives in earlier years.

In many reports of this venture it is erroneously stated that it was almost called off because shortly before the proposed start Donald MacDonald died after being thrown from his horse.

This is not so. Although this was how MacDonald did meet his end this did not occur until 1887. The great trek departed from Clifford's Creek on March 26 1883, with Charles MacDonald in command, Will MacDonald, Jim McGeorge, Peter Thompson, Jasper (Jimmy) Pickles and with young John and Duncan McKenzie assisting as far as Dubbo, where Donald McKenzie would replace his two brothers. Dan MacDonald would eventually join them later on the trek.

They took a route which took them across the Great Dividing Range to Bathurst, then Orange, Dubbo and Bourke. In northern New South Wales they acquired 500 head of cattle from Samuel Marsden to supplement the 675 cattle and 46 bullocks they had started with.

At the Queensland border they found that because of drought conditions in Western Queensland, the Government had imposed a poll tax on every beast entering the state, causing a serious depletion of their finances.

Once into Queensland they faced severe drought conditions, hostile natives and even more hostile landholders who were resentful of such a large herd passing through and thus adding to their own problems.

Near Winton on the Diamantina Channel country they were forced to bring the drive to a halt, reaching an agreement with the manager of Eldersley Station to camp on a muddy stretch known as the Nine Mile Water Hole.

There a clash of personalities between Charles MacDonald and Donald McKenzie came to a head with Donald deciding he had had enough of the venture, heading back to New South Wales. With money running out, Charles had no option but to pay off Jim McGeorge and Jasper Pickles, leaving only him and his brother Will to handle the quickly diminishing mob. They were three months at the Nine Mile Water Hole before rains came and by then they had lost half the herd.

While Will nursed the diminished herd, Charles rode back to a point where he could wire for more money to hire a replacement drover, who lasted only until they reached the MacArthur River where he succumbed to malaria. The brothers managed to hire a Chinese cook as a replacement, but he too became a casualty of the almost incessant attacks by Aboriginals when he was speared in the leg.

About this time they also lost one of their wagons which

fell apart. They were too weak and exhausted to make any attempt at repairs so simply abandoned it.

Hearing of their plight, two stockmen Charlie and George Hall joined them for a while and got them to a point near the Overland Telegraph Line in the Northern Territory. Here tragedy struck again when Charles MacDonald went down with a severe attack of malaria.

They roped him across a horse and Charlie Hall set out for the nearest point of civilisation, the small settlement of Palmerston (now Darwin). On the way he met up with two stray prospectors who agreed to take the patient to Palmerston where he was treated and sent by boat to Sydney to recuperate.

Charlie Hall rejoined the team and they continued their trek, but more trouble struck at Victoria River Willaroo Station where George Hall was struck down with malaria. The Hall brothers were replaced by another stockman, Joe Edmonds who helped Will MacDonald get the herd across into Western Australia. There they met up with the Duracks. Will was determined to press on so Michael and John Durack helped him to get the mob to the Ord.

Leaving the cattle there, they rode into Wyndham where Will was astonished to find his big brother Dan awaiting with much needed funds and the good news from Cliffords Creek that Charles had almost recovered.

Dan rode back to the Ord with Will who then went down with malaria. Dan and Charlie Hall took him to Palmerston and put him on a boat to Sydney. He spent Christmas 1885 at sea and being a tough young fellow, was almost recovered from illness by the time he reached Sydney and was met by Charles.

Within weeks the two were on a boat back to Palmerston where they hired horses and caught up with the herd now being slowly moved down the Kimberleys by Joe Edmonds and a black youth Edmonds had enlisted to help him - Dan MacDonald having gone off on other business.

At a leisurely pace they pushed the small herd south and eventually reached their long sought destination. Charles recorded the event briefly in his diary:

Arrived here June 3rd, and called it Fossil Downs.

The journey had taken three and a quarter years and at its end only 327 cattle and 13 horses remained.

There was no time for reflection and the next day Will left with their remaining wagon for Derby to acquire urgently needed supplies. This task was carried out successfully with the faithful1 old wagon becoming the first and only vehicle of its kind to have made a crossing of the entire continent.

Charles and Will settled down to run their new empire of Fossil Downs - a dream at least partly fulfilled.

In one way, their timing was perfect because the arrival coincided with a major gold strike at Hall's Creek which saw a flood of miners engulfing the district in their search for the elusive metal. The Halls Creek lodes petered out after a few years but in that period Fossil Downs received a welcome addition to its cash flows from the stock sold to feed the miners.

But there were downs to match the ups and in 1894 two events occurred to threaten the existence of the still struggling enterprise. At the beginning of that year the "wet" brought much heavier than normal rains, causing extensive flooding and great stock losses. Later that year a greater threat was to loom in human form with the outbreak of the so-called Kimberleys War.

This started on the night of October 31 1894 on the Lillimooloora Station in Bunubun Country, north-west of Fossil Downs. A star blacktracker named Jandamarra (also known as Pigeon) shot his superior officer Constable William Richardson while the latter was sleeping. He freed the 17 chained Aboriginal prisoners they had taken in previous weeks and then declared a state of war aimed at driving all white settlers out of Bunuban and neighbouring lands. This was no spur of the moment uprising but a very carefully thought out and executed plan by a skilled tracker and marksman, with a considerable arsenal of seized weapons and a large and enthusiastic band of followers.

Jandamarra had a concise programme mapped out and had drawn up a list of stations to be attacked and wiped out. These were mainly stations with a bad record of brutal treatment of Aboriginals. Fossil Downs was also on the list because several years earlier Charles MacDonald had been one of a number of Justices of the Peace appointed in the Kimberleys. These justices held unprecedented powers to sentence Aboriginal offenders to gaol terms of up to 3 years, or order floggings of up to 50 lashes. They also had power to issue police warrants to arrest and could validate two-year contracts for bonded black labour. In effect they became extended arms of the local police and were clearly prime targets in the eyes of Jandamarra and his followers.

Fortunately for the MacDonalds, Jandaramarra never did get down to Fossil Downs.

In a very early strike Jandamarra had a major success when his forces seized a wagon supply convoy heading north from Derby, killing the 2 whites in charge and seizing a huge haul of guns, ammunition and general supplies. Unfortunately for him the contents also included large quantities of liquor and his forces staged a wild party celebrating over several days and totally out of his control. Several of his followers were killed in alcohol-induced fights. More seriously for Jandamarra, valuable time was lost which should have been used in training his rough forces in how to use the guns they had seized.

News of the happenings had quickly reached Derby where the police were able to organise a volunteer force, mostly of armed settlers, to come after the rebels. Alerted to the advance of this force, Jandamarra retreated with his forces to the Windjana Gorge, where they should have been safe in the honeycomb of connecting caves and tunnels. A section of the police force, led by blacktrackers still loyal to them, managed to surprise and scatter the rebels into caves which were not connected.

Jandamarra could easily have withdrawn the bulk of his band into the safety of the cave system, where the police would not have dared followed, but instead chose to fight it out, with only 2 followers capable to firing guns. He was seriously wounded in the ensuing battle and several of his key followers were killed or captured. Carrying the almost fatally wounded leader, the band managed to escape from the area through secret cave exits. Jandamarra was taken to his wife and mother who nursed him back to health over several months. His followers had all headed north for various bolt holes in the wilds of the Leopolds.

The rebellion was temporarily squashed but by no means broken as when Jandamara recovered he too went to the Leopolds and regrouped his forces, who had lost most of their weapons and ammunition in the battle of Windjana Gorge. Nevertheless over the next two years he was able to wage a guerilla-type war, staging lightning raids on stations.

In that time hostilities only came close to Fossil Downs once, and then not from Jandamarra's forces. The Western Australian Government had responded quickly to the initial uprising by sending Police Inspector William Lawrence, then stationed at Roebourne, to the Kimberleys to take charge of a military style operation against not only Jandamarra, but any natives who might be sympathetic to the rebel cause. His instructions from Police Commissioner Phillips in Perth were quite explicit:

The natives in the West Kimberley have broken into open hostility towards the whites. The Police there being too weak to cope with them, you are to proceed to Derby, taking two Constables, specials if necessary, and six good trackers with such horses, arms and

ammunition as you can command. Upon arrival you are to assume
command of the whole force and direction of the operations against
the natives. In doing so you must be guided by circumstances and
your own judgment. You must understand that the object of your
mission is to free the district in a decisive manner and act promptly
in the matter,

Inspector Lawrence was a tough, seasoned operator who quickly organised a small but effective force after his arrival in Derby. By then the battle of Windjana Gorge was over and all was quiet throughout the Kimberleys. It was thought that Jandamarra had been killed at Windjana and his body carried off, but it was also known that a large part of his force had escaped to the Leopolds.

With no one to actually fight, Lawrence devised a campaign of terrorising any remaining blacks who might be sympathetic to the rebels. His first strike in this campaign was in the Margaret River area on the southern boundary of Fossil Downs.

This was the home of the Gooniyandi people, who had little contact with the Bunubans and no sympathy at all with the rebel cause. Inspector Lawrence was not about to let a little matter like that deter him from his duty. A party of about 40 Gooniyandi people were camped in the then dry river bed of the Margaret River and were sleeping when Lawrence and his men swooped down on them in a typical dawn raid, shooting as they plunged into the group on horseback. It was all over in a matter of minutes, and Lawrence in his report on the incident recorded twelve dead and many wounded. He then gathered the remaining women and children together and brusquely ordered them to flee to the Leopold or be shot too.

Such was justice administered white man style in the Kimberleys in the 19th Century.

No further violence occurred on or around Fossil Downs

during the ensuing war of attrition, but like all Kimberley stations in that period, it had to remain as a mini fortress, constantly on full alert in case Jandamarra came along on one of his night lightning strike raids.

The Kimberley War ended in April 1897 when Jandamarra was finally tracked down, wounded then shot dead. His head was cut from his body and sent to Perth for display. It was later shipped to London for display and eventually was acquired by a prominent English arms manufacturer as a trophy.

Its present whereabouts is unknown.

The whole sorry, sordid story of this uprising occurred because the settlers were never prepared to negotiate with the indigenes over their land.

They simply took it, with Government sanction.

In the end though, Jandamarra did have a victory of sorts because in 1992 the Federal Government purchased Leopold Downs Station and quietly, handed it back to the original owners, the Bunuban People.

Fossil Downs saw many changes in the years that followed the Kimberley War. Around the turn of the century the McKenzie family, which had never been actively involved in the management of the property, sold their interests in it to the MacDonalds.

Charles MacDonald, who never married continued to manage Fossil Downs, refusing the offer of a seat in the Upper House of the Western Australian Parliament. When he died in 1903, Will MacDonald, who had married Ida Oliver, took over the running of Fossil Downs, but he too died in 1910, leaving a widow and a son.

Over the years, Dan MacDonald had helped out at Fossil Downs but was away for long periods searching for gold and attending to other interests. With the death of Will, he took over the station and in the same year married Edith Maude

Mitchell, daughter of Judge Mitchell, the last Administrator of the Northern Territory when it was under the control of South Australia. The couple had three children William (Bill), born in 1911, Archibald and Jean.

In the late 1920's Sidney Kidman, the famed "Cattle King", bought a half share in Fossil Downs for 75,000 pounds, but this led to problems, and on March 13 1928 the property was offered for sale without reserve at public auction.

Particulars provided to would-be purchasers described Fossil Downs as comprising 1,064,633 acres held as pastoral leases and at that time running about 22,800 head of cattle, 200 horses, and 50 donkeys. Dan MacDonald was the successful bidder at the sale, so Fossil Downs was again back in full control of the family which founded it.

The Great Depression brought fresh problems to Fossil Downs as Dan MacDonald had great difficulty paying the instalments due to Kidman. He was rescued by his brother Duncan, who up to that period had played no role in the property. Duncan became a silent partner, visiting Fossil Downs only occasionally. He contracted malaria and died aged 54.

Dan then took his son William (Bill) into partnership and together they rode out the Depression years, before Dan died in April 1939, aged 77.

Just prior to Dan's death an event occurred which was to dramatically change the style and fortunes of Fossil Downs.

On a ship taking him from Fremantle to Sydney, Bill MacDonald met up with a quite remarkable woman, Maxine Darrow, daughter of Judge Darrow. An extremely beautiful young woman, Maxine had been educated at Kirribilli convent, and on leaving had done some modelling and also worked for Warner Bros Motion Pictures. By the time she met up with Bill she was a well known Sydney socialite in her mid-twenties.

The couple were married in Sydney late in 1937 and Bill

MacDonald brought his bride to Fossil Downs on New Year's Day, 1938.

In his earlier days Bill MacDonald had studied architecture and the couple set about building a dream homestead of cement bricks and blackheart timbers, one of Kimberleys finest mansions, though not completed until after the war. World War 11 brought many changes to Fossil Downs. After Japan entered the war, most women were hastily evacuated from the Kimberleys, but Maxine refused to leave and became an aide to Bill when he organised the West Kimberley Volunteer Defence Corps, learning to handle a bren gun and hurl grenades.

After Major General Gordon Bennett escaped from Singapore early in 1942 he was assigned to the Kimberleys to take charge of resistance forces there as a Japanese invasion of northern Australia was expected at any time. He made Fossil Downs his headquarters and Maxine worked as coding officer for the staff.

Hers was a very isolated position as one period of 6 months went by without her sighting another white woman. Plans were prepared for the natives to take her deep into the Leopolds and hide her in the event of an invasion. All able males were also to head for the Leopolds where they were instructed to wage a guerilla war against the occupying Japanese forces. Shades of Jandamarra!

After the war, the job of completing Fossil Downs homestead continued but Bill MacDonald suffered a series of heart attacks resulting in the outside running of the property falling mostly on the shoulders of Maxine.

Bill MacDonald died in 1963 and for the next quarter of a century Maxine MacDonald ran Fossil Downs with all the finesse and efficiency of a true MacDonald. She died in 1988 and Fossil Downs is now owned and run by her daughter Annette (Mrs Henwood). It is the only one of the great 19th

Century Kimberley stations to have remained in the same family hands for all that time.

If you are passing through Fitzroy Crossing any time call in at the Fitzroy River Lodge, and see the great life size portrait of Maxine MacDonald hung at the entrance to their Maxine Restaurant - tribute to a city socialite who became a Cattle Queen in the process finding her own piece of paradise.

She once observed that with the Kimberleys, you either hated them or you loved them. She loved them from the day she set foot on Fossil Downs, and she loved it throughout her near half century reign , carrying on the great traditions of her husband's father and his brothers, who in 1883 set out to find their own Garden of Eden on the other side of a vast continent, and against all the odds, succeeded.

36

Hopping to Paradise

Next time you down a pint of beer spare a thought for one of its main ingredients - hops. They may well have come from Rostrevor, one of the nation's leading hop farms, located in a scenic paradise created in the19th Century.

Located in the beautiful Ovens Valley in the shadow of Victoria's Mount Buffalo, Rostrevor was born out of one of Australia's darkest chapters in the heady days of the gold rushes.

In the early 1860s the troubles of Lambing Flat and in particular the disgraceful events of Sunday, June 30 1861 are always cited as being the worst example of racial intolerance on our soil.

This was when some 3000 members of the Miners' Protective League mustered at Tipperary Gully with the deliberate intent of driving 1200 Chinese miners from the Lambing Flat fields (later renamed Young) in Central New South Wales. In a day of tragedy they brutally bashed Chinese miners, with pickaxes and iron bars, stealing and burning all the possessions in the process. It was late evening before troops and special constables sworn in by Commissioner Griffin, were able to restore some semblance of control over the ugly situation.

The real miracle of that sad day was that none of the Chinese were actually killed. Despite many rumours to the contrary, not a single authenticated death of a Chinese miner was recorded that day. In fact the only casualty was of a white miner in the clash with troopers that evening. In the long term the Chinese were not driven permanently from Lambing Flat and some 700 actually received some Government compensation for their losses on the day.

While the Lambing Flat riot was a disgraceful event, it was by no means the worst race riot on the goldfields of Australia.

Five years earlier down on the Ovens Valley field of Victoria the beauty of the setting failed to dampen the ardour of the participants.

Gold in payable quantities was first discovered in the Ovens Valley in the rugged Buckland River area in 1853 by an American prospector Henry Pardoe. He was one of a group of 70 Californian miners who chartered a ship out of San Francisco to this new gold rush.

Pardoe's discovery sparked an instant rush to the Ovens Valley and by 1856 more than 6000 miners, including 2400 Chinese, were in the valley jostling for the ever decreasing "finds". This was a familiar pattern on all the Australian goldfields and tensions between the white gold seekers and the patient, hard-working fossicking Chinese, increased.

In the early years of settlement the Ovens River had been known as the Burwang River, but in 1824 it was renamed by Hume and Hovell after Brigadier Major J. Ovens, who was then private secretary and chief engineer to the Governor of New South Wales (which included Victoria) Sir Thomas Brisbane.

I t runs east-west along the northern face of Mount Buffalo. The Buckland River and Valley where the major gold strikes occurred is a tributary of the Ovens River and was named after John Buckland, an early settler in the area.

By mid-1857 the numbers of white miners had diminished considerably though most of the Chinese remained as there were still adequate pickings for them along both the

Ovens and Buckland Rivers.

The ill-feeling between the two groups came to a head on July 4 1857 when the remaining Americans gathered at Tanswell's Hotel on the Buckland diggings to celebrate American Independence Day. Fuelled by liquor, the leader of this group, John Thomas Bell, urged the miners to run the Chinese right off the Ovens and Buckland fields. He found a willing response and soon 120 miners, mainly Americans, had armed themselves with crowbars and other weapons. They marched on nearby Loudon's Flat, which contained the smallest of the Chinese groups, attacking every Chinaman, stealing and burning all their possessions. The sole policeman in the area, Constable Duffy, tried in vain to reason with the mob.

The routed Chinese fled down-stream to Stony Point, where some 800 of their countrymen were camped. Spurred on by their success, or excesses, at Loudon's Flat, the militant miners pursued the fleeing Chinese. At Stony Point, there was some resistance but so fierce was the assault that the Chinese caved in and fled as best they could across the river wherein a number drowned. Some terrified Chinese fled in the opposite direction and took refuge on the Mount Buffalo plateau where they all perished in the bleak winter conditions. Their bones and pigtails were discovered many years later in a place promptly given the name Skeleton Gully.

At the main Chinese camp the survivors, now numbering well over2000, initially offered passive resistance and refused to move, but such was the fury of the attack that they too soon were forced to flee to Porepunkah some 20 miles away. In the following days they managed to struggle out of the Ovens Valley to Beechworth , where most of them settled and eventually died. At Beechworth there are some 3000 Chinese graves, eloquent testimony to the grim events of July 1857 - perhaps the major effort of "ethnic cleansing" to be carried out in Australia.

When news of the riots reached Beechworth Superintendent Robert O'Hara Burke (who later was to die so tragically at Coopers Creek with William John Wills) set out with a detachment of police for the Buckland. They marched the 60 miles in 24 hours but at all the mining sites they found no humans, only burnt or abandoned huts, tents and belongings. A further search on the Upper Quartz Ridge unearthed 300 Chinese who had taken to the hills and were in dire straits.

John Bell, who had incited the whole affair, and several of his henchmen had disappeared. Police eventually arrested 12 men, 4 of whom received light sentences of 9 months gaol on charges of rioting. No charges of theft could be made to stick because at that period the Chinese could not give evidence in court unless they had taken out residency tickets.

Among the Chinese who had been so brutally evicted from the Buckland Valley on that July 4th was an unusual individual, William Pan Look, the Chinese storekeeper and gold buyer at the main camp, whose stock was looted by rioters.

He was different to the other Chinese on the fields as he was a Christian having been converted by Roman Catholic missionaries in China before coming to Australia.

With his fellow countrymen he initially fled to Beechworth, but when order was restored and a number of them returned to the diggings he went with them, rebuilt his store and started afresh.

However, the trade proved unprofitable due to the small numbers of miners and he moved back to Beechworth, and later to Melbourne. He married an Australian girl and the couple had four sons, Ernest, Alfred, Frank and William Thomas, who were destined to have a considerable impact on the district which had been so unfriendly to their father.

In 1890 the Pan Look brothers returned to the Ovens Valley to work for a Chinese tobacco and hop grower, Ah Sue. The brothers saved their money and 3 years later pooled their resources to buy Ah Sue's 20 acre farm at Black Springs, now renamed Eurobin. In 1893, their youngest brother, William Thomas, was then aged 14, joined them and was to prove to be the dynamic force in the family in the decades ahead.

In those days both tobacco and hops were experimental crops but the brothers survived and in time acquired 8 properties adjoining their original modest holding, They ended up with 1500 acres of prime land with 3 miles of river frontage bisected by the Ovens River. They named this property Rostrevor, and also changed their family name slightly to Panlook.

Two of the brothers, Ernest and Frank, left to pursue other interests, but Alfred and William soldiered on, continually experimenting with new varieties of both tobacco and hops.

There was a big breakthrough for all the hop growers in the Ovens valley around the turn of the century when Donald Gow, a Harrietville dairy farmer, imported from America a relatively new variety of hops, Californian Cluster, This proved to be superior to the English varieties hitherto grown in the valley and in the next few decades all the Ovens Valley hop growers, including the Panlooks, changed to it.

Under William Panlooks' guidance Rostrevor expanded rapidly until it had more than 100 acres of Californian Cluster hops under cultivation but the small kilns and irrigation machinery could not cope with the output.

They estimated that they needed at least 200,000 pounds to undertake the mechanical expansion needed - an amount far beyond their resources.

In 1919 William and Alfred formed themselves into a company, Panlook Brothers Pty Ltd, with William as the general manager. William met Thomas Mitchell, the livewire manager of Henry Jones and Company which at that time was marketing agent for most of the Tasmanian hop crops. Mitchell in turn introduced the Panlooks to Sir Henry Jones, the founder of the company, After inspecting the Rostrevor property, Jones and Mitchell, decided to take a major interest in the Panlook enterprise, injecting into the company the much needed capital for expansion.

It was a very successful partnership and the Rostrevor Hop Gardens, as they became known in the 1920's, became the largest hop gardens in the Southern Hemisphere, producing an annual harvest of enough hops to brew 20,000,000 gallons of beer, at that time more than 10% of Australia's total output. Rostrevor not only became one of the major industries of the Ovens Valley, but each year it became a wonderful haven for some 600 hop pickers who gathered there for the long picking season from mid-February. The work was not nearly as strenuous as other seasonal jobs, and many families went each year for a working holiday, with women making up half the picking teams. They were housed in comfortable accommodation and had a general store, canteen, post office and social hall.

This ideal mix of holiday and work in a delightful scenic setting lasted until the 60s when mechanisation of picking and processing took over, greatly reducing the numbers of the former holiday-workers. Only a lucky minority these days get to enjoy the work pleasures of yesteryear.

William Panlook remained as an active manager until he retired in 1963. He died on September 3 1965 at the grand old age of 86.

Rostrevor remains the great hop showplace of the Ovens Valley, though not now in Panlook hands. It has contracted since the heady Panlook days though it is still the largest Hop Gardens on the Australian mainland (there are two slightly larger hop farms in Tasmania), And there is still more than a 30% chance that the next glass of beer you down will include in its content the flavour of hops grown in a veritable Garden of Eden setting established a century ago by Chinese entrepreneurial skills developed out of one of Australia's blackest episodes —a failed attempt at ethnic cleansing in the Ovens Valley in 1857.

37

An Australian Xanadu

It must be acknowledged that Ghenhis Khan (1162-1227) wasn't the sort of fellow you would want to have as a near neighbour. As Mongolia's number one warlord in the 13th Century he caused a fair amount of chaos and loss of life wherever he led his troops.

When, in the year 1212, China refused to pay tribute, he simply overran and then occupied it, before turning his attention westward to expand the Mongolian Empire to the Black Sea, swallowing up in the process Korea, Persia, Armenia a fair slice of Russia and assorted other minor kingdoms. His tactics were of the slash and burn variety and he was the first recorded warrior to use germ warfare by the simple method of throwing bodies of plague victims over the walls of the towns and cities he was besieging, thus hastening the end of the inhabitants. Some of this plunder and pillaging of countries with more civilised ways than was to be encountered on the Mongolian steppes must have rubbed off on him, because his grandson Kublai Khan (1216-1294) was quite a civilised chap by the standards of the time.

Kublai Khan became absorbed with the ancient cultures of China and eventually proclaimed himself Emperor, the first in the Yuan Dynasty. He was a liberal -minded ruler who fostered both the arts and commerce and established Lamaistic Buddhism as the state religion yet was tolerant of other faiths.

He is perhaps best remembered for building a Palace at Xanadu (or Shanadu) as part of a great mountain summer retreat for himself and succeeding Emperors. Xanadu, is located north-west of the capital of China (which we now know as Beijing) to the south of Zhangjiakou, in the territory which the Chinese call Inner Mongolia, but which the Mongolians more rightly refer to as Outer Mongolia.

Under Kublai Khan's guidance China became the richest and most culturally advanced country of the 13th Century and Xanadu became a mythical place of beauty and harmony where the arts and culture flourished. When Marco Polo visited it in his travels he marvelled at its wonders, inspiring Samuel Taylor Coleridge to pen a poem in homage to the city.

Australia, alas, has never had a leader of Kublai Khan's statue, vision and learning, so we lack a summer retreat of Xanadu standard yet some individuals have managed to carve out for themselves some very impressive summer retreats along our coastline. One of these exotic creations might, just might, qualify for the title of a mini Australian Xanadu.

Its name is Thubbul, part of a property settled and so named by the D'Arcy family in the 1850's and held by that family for a dozen decades for varying agricultural purposes, ranging from timber cutting to general farming and, at one stage, to maintain a pea growing venture.

As with most properties held by the one family over an extended period, its size and usage fluctuated with markets and family fortunes. When the D'Arcy family finally parted company with Thubbul in the early 1970's the property comprised a hundred hectares of rocky forested headland, located near the mouth of the Murrah River, south of Bermagui, in the Parish of Murrah, in what was then the Mumbulla Shire Council - but is now part of the expanded Bega Shire Council.

The property is very isolated, lacks formed roads or any usual amenities such as connections to water, sewage or the electricity grid.

This was the piece of virtually untouched paradise that was acquired in a joint effort by the prominent Sydney architect Philip Cox and family friends Willy Ferguson and Wesley Stacey.

This Sydney trio made their purchase to have for themselves a wilderness area retreat for their families, and friends, in the long summer vacations and other school holiday breaks. Their idea was simply to go camping in these periods in their own piece of isolated coastal paradise.

But, as Robbie Burns was fond of saying, the best laid plans of mice and men gang awry, and Thubbul took on a life of its own and developed in a way far distant from the plans of the trio of owners.

What happened next is best told in *A Place on the Coast*, by Philip Cox (with help from co-writer Janet Hawley) accompanied by an array of quite magnificent photographs by Patrick Bingham-Hall, published in 1997 by the Five Mile Press,

It so happened that the members of all three families involved were keen gardeners which meant that they could not resist the idea of converting some of that lovely space they owned into gardens, even though they would be on hand only occasionally to tend to their plants.

Philip Cox gives credit to the green-fingered Alison Ferguson for launching into the gardening venture, which in time led to the creation of three separate but connected gardens of a mixture of native and introduced plants, shrubs and trees, and eventually even very productive vegetable patches.

It was a daunting undertaking by any standards. In winter that part of the South Coast is buffeted by storms and high winds blown up from the Southern Ocean, and being on a headland Thubbul was subjected to constant salt water sprays fatal to plantings. The giant stands of trees gave some protection from elements and the use of walls and selection of hardy plants enabled the ambitious gardeners to conquer nature, making the gardens one of the showpieces of the property.

No buildings had been planned for Thubbul but after a while a small shed was erected to store tools and camping gear. Alas, this provided no protection for their goods and chattels as vandals repeatedly broke in to the shed. Something more was needed to keep the itchy-fingered tribe at bay, so the shed was incorporated into a pavilion with fireplace.

This worked and from then on more pavilions were added and gradually took shape over the years into a complex of rooms for eating, living and sleeping purposes. All were built to a standard format of low flat roofs, to harmonise with the surrounding bush, with glazed walls erected around bush timber poles. The original floors were of brick but these proved difficult to clean, and were replaced with concrete floors tiled with dark slate. As the property was not connected to the electricity grid solar panels were used to provide basic lighting. Most cooking was carried out on barbecues or a wood fired stove. For the large dining room with its massive fireplace a huge honey coloured slab of Norfolk Pine was brought from Norfolk Island and made into a spectacular dining table.

When completed the complex with its various additions covered some 450 square metres and included 6 bedrooms, 3 bathrooms, a kitchen, a dining rooms, a day/music room, a study, and a boatshed with living room extensions. But even this impressive spread of structures and the combined gardens only occupied one and a half hectares of the 100 hectare property - the rest being mostly heavily forested virgin bush. Thubbul eventually became such an enchanted retreat that Cox and his family spent more and more time there - he even added a study for his architectural work.

And over time more and more of his friends from the Sydney and Melbourne cultural scene - artists, writers, photographers -visited and spent long off-season periods working or recharging their artistic batteries. Thubbul gradually became and all year round artistic retreat, a kind of minor Aussie Xanadu!

Yet Gardens of Eden, irrespective of their size or location, have the unhappy knack of attracting serpents to their patch. And this is what happened to Thubbul in 1997 when a local strolling along the adjacent beach saw perched high on the cliff face a whale-watching platform. On further exploration he discovered a boatshed complete with built-in accommodation.

On making enquiries at the Bega Shire Council he found that permission had not been granted for these two structures, nor for most of the remaining Thubbul main buildings - except for one original pavilion erected some twenty years earlier.

By his inquiry he had really set the cat amongst the environmental pigeons, causing severe embarrassment to the Shire Council because the Thubbul land was zoned 7 (f) under the Shire's Environmental Plan which meant that any development had to be sanctioned both by the Council and the New South Wales Department of Urban Affairs and Planning.

Council referred the matter to its Planning Department. In due course the officers of this department came up with the recommendation that the whale-watching platform and the boatshed on Thubbul should be demolished but as the main buildings were not in breach of Council regulations, Philip Cox should be allowed to lodge a retrospective development application for the 222 square metres of buildings already erected in the central complex.

In most rural councils this sensible recommendation would have been adopted without dissent, but some local politics came into play and a majority of councillors who had probably not heard of Kublai Khan or Xanadu, rejected the advice of their own Planning Department. They engaged in a fairly typical cutting down to size Tall Poppy exercise, insisting that the buildings all be razed. They did however, agree to a deferral of this fairly drastic action pending a legal challenge by Philip Cox.

The Land and Environment Court considered the matter at some length and finally brought down a finding in favour of Cox. The old boatshed and its add-on bedroom had to go, but the main buildings at Thubbal could stay. This was exactly what the Council officers had recommended in the first place. It was a case of commonsense prevailling for once. The Australian Zanadu was saved from the bulldozers with the Pecksniffians parading their high priciples in vain.

In August 1999 the NSW Government sacked the Bega Shire Council, giving its reason as vindictive behaviour, bad language, poor management practices and cronyism on the part of its councillors, and appointed an Administrator.

> *In Xanadu did Kubla Khan*
> *A stately pleasure-dome decree*
> *Where Alph, the scred river, ran*
> *Through caverns measureless to man*
> *Down to a sunless sea.*
> *So twice five miles of fertile ground*
> *With walls and towers were girdled round*
> *And there were gardens bright with sinuous rills*
> *Where blossom'd many an incense-bearing tree;*
> *And here were forests ancient as the hills,*
> *Enfolding sunny spots of greenery.*
>
> SAMUEL TAYLOR COLERIDGE

38

The Global Village

"It is bad enough to know the past; It would be intolerable to know the future". W. Somerset Maugham.

As previous chapters have examined attempts of individuals or groups to find their way to Paradise, perhaps it would be fitting to examine how such attempts may be undertaken in the future. Unless of course you share the sentiments of Somerset Maughan quoted above. If you cannot bear to risk a look into the future, then gently put this volume down and go on with some other more comforting reading!

Lack of a crystal ball makes the task of predicting the future difficult, but some pointers from the past do provide a few clues. One thing that has been established beyond any doubt from past history is the fact that the male half of Homo sapiens is the most destructive species to have ever inhabited Planet Earth. In the few hundred thousand years he has been more or less in control of the planet he has managed to destroy most of its rainforests, wreck; its eco systems and generally stuff up the environment. As a result most of its beauty spots which might qualify as possible Gardens of Eden are fast disappearing and may well all be extinct by the middle of the 21st Century at the present rate of destruction.

This will pose considerable problems for those members

of Homo sapiens who are still around and in search of personal or group Utopias in which to take refuge from the maddening crowd.

If all the physical beauty spots have been destroyed by the developers, where can they turn, leaving aside such unlikely destinations as the Moon, Mars or Venus? Marshall McLuhan may have left us a clue here. He was the Canadian Professor who some decades back, at the very start of the Electronic Age, declared that we all were or soon would be living in The Global Village.

The pundits of the day, of course, try to ridicule the Professor and his then unorthodox thoughts out of court, but time has proven McLuhan spot on. We DO live in a Global Village.

Television gives a demonstration of this easy to understand.

In the Vietnam and Gulf Wars battles were brought right into our living rooms as they were being fought, complete with all the blood and gore and body bags It was a sobering experience not only for the millions of viewers, but for the generals and the politicians who saw to their utter dismay that they had lost their grip on the situation.. No longer would their propaganda work. No longer would their lies and evasions stand up as they did in the days of the old completely controlled black and white print media. Colour television may well have put paid for ever to large scale warfare, though no doubt small scale skirmishes will continue to provide regular doses of the modern equivalent of the Roman Circuses, with their lions and victims keeping the ratings up.

With the freeing up of the world banking systems, the advent of electronic transfer systems and the spread of credit cards, governments have lost control of their monetary system. The Gold Standard and other artificial control devices have become as obsolete as the dodo, while other , more menacing nasties, await our controllers around the corner.

It seems clear from the present trends that Day Dreamers of the 21st Century will have to find their Utopias not in the physical sense as in the past, but in the rapidly developing electronic age. There appears to be two quite different paths they can tread here, one cerebral and one of a distinctly intellectual character.

Down along the cerebral path lies Virtual Reality, still in embryonic form, but with enormous possibilities for expansion in the decades ahead.

The seeker of Paradise who turns to Virtual Reality will have a thousand options to match his wildest dreams. He or she will be able to travel wherever the mind cares to wander with any companion(s) of choice and in any circumstance. Journeys will only be limited by the imagination of the traveller. Of course such adventures may have their hazards. They may become addictive far beyond that of present day opiates, but then the search for Paradise has always been a risky pursuit!.

The other path to Paradise I mentioned will provide mental stimulation to the searcher, rather than the glorified bouts of cerebral masturbation administered by the Virtual Reality process, The mental path leads to the Internet, the most subversive invention yet devised by mankind. Now only in its infancy, and being used as a toy to play games, as an educational tool and an electronic market place, its role of the future will be as a destroyer and maker of governments, and the instrument that will bring power to the people of the world for the first time in human history. Whether they use that power sensibly is another matter.

From the time Homo sapiens organised himself into villages, towns, cities and finally states, power always rested in the hands of a few, sometimes priests, sometimes kings or despots and in modern times by governments who controlled ideas and the means of communicating them.

What those in power have always feared most are ideas. Ideas contrary to their own thinking or which threaten their power. For thousands of years they maintained power because they controlled the flow of ideas by censorship and more drastic devices. The invention of printing was a threat, but was kept in check for centuries by illiteracy and censorship.

The 20th Century saw many changes of the power structures but so long as powerful allies controlled all major media forms the status quo has been maintained without the need for overdue censorship.

The Internet has changed all that because it cannot be controlled or censored. Computers are such a part of every day life in all developed countries that they, the evil instruments which hold the Internet in their bowels, cannot be discarded.

Whether they like it or not, every developing country is wedded to computers - and with them the Internet. Subversive ideas will be increasingly fed into it anonymously and will defy the efforts of the best brains of the CIA, KGB, MI5 or ASIO to trace them. Anonymous players in Tierra de1 Fuego will be able to put their subversive thoughts on to the Internet to have them picked up and read within minutes by thousands of equally anonymous surfers around the globe.

For the first time in history our masters - the politicians, the power brokers, the billionaires will all be helpless - totally castrated by the ideas flowing out of control from the Internet. Good ideas. Bad Ideas. Subversive Ideas. Ideas out of control. How the people in power will cope with this anarchic situation is anybody's guess. There has been no precedent in history. No time when ideas actually flowed freely within and across boundaries. Where will the Paradise seekers stand in this coming age of Internet-created chaos?

If they join the Paradise Club and enrol on the Internet, it should expand their education rapidly since they will be exposed for the first time in their lives to a barrage of ideas, many of them original, thought provoking. Since we use only part of our brain capacity as we go through life , there is plenty of spare grey matter to take on board all this new input. In turn that should provide a lot of stimulation of the brain , resulting in the Surfer taking an active and positive role by producing and promoting new ideas to join the others on the Internet. In time the Surfer may find such stimulation to be the ultimate Utopian goal of Homo sapiens.

If pieces of Paradise are going to be more difficult to locate in the 21st Century what are we to make of Andy Warhol's claim: *In the future everyone will be famous for fifteen minutes.* This notion of course is nonsense given the fact that the world population is around the five billion mark. Forests would vanish and the airwaves would be clogged with efforts to publicise heroes by the billion.

By definition, heroes are an exclusive breed, though as Oliver Wendell Holmes Jr pointed out in 1882 in his farewell lecture to the Harvard Medical School, there are 3 occasions in life when everyone plays a chief personage role of the hero: at his/her own baptism, wedding and funeral. Except of course, heathen bachelors and spinsters who get to play the hero role only once - at their funeral.

In 1922 HL Mencken made the observation that the chief business of a nation, as a nation, is the setting up of heroes, mainly bogus. This was Mencken at his cynical best, simply pointing out the fact that kings and governments had long been in the business of creating heroes for their subjects to admire to draw their attention away from the follies and inadequacies of the said kings and governments.

Things have changed a lot since Mencken penned those words. These days kings are in short supply and don't seem to create anything except hair-brained offspring, while governments, at least in the western world, seemed to have gone out of the hero-creation business. Or perhaps they were simply overtaken by the superior techniques of the opposition forces; initially by Hollywood, and in more recent years by television, the press tabloids and the women's magazines; all aided and abetted by that modern phenomena, the paparazzi. In the future these forces may well be superseded by new technologies such as the Internet in the hero-creation business.

One thing we can be absolutely sure of is that the hero business is not going to fade away in the 21st Century - the profits it generates are too vast for that to happen.

Back in 1836 Thomas Carlyle observed: *Hero worship exists, has existed, and will forever exist, universally among mankind.* Why is this so? The probable explanation is that early in life most people come to the realisation that through circumstances or the lack of basic talents, they are never going. to achieve hero status among their fellow men and women. So they transfer their dreams to one or more of the heroes in their field of interest, whether it be sport, entertainment, fashion, or simply some shooting star the media has created overnight.

And the masses need this endless fodder served up by the multi-media outlets because hero-worship has become the modern soporific, far more addictive than nicotine or heroin, providing the necessary daily "fix" for the "user" to get through the pains and trauma of modern life. It also eases the burden of knowing that the chances of finding ones personal paradise is receding with every passing year.

If you can't live in your own Garden of Eden, you can always dream away in the shadow of a hero or heroine who has apparently achieved this goal. For, as Jonathan Swift observed in his *Cadenus and Vanessa* (1713):

> *Whoe'er excels in what we prize,*
> *Appears a hero in our eyes.*

ACKNOWLEDGEMENTS:

I received help from many people while putting this book together. Many I can't thank personally because they were unknown faces in libraries and archives such as the staff of the State Library of NSW and the adjoining Mitchell Library - very knowledgable folk who, if they don't know the many trick questions directed at them can usually be relied upon to steer the researcher in the direction where they may be found.

My thanks also to the librarians at the *Bulletin* and the *Sydney Morning Herald* who helped with specific queries, and the archival officers at the Australian Broadcasting Corporation. Up in Cairns, very hard working archival officers of the *Cairns Post* helped me in 1996 and again in 1998 to unlock some of the vast amounts of north Queensland history buried in their files. I am also indebted to the staff of the Cairns Library and Gill Jenner of the Cairns Historical Society, while the library staff of the Cairns campus of the James Cook University generously gave me access to their computer files for several days in 1996 when city-based computers were "down".

Also, many people in the Cairns district helped me with my research into the life of Cedar Bay Bill and the Police raid on Cedar Bay in 1976. Chief helper in this enterprise was Colin Burns of Bloomfield River, but valuable information also came from Ron Edwards (Kuranda), Eugenie Navare (Cairns), Don Croft (Ayton) and a large number of other contacts who requested anonymity given the fact that the raid is still an extremely sensitive issue in the Cairns area. For the remarkable Panlook story (Hopping to Paradise) I had great help from Barry Brebner (Dubbo), Graham Hughes (Manager of Rostrevor Hop Gardens), Chris Dormer (Curator of the Robert O'Hara Burke Museum, Beechworth), Jean Ellis (Myrtleford) and the Myrtleford Library Staff.

I am deeply indebted to my old friend Bob MacDonald (Dubbo) for making available family records enabling me to compile a definitive article on Bob's family members' cattle drive from one side of the continent to the other to establish Fossil Downs in the Kimberleys (still in MacDonald family hands). Bill Metcalf of Griffith University was a great help with his specialty - modern communes; Lynette Rayner of *The Australian Market and Fairs Magazine*, helped with information on the Australia-wide explosion of craft and art markets in recent years. Other helpers insisted on anonymity for varying reasons including an individual who was able to supply me with a huge amount of material for the chapter on the South Australian Village Settlements. To all these people, named and anonymous, my thanks again for your help in putting together this volume on the search for an Australian paradise.

Bill Hornadge

Bibliographical notes:

Gener'al reference sources.

The Australian Encyclopaedia.
The Australian Dictionary of Biography.
The Macmillan Dictionary Of Biography.
Webster's Biographical Dictionary.
The History of Paradise, by Jean Delumeau (Continuum USA 1992).
Strangers In Paradise, by Martin Sutton. (A & R 1995).
Mitchell Library (Sydney) Australasian Reference Section.
The Nelson Dictionary Of World History.
The Macquarie Dictionary.
Magazines: *Grass Roots*, *Earth Garden*, *Nation Review*, *Oz* (both Australia and the UK) and *Private Eye* (UK).

Chapter Sources.

IN THE BEGINNING.

Discovery : The Quest for the Great South Land, by Miriam Estensen (Allen & Unwin 1998).
The Secret Discovery Of Australia, by Gordon McIntyre (Souvenir Press 1977).

EARLY SETTLEMENT PLANS.

Some Proposals For Establishing Colonies In The South Seas, by George Mackenass. Self-Published 1943.

THE MATRA PLANS.

Some Proposals for Establishing Colonies In The South Seas, by George Mackanass. As above.
James Mario Matra, by Alan Frost (Miegunyah Press 1995).

PARADISE LOST.

The History and Description of Sydney Harbour, by PR Stephensen (Rigby 1966).
Sydney's First Four Years, by Captain Watkin Tench (A & R 1961).
Triumph of the Nomads, by Geoffrey Blainey (Macmillan 1975).

Dispossesson :Black Australians and White Invaders, by Henry Reynolds (Allen & Unwin 1989).

The Future Eaters, by Tim Flannery (Reed Books 1994).

Guns, Germs and Steel, by Jared Diamond (Cape I997).

AN ISLAND PARADISE.

Lord Howe Island, by Harold Rabone (Austris 1972).

Discovering Lord Howe Island, by Jeane Edgecombe and Isobel Bennett (Pacific Map 1978).

Lord Howe Island, by Alan and Valrie Finch (Rigby 1967).

VAN DEMONS LAND.

The Lost Australia of Francois Peron, by C Wallace (Nottingham Court Press (UK) 1984).

The Fatal Shore, by Robert Hughes (Collins-Harvill 1987).

Black War, by Clive Turnbull (Cheshire-Landsdowne 1965).

The History of Tasmania, by John West (A & R 1971).

The World of Olegas Truchanas, by Max Angus (Olegas Truchanas Publications Committee 1975).

THE EARLY SETTLEMENTS.

Journal and Proceedings Vol. 1 Part 1 of The Western Australian Historical Society.

NEW ITALY.

New Italy, by Frederick Chudleigh Clifford (Government Printer Sydney 1889).

Phantom Paradise, by JH Niau (A & R 1936).

THE PARAGUAY COLONIES.

A Peculiar People: The Australians in Paraguay, by Gavin Souter (Sydney University Press 1968).

With Lane In Paraguay, by Don Gobbett and Malcolm Saunders (Central Queensland University Press 1995).

Where Socialism Failed, by Stewart Grahame (John Murray (UK) 1912).

Paradise Mislaid: In Search of the Australian Tribe in Paraguay, by Anne Whitehead (University of Queensland Press 1997).

The Working Man's Paradise, by John Miller (William Lane) (Sydney University Press 1980).

The Lanes of Cosme Colona Paraguay, by Clarrie Beckingham. Self-published 1993.

Cosme Monthly 1897-1899.

THE QUEENSLAND CO-OPERATIVES.

The Gayndah Communes, by Bill Metcalf (Central Queensland University Press 1996).

THE VILLAGE SETTLEMENTS.

The Village Settlements on the River Murray in South Australia 1894-1909, by DB Mack. Self-Published 1994.

Article 'A Great Social Experiment - Village Settlements In South Australia', by Rev. J Berry (Adelaide) in *Review Of Reviews* (London) April 20 1895.

THE SPIRITUAL FACTOR.

Without Sin : The Life and Death of the Oneida Community, by Spencer Klaw (Penguin (USA) 1993).

Religions in Australia, by Tess Van Sommers (Rigby 1966).

A History of Buddhism in Australia 1848-1988, by Paul Croucher (New South Wales University Press 1989).

The Hahndorf Walkers and the Beaumont Connection, by ER Simpson (Beaumont Press 1983).

Hahndorf : A Brief Look at the Town and its History, by Anni Luur Fox (Fox Publishing 1977).

With Dew On My Boots : A Childhood Revisited, by Colin Thiele (Walter McVitty Books 1997).

THE SECOND COMING.

Krishnamurti's Talks Ojai-California (USA 1949).

Tales of a Big Country, by Keith Wiley (Seal Books 1977).

THE ISRAEL OF OZ.

An Unpromised Land, by Leon Gettler (Fremantle Arts Centre Press 1993).

Chosen: the Jews in Australia, by Hilary Rubinstein (Allen & Unwin 1987).

Edge Of The Diaspora: Two Centuries of Jewish Settlement in Australia, by SD Rutland (Brand1 & Schlesinger 1997).

Hebrew, Israelite, Jew : The History of the Jews of Western Australia, by

David Mosserson (University Of Western Australian Press 1990).
The Jewish Encyclopaedia (Ref: Birobidzhan).
From Assimilation To Group Survival, by PY Meding (Cheshire 1968).

BOB'S KIBBUTZIM PLAN.
Robert Hawke: A Biogrephy, by Blanche D'alpuget (Schwartz 1982).
Article 'Kibitzing Hawke's Kibbutzim' by David Hirst, *Weekend Australian*
June 25-26 1983.

THE YEPPOONESE WAR.
A Hack's Progress, by Philllp Knightley (Cape (UK) 1997).
Rockhampton Bulletin and Brisbane *Courier Mail* 1978-1991.

MAKE LOVE, NOT WAR.
Hippie Hippie Shake, by Richard Neville (Minerva 1996).
Out Of My Mind, by Richard Neville (Penguin 1996).
Article 'Ferals' by Max Whittaker, *Australian Magazine* February 17-18
1996.

GOING TO POT.
A Treatise On The Culture Of Flax And Hemp, by Dr Francis Campbell.
Self-Published 1846.
Article in *Ken* magazine, Chicago (USA) December 15 1938.
Article 'A Potted History' by John Jiggens, *Good Weekend* (SMH) March 2
1996.

MODERN COMMUNES.
From Utopian Dreaming to Communal Reality, by Bill Metcalf (University
of New South Wales Press 1995).
Communes in Rural Australia, by Margaret Munro-Clark (Hale & Iron-
monger 1986).
Article 'Where the Drop Outs are' by John Lindblad, *Bulletin* March 27
1976.
Article 'Dropping Out - How to avoid the pitfalls' by John Lindblad,
Bulletin April 4 1976.

SYDNEY OR THE BUSH.
The Book Of Earthly Delights : Living in the Bush with Neil Douglas and

Abbie Heathcote (Compendium 1976).

Article 'Your Money or your life' by Louisa Hatfield, *Sydney Morning Herald* January 15 1996.

Article 'Revolt of the Wage Slaves' by Deidre Macken, *Sydney Morning Herald* May 30 1998.

Article 'Quitting the rat race' by Sacha Molitarisz, *Sunday Herald* September 28 1997.

Article 'Bush Whacked' by Alex Burke, *Sydney Morning Herald* December 30 1995.

Article 'Olive went Bush' by Janet Hawley *Good Weekend* (SMH) May 16 1998.

ISLAND HIDEAWAYS.

Article 'Life on an Island' by Deborah McIntosh, *Sun-Herald* September 27 1998.

DROP-OFF SPINOFFS.

The Australian Markets And Fairs.

Article 'Coffin Up' by Bruce Montgomery, *Australian Magazine* October 11-12 1997.

Article 'Death becomes them' by Emma Tom, *Sydney Morning Herald* December 7 1996.

PARADISE FOR SALE.

Bulletin July 8 1898.

Article 'Private Property' by Denise Ryan, *Sun-Herald* January 18 1998.

Article 'A drop in the Ocean' by Graeme Orr, *Bulletin* December 29 1998.

THE BEACHCOMBER

Confessions of a Beachcomber, by EJ Banfeld (Unwin (UK) 1910).

Last leaves from Dunk Island, by EJ Banfield (A & R 1912).

CEDAR BAY BILL.

Cairns Post various Law Reports 1963-4.

Article 'Cedar Bay Bill makes his final journey home' by Margaret Mackay-Payne, *Cairns Post* October 8 1987.

Escape to Adventure, by Georg Von Konrat (Davies (UK) 1963).

SHOOTING UP IN PARADISE.
Cairns Post. Various News Stories And Articles.
Feature Supplement on Cedar Bay Raid in *Brisbane Sunday Mail*, August 30 1998.

THE NOBLE SAVAGE.
Article 'The Outsider' by Frank Robson, *Good Weekend* (SMH) November 21 1998.
Article 'Alive and well - Our very own Tarzan' by Sally Macmillan, *Sunday Telegraph* July 7 1996.

ON THE BEACH.
South Seas Paradise, by Julian Hilas (Robert Julian Dashwood) (Hale (UK) 1965).
Castaway In Paradise : The Incredible Adventures of true life Robinson Crusoes, by Lucy Irvine (James & Simmons (UK) 1963).

OVERLANDING TO PARADISE.
Fossll Downs : A Saga of the Kimberley, by Gordon Mckenzie. Self-published 1995.
Burn To Billabong : Macdonald Clansfolk 1788-1988, by Nancy Macdonald (Portfolio Design No Date).
The Overlanders, by Gary Hogg (Hale (UK) 1961).
Bulls And Boabs : Kimberley People And Places, by Athol Thomas (St George Books 1981).
King of the Kimberley, by Rocky Marshall (Wahratta Enterprises 1988).
Outlaws of the Leopolds, by Ion L Idriess (A & R 1952).
Jandamarra and the Bunuba Resistance, by Howard Pedersen with Banjo Woorunmurra (Magabala Books 1995).
In the Tracks of the Cattle, by Jeff Carter (A & R 1968).
Northern Patrol, by RH Pilmer (Hesperian Press 1998).

HOPPING TO PARADISE.
Myrtleford : Gateway to the Alps, by Kay Robertson (Rigby 1973).
Beechworth : A Titan's Field, by Carol Woods (Hargreen 1995).
Beechworth Cemetery, by Ian Hyndman (Bethel Publications 1992).
The Hop Industry in Australia, by Helen Pearce (Melbourne University Press 1976).

Bush Battlers, by Jeff Carter (Seal Books 1977).

Sojourners, by Eric Rolls. (University of Queensland Press 1992).

Citizens, by Eric Rolls (University of Queensland Press 1996).

The Mount Buffalo Story 1898-1998, by Dan Webb and Bob Adams (Miegunyah 1998).

Rediscovering Victoria's Goldfields, by John Bechervaise (Pitman 1980).

Article 'Discovery of the Buckland' by LD Walker, in *The Alpine Observer* November 20 1953.

Report headed 'The Buckland Riot' in *The Ovens and Murray Advertiser* July 8 1857 and further report 'White Australia' in the issue of July 15 1857.

Regulations for the Chinese on the Gold Fields, published to the (Victorian) Legislative Assembly on March 19 1856 with further amendments June 11 1857 and July 14 1857.

Report on Victoria Buckland Riot, to the Clerk of Assembly on April 28 1858 by Members of the Board of Inquiry, Camp Beechworth, December 31 1857.

AN AUSTRALIAN XANADU.

Roads To Zanadu : East and West in the Making of the Modern World, by John Mereon (Child & Associates with ABC 1989).

A Place on the Coast, by Philip Cox with Janet Hawley (The Five Mile Press 1997).

THE GLOBAL VILLAGE.

Visions : How Science will revolutionise the 21st Century, by Michio Kaku (Oxford University Press 1998).

Article 'The Future isn't what it used to be' by Richard Neville, *Good Weekend*, (SMH) May 16 1998.

Article 'Brave New Suburb' by Chris Moriarty, *Bulletin* January 16 1996.

The Age of Unreason, by Charles Handy (Arrow 1995).

Next : Trends for the Future, by Matathla & Salmnan (Macmillan 1998).